PRAISE FOR *CRIME SCENE ASIA*

A fascinating book. This is an easy to read compendium of some of the most interesting and important criminal cases in Asia and Australia over the last decades, revealing the difficulties, successes and trials and tribulations associated with complex forensic science and medical evidence in the court room.

— Forensic pathologist Johan Duflou
Clinical Professor at the Sydney Medical School
of the University of Sydney, Australia

An irresistible read. Gripping tales of the relentless pursuit of truth through forensic science, no matter the odds.

— Dr Raquel del Rosario-Fortun
Professor at the University of the Philippines-College
of Medicine, the Philippines

Liz Porter takes great pains in understanding complex scientific evidence and presents it with such clarity. It is a well-researched and presented book of criminal cases, which is fascinating to read.

— Dato' V Sithambaram
Eminent criminal lawyer, Malaysia

An absolutely fascinating read: Liz Porter has a journalist's eye for detail and a storyteller's ear for narrative. Put them together and we have a superbly told series of tragic (and sometimes tragicomic) true stories leaving the reader stunned by the way ordinary lives can drift into extraordinary drama.

— Nury Vittachi,
Author and Chairman, Asia-Pacific Writers and
Translators Association, Hong Kong

CRIME SCENE ASIA

CRIME SCENE ASIA

WHEN FORENSIC EVIDENCE BECOMES THE SILENT WITNESS

Liz Porter

Marshall Cavendish
Editions

Published by Marshall Cavendish Editions
An imprint of Marshall Cavendish International

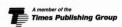

A member of the
Times Publishing Group

Other Marshall Cavendish Offices:
Marshall Cavendish Corporation. 99 White Plains Road, Tarrytown NY 10591-9001, USA • Marshall Cavendish International (Thailand) Co Ltd. 253 Asoke, 12th Flr, Sukhumvit 21 Road, Klongtoey Nua, Wattana, Bangkok 10110, Thailand • Marshall Cavendish (Malaysia) Sdn Bhd, Times Subang, Lot 46, Subang Hi-Tech Industrial Park, Batu Tiga, 40000 Shah Alam, Selangor Darul Ehsan, Malaysia

Marshall Cavendish is a registered trademark of Times Publishing Limited

National Library Board, Singapore Cataloguing-in-Publication Data

Names: Porter, Liz
Title: Crime scene Asia : when forensic evidence becomes the silent witness / Liz Porter.
Description: Singapore : Marshall Cavendish Editions, [2018]
Identifiers: OCN 1003154361 | 978-981-4634-32-8 (paperback)
Subjects: LCSH: Forensic sciences—Asia. | Murder—Investigation—Asia. | Criminal investigation—Asia.
Classification: DDC 363.25095957—dc23

Printed in Singapore by Markono Print Media Pte Ltd

For my darling daughter Alice.

In memory of my late mother, biochemist Rose Porter (1916–2005). How I wish she were still here to talk to about life, books and science.

And for my good friend Herbert, who read so many versions of the openings of the stories in this book and always remained enthusiastic and encouraging.

CONTENTS

FOREWORD

It was a book that led me to the world of forensic medicine: *Dead Men Tell Tales*, a 1968 Pan paperback by Jurgen Thorwald. A book in the true crime genre, it left me starry-eyed about the power of forensic science and medicine to catch murderers: a riveting read for a sheltered schoolboy. When I have been back to it, I can recall my excitement; but, predictably, it reads now like a pale impression of reality.

Fast forward almost 50 years to the gripping cases in this collection and to Liz Porter's extensive research and wonderfully engaging style. The way she handles their many aspects, some of which are nicely nuanced, demonstrates respect for how sophisticated consumers of contemporary forensic fare have become. Her cases each have their own special mix of suspects, crime scenes, police, lawyers, judges, scientists, doctors, psychologists and psychiatrists; these interact in their own way to finally result in a verdict. The vagaries, the uncertainties along the way are on brilliant display here too – but ultimately all is distilled to one of two formal outcomes: guilty, or not; and, on a number of occasions, both.

Examination of the scene is a crucial component of the evaluation of virtually all serious crime. It is only by re-creating what happens at the scene that the court can come to conclusions about the actions of the accused. Such conclusions might be arrived at via corroboration of the evidence of other witnesses (as well as the accused), inferences drawn simply from the evidence and nothing else, and in murder cases, these include inferences about the state of mind and intentions of the accused. The terrible Singapore case of the missing eight-year-old girl captures all of this, and additionally captures the tension of the high stakes associated with a capital case. The accused, after being convicted despite having a low IQ and possibly mental illness (and therefore arguably not responsible for his actions) was sentenced to death. The sentence was upheld 2:1 on appeal, and carried out.

The forensic science and medical evidence in *Crime Scene Asia* is fascinating in itself, as are the accounts of the police investigations. But what sets this book apart is seeing how that evidence is used in court by the prosecution and then challenged, or alternative forensic evidence introduced by the defence. The reader hears from the experts, but also experiences the lawyers, facing each other on a tightrope trading blows, where a wrong step or a change of stance can – and does – send them crashing to oblivion below. This type of writing, setting the expert evidence in the advocates' framework, is new and is possible because Liz Porter, on the evidence of *Crime Scene Asia*, has a collection of gifts which not all authors in the genre may have acquired: background investigative, forensic and legal knowledge, insight and research and writing skill.

The Asian setting for the cases is obviously a distinctive feature of the book. The cases from Singapore, for example, involve trials by judge alone. Ultimately, juries are a crucial protection for citizens, and generally they are dispensed with as an efficiency measure. Trials are easier and cheaper without them, although the results, in my view and supported by examples in this book, are not necessarily more reliable. In addition, a number of Asian countries have capital punishment. I have been forever grateful not to work in such a jurisdiction. The possibility of execution in a number of the cases in this book adds a further stressful dimension to the accounts which many readers will not be familiar with. But there are also examples of wonderful and heart-warming results from some non-criminal case applications of forensic DNA, and others – for example, an extraordinary parentage testing case from the Philippines – producing real insights into the way people live.

One of the great things about *Crime Scene Asia* is that Liz Porter is not painting a simple, two-dimensional utopian picture of perfectly precise justice. The Innocence Project is clear evidence that criminal trials (in the United States at least) can be flawed without those responsible for the process being aware: wrong executions and wrong convictions haunt American (and almost certainly other countries') death rows and prisons. She has examples of flawed forensics leading to wrong convictions, and to convictions where real doubt exists but which still stand. Being associated with such a case (or, God forbid, such cases) is the stuff of nightmares for most of the players in the courtroom drama: judge, barristers, expert witnesses and, yes, usually police. There are also, however, clear cases of corruption, incompetence and poor performance, the criminal trial anywhere being a human enterprise.

Without giving the game away there are cases in the pages which follow beautifully showing:

- Forensic evidence clearly corroborating otherwise purely circumstantial evidence
- The complexities of autopsy and forensic science evidence being tied to the mental state of the accused
- That technically perfect DNA analysis, identifying accused individuals who have left biological material at crimes scenes, can be easily misinterpreted and used to wrongly convict them

- That technically perfect chemical evidence of explosive material on the hands of an accused can have an innocent explanation
- The potential for an over reliance on confession evidence to result in injustice
- The importance of prosecution expert witnesses agreeing to reasonable propositions put to them by the defence to avoid injustice
- Independent courts and judges throwing out clearly wrong prosecutions, making wrong convictions, and making good judgements too
- That what objectively is an accident could be a murder depending solely on one's interpretation of the surrounding circumstances
- And many other striking examples of crime scene and forensics operating in investigations and trials.

Crime Scene Asia sets a new benchmark in criminal investigative, forensic science and forensic medicine story-telling. The cases are each dramatic in their own way, and thus make compelling reading. For those who are interested in the issues, the detail allows the reader to identify them and think them through. *Crime Scene Asia* thus also works at deeper levels. Quite simply, Liz Porter is to be congratulated – she has written a winner.

Stephen Cordner
Professor of Forensic Pathology
Monash University, Australia

AUTHOR'S NOTE

I was sitting in a café in Sydney, transfixed, as former Hong Kong-based barrister Peter Lavac told me the story of a former client, a truck driver called Chan, who, in 1997, managed to get himself enmeshed in what appeared to be a plot to blow up Hong Kong Island's stone-walled Stanley Prison. The key plotters, Lavac was telling me, were two of the former British colony's most notorious gangsters. One was a guy called Big Spender, nicknamed for the lavish lifestyle he funded with his armed robberies and kidnappings.

Lavac's client, Chan, was only a minor player in this criminal big league. But he was in serious trouble nevertheless. Police had raided the rural hideout that Big Spender had set up to store his explosives: a load big enough to flatten a whole block in Hong Kong's Central Business District. Chan's story was that he had only been a delivery boy. Specifically, he said he had been hired to deliver a truckload of empty barrels.

Chan had just finished dropping off these barrels when police swooped. He was arrested and the results of forensic testing of his hands and clothing suggested that he had had closer contact with the explosives than a mere delivery boy should have had. So the Hong Kong police were treating him as a dangerous terrorist.

Lavac was telling me this story because its hero, in the end, turned out to be a forensic scientist. And when I had been working on my two previous books, cases where the forensic scientist is the hero were always the ones I was looking for.

But was I actually writing a book? By the time I met Peter Lavac, I wasn't sure.

I had lined up my chat with Lavac some months earlier. At the time I had certainly been trying to work on a book: one with the working title, *Asia – forensic science casebook*.

I had come up with the book idea in Singapore, when I was there for the 2014 conference of the Asia-Pacific Writers and Translators Association and had been on a panel talking about crime writing. I had been reading a collection of local crime fiction called *Singapore Noir* and noted that there was also a *KL Noir* and a *Hong Kong Noir* in the series. But there seemed to be a dearth of local true crime. One bookshop I visited had a floor-to-ceiling wall of shelves devoted to books on "feng shui". Its true crime section had three sparse shelves and nothing much local. But I did find a local prosecutor's memoir (published by Marshall Cavendish, whom I soon identified as the local publisher with an interest in true crime-related topics).

At the APWT session on crime writing, I floated the idea of doing a local forensic science casebook – and received an enthusiastic response.

I had two more days left in Singapore so I did a quick Google, came up with a staff list for Singapore's national forensic sciences agency, the Health Sciences Authority (HSA), and fired off an email.

I was gratified to get a prompt reply and an invitation to come in for a chat. Later that day I spent a delightful hour and a half with a forensic scientist whom I won't name because I don't want to embarrass him. Suffice to say that I walked out on to Outram Road with a notebook full of case ideas and books to read.

When I arrived home to Melbourne I contacted Marshall Cavendish about my idea. The publishers liked it – and I had a deal.

I then began work on the new book in much the same way I had started my previous two forensic science books, *Written On*

The Skin: an Australian forensic casebook and *Cold Case Files: past crimes solved by new forensic science.* That is, I contacted a long list of scientists. Sometimes I had cases in mind that they had been involved in and that I wanted to include. Or I wanted to ask them if they had a particular case where (a) the back story was interesting and (b) the forensic science work involved had been both dramatic and effective, in that it had either solved a mystery, won police a conviction or helped a defence lawyer exonerate a falsely accused client.

This process had worked very well for my two previous books. Both police and scientists were always willing to talk to me, and happy to participate in the whole book development process. They checked the copy that I sent them for accuracy and even took a last look at the page proofs before the book was printed.

Even when I was researching my first book, *Written On The Skin*, my approaches were welcomed. The scientists and police I interviewed were mainly from the state of Victoria where I live, and many of them had probably read the articles I had written as a reporter for the Melbourne paper, *The Sunday Age*. So I suppose I was a known quantity.

By the time I got to my second book, the process went even more smoothly. I emailed scientists and police from around Australia, the UK, and the US (where I contacted an officer from the US Bureau of Alcohol, Tobacco, Firearms and Explosives out of the blue to ask about a case in which its ballistics database had tracked a gun used in a drive-by shooting). None of them had ever heard of me. But I would send details of my first book, assure them of my *bona fides* and my respect for accuracy and promise that they would get to check the copy. And off we would go.

I assumed that this new Asian casebook would proceed in the same fashion.

But by mid 2015, everything (except the publishing deal) had started to fall apart. The HSA scientist told me he would love to help but his boss didn't think it was a good idea. A Singaporean scientist in private practice, whom I had thought would help me, backed out.

I had also emailed Hong Kong government scientists but received no response. A Thailand-based forensic pathologist, Dr Porntip Rojanasunan, was friendly but difficult to contact. In any event, I found that most of her cases did not really fit my criterion for inclusion as they didn't have (from my viewpoint) a satisfactory denouement in court.

Meanwhile, I talked to various forensic science contacts in Melbourne, who emailed their Asian-based colleagues. Most of the time, I received polite initial replies from these scientists but silence usually fell once I started making enquiries about specific cases.

Another contact I had pinned some hope on was UK-based forensic scientist Sheilah Hamilton. She had been a government forensic scientist in Hong Kong and hadn't seemed shy about talking to the media. She also seemed to have worked on lots of interesting cases. We emailed a little and then I finally arranged to talk to her on the phone.

That's when she gave me the bad news. She did not want to be in my new book as she was thinking of writing her own. Yet she did not shut me down completely. We had talked about an interesting case involving forensic traces of explosive and she had mentioned the name of the barrister on that case, a Peter Lavac. She told me that he would probably be happy to talk to me about it.

Perhaps he would, I remember thinking. But that was one case. I had also had a friendly response from former Australian Federal Police scientist David Royds. I knew that his role in the successful forensic investigation into the 2002 Bali terrorist bombings had been particularly dramatic. I was also aware that he would be able to give me a thorough rundown of both the Indonesian and the Australian sides of the operation. This was going to be handy because the Indonesian scientists on my list had also not replied to my emails.

I had two cases. I needed 16. It was definitely time to officially lay this book idea to rest.

But barrister Peter Lavac proved so easy to find. He was no longer working in Hong Kong. In fact he was working in Sydney, and I was going to be there for a conference for my one-day-a-week job as media officer for a Melbourne-based legal research organisation.

So I arranged to meet him. I told him about my apparently doomed plans for the book and that I was about to call the publisher and abandon it. But he was willing to have a chat about the case anyway.

We spoke for about an hour and I taped about thirty minutes of our chat.

I certainly didn't change my mind about the book that night.

But in subsequent weeks I found my thoughts returning to Chan and The Big Spender. It was such a good story, and I really wanted to be able to tell it. So I listened to the tape and had a go at drafting a story outline. Meanwhile I considered the literal meaning of "forensic": "to do with a court". I reminded myself that lawyers, as well as scientists, could be good sources of cases decided by forensic scientific evidence.

I realised I could still write the book. I would just do it by talking to lawyers instead of scientists. So, once again, I began looking for cases. But this time, on my own. I searched the database of Hong Kong's *South China Morning Post*, Malaysia's *New Straits Times* and Singapore's *The Straits Times*. After all, few cases with interesting forensic evidence escape the notice of newspaper court reporters. I also searched worldlii.org, the world database of court judgements and information.

With the Singapore cases, one criminal lawyer's name kept coming up: Subhas Anandan. When I first started thinking about this book, he was still alive. Sadly he died in January 2015, but his colleague and nephew Sunil Sudheesan was still in practice.

I emailed Sunil, asking for information and telling him I was heading for Singapore. He replied with an invitation to lunch and, later, a vast e-bundle of documents. He also told me about a case where the evidence of Australian forensic pathologist Professor Johan Duflou had saved one of his clients from the hangman's noose. Duflou had also been an expert witness in the trials of Ram Tiwary, a Singaporean jailed for murder in Sydney and later acquitted – and whose case, my publishers suggested, might be an interesting one for me to look at.

Over at the Singapore Police Force Public Affairs Department, the Head of the Media Production and Liaison Unit, Superintendent Jimmy Law, was also very helpful. He pointed me in the direction of two cases ("Death in Bukit Batok Nature Park" and "The CCTV Camera's Eye Sees All") where the forensic science work had been so dramatically successful that the police had made Crimewatch TV episodes about them and put them on YouTube.

In Malaysia, I had the help of eminent criminal lawyer Dato' V Sithambaram ("Unknown Male One") while HK criminal lawyer Gary Plowman, SC, gave me a lot of time, explaining the background of a case in which a man was charged with murder after his car exploded, killing his wife ("Murder or Accident?"). Gary also put me on to Hong Kong's Judge Audrey Campbell-Moffat, SC, of the Court of First Instance of the High Court, who was kind enough to talk me through the forensic evidence in a case she prosecuted ("The Body in the Couch").

In the meantime I kept reading *ForensicAsia*, the newsletter of the Asian Forensic Sciences Network. Occasionally it featured case reports from scientists whose work I needed to describe. But the group's organisers had also ignored my emails. One of the Philippines-based scientists whose work was published in it, Dr Maria Corazon de Ungria, responded to my message to her via Twitter. So did her colleague, forensic pathologist Dr Raquel del Rosario-Fortun, who replied to my email. Three cases came out of those conversations: "A Surprise Paternity Test Result", "Solving a Giant Genealogical Puzzle" and "The Marivic Genosa Case".

In the end I had enough material for a proper casebook, with 16 cases spread across Singapore, Malaysia, Hong Kong, the Philippines and Indonesia.

The book that resulted, *Crime Scene Asia: when forensic evidence becomes the silent witness*, is like my two earlier forensic science books, in that it's a casebook of real-life examples of the way forensic science is used to solve crimes, convict criminals and exonerate the falsely accused.

And, as with those previous books, I couldn't have done it without huge assistance from a dozen other people. The lawyers I mentioned above helped me by talking to me and then checking what I had written and making corrections and additions. In this respect I am also particularly grateful to scientists David Royds, Professor Johan Duflou, Dr Raquel del Rosario-Fortun and Dr Maria Corazon de Ungria, as well as to Melbourne forensic pathologist Dr Byron Collins and an anonymous Australian police scientist (who knows who she is). Sydney criminal lawyers Tim Game, SC, and David Dalton, SC, were also kind enough to read my draft of the Ram Tiwary case and make comments that were a great help to me.

I would like to thank my publisher Melvin Neo, and Violet Phoon who helped edit my book. Both have been an absolute delight to work with. And I am enormously indebted to Professor Stephen Cordner, Professor of Forensic Pathology (International), at Monash University and Head of International Programmes, Victorian Institute of Forensic Medicine for doing me the honour of reading my manuscript and writing its Foreword.

Liz Porter
Melbourne, Australia
November 2017

THE CASES

Case One
DEATH IN BUKIT BATOK NATURE PARK

When a morning jogger found an unidentified woman's body in a beautiful Singapore nature park, police were stumped. Who was she? No relative or friend had reported her missing. All police had to go on was a series of dental implants in her teeth. Through a combination of great forensic work and tireless door knocking, the dead woman's dentist was identified. But why had she been killed? The victim's work colleagues had no idea and her mobile phone had disappeared. Inspector Kelvin Kwok obtained her phone records and his team of investigators got to work. The phone was still in use. And three numbers had been called repeatedly in the days since her death. Was the killer the caller?

The green woodlands of Singapore's Bukit Batok Nature Park comprise what travel guides like to call "an oasis of calm" in a frenetically busy city. The 36-hectare park boasts lush greenery and abundant birdlife, while the clear waters of its lake are home to several species of fish and two varieties of freshwater turtle. Its undulating paths draw joggers; its serenity attracts birdwatchers and nature lovers. And, as became apparent one day in 2008, its leafy hollows also make it an appealing venue for a killer in need of a place to dump a body.

As the murderer in question had hoped, his victim lay undiscovered for several days. Then, on the morning of October 20,

2008, the dawn birdcalls were drowned out by the whoop of police sirens. At 7 am a jogger had been making his way along Lorong Sesuai, a small road that leads into the park from busy Upper Bukit Timah Road, when he came to a sudden halt, nostrils twitching.

It was the time of year when an optimist might hope to catch the last whiff of the night-blooming sweetness of the park's native Tembusu tree. But the odour the jogger could smell was sharp, unmistakable and strong enough to banish the usual ferny freshness of morning. His nose led him to a decomposing body lying in vegetation at the bottom of a heavily wooded slope.

Fortunately the man had his phone on him. Soon, two police cars were screeching to a halt on Lorong Sesuai. After a quick look at the body, the officers unrolled the crime scene tape and began calling in the forensic artillery.

By mid-morning the area was swarming with crime scene investigators. A photographer recorded the tyre marks that could be seen at the top of the slope. His camera also captured traces of yellow paint embedded in a damaged tree trunk. Other officers searched the undergrowth, bagging orange and black plastic fragments they found at the base of that tree. It seemed logical to assume that the same car that had left the tyre marks had also run into the tree. Judging by the 1.2 m to 1.3 m distance between the left and right tyre tracks, a small vehicle was responsible.

Neither shoes nor bag nor wallet were found on or near the body. So it seemed likely that the victim had been brought to his or her final resting place in that car.

None of the officers touched the body, which was clad in a beige polo shirt and black pants. They were waiting for forensic pathologist Dr Paul Chui. As is customary, he wanted to examine the body *in situ*. It would then be transported to the mortuary at the Health Sciences Authority's Centre for Forensic Medicine for him to carry out an autopsy. The Health Sciences Authority (HSA) is the country's national multidisciplinary scientific regulatory agency. Its Forensic Science Division provides forensic science services to law enforcement agencies, hospitals, private organisations and individuals across Singapore.

What could the forensic pathologist say?

From his preliminary examination, the forensic expert judged the body to be that of a woman aged between 25 and 45. Running his gloved hands gently over her head, he could feel damage on its left side – probably caused by a heavy blow. He guessed she'd been dead for about four days. Certainly she was far too decomposed to be identified visually. As with all badly decomposed bodies, the best clue to her identity would be her teeth.

Later that day, his autopsy examination confirmed that she was female, had been about 1.53 m tall and had suffered blunt force trauma to her head. But the woman's body told him nothing else that would help the police find her killer.

For a start, who was she? If she were a local, then she had no close friends or family. Two days after the discovery of her body, there had been no reports lodged with police about a missing woman. Taking Dr Chui's estimate that she had been dead for four days, she had now been missing for almost a week.

Might she be a tourist? Did her friends and family think she was away? Or was she a loner?

An appeal to the media

The woman had been wearing silver and yellow rings on her left and right ring fingers respectively and a Seiko watch on her left wrist. A silver chain hung around her neck. Although none of these items were distinctive, the police took the unusual step of having them photographed for the press. The pictures appeared in the papers three days after the woman's body had been found.

"Who do these belong to?" was the headline. The only other external clues to the mystery woman's identity were the traces of yellow paint on the tree and fragments of plastic found near her body.

Earlier that year, Singapore police had set up the island nation's first Vehicle Paint Database to help trace vehicles involved in hit and run accidents and terrorist car bomb attacks. Logging on to it, HSA forensic chemists found that the yellow paint on the tree did not match any of the paints on the database. But the pieces of clear orange plastic found at the crime scene looked to have come from the housing of a car light while the fragments of black plastic appeared to be part of the number plate.

No Japanese-made cars that came in yellow had orange light housing. It seemed likely that the car in question was a Chery QQ – a Chinese make of car. If the woman – or her killer – had one of these, the location of the fragments suggested the car had been used to transport her body to the nature park.

Secrets in the teeth

The detectives at Singapore's Criminal Investigation Department (CID) were counting on the X-rays of the dead woman's teeth to solve the mystery of her identity. Taken after the autopsy, these radiographs documented extensive dental work, including crowns, implants and bridging. This victim had spent many hours in her dentist's chair. Unless the work had been done overseas, one of Singapore's more than a thousand dentists would be able to recognise his or her work.

The dental implants themselves, meanwhile, contained valuable information. Each was stamped with a serial number, its digits so tiny that they could only be read through a microscope. These numbers indicated that the implants had been supplied by the global company Straumann, Switzerland-based but with a Singapore branch that sold the implants directly into Asia. A check with the company established that the implants in the dead woman's mouth were part of a batch imported between January and June in 2007 and despatched to a long list of local dental surgeries.

The CID's special investigation team assigned to this case had more than a dozen members. Its leader, Inspector Kelvin Kwok, handed each member a copy of the dead woman's dental X-rays, along with a list of names and addresses, several pages long. These were the details of all the dentists who had ordered Straumann implants after January 2007.

Three days of door knocking

This search would be a tedious process, Kwok reminded his troops. The only information that the officers could give the dentists was that they were looking for an Asian female patient, aged between 25 and 45. But finding the right dentist would unlock the secret of the dead woman's identity. And that would bring the team one step closer to finding her killer.

This systematic approach worked. After three days of door knocking, one of the dozens of dentists interviewed recognised the dental X-rays. He had spent many hours with their owner. She had needed a crown and a root canal treatment on one tooth, along with a metal filling in the neighbouring tooth.

The patient's name was Choo Xue Ying and she was 47 years old.

"When she first came to see me," the dead woman's dentist said, "she had severe tooth decay. Three teeth had to be extracted and she requested dental implants."

Back at CID headquarters, Kwok briefed the team on the little that was known about the dead woman. The key detail was that she had been working as a property agent for the giant realtor Propnex. After a visit to the company's office, where she had been one of many hundreds on the books, it was easier to understand why her colleagues had not reported her missing.

"Jennifer", as she was known at work, was very much a solo operator. In fact she had not set foot in the property agency's headquarters for some months.

As the forensic officers who had examined the paint fragments had suggested, she also owned a little yellow Chery QQ car. Judging from the pieces of damaged plastic found at the scene, that car was likely to have a broken signal light. If Jennifer Choo had been driven to the scene in her car, or killed in it, the vehicle would be a rich source of forensic evidence.

The search for the car

It was Monday October 27 – and only four days since Choo's body had been discovered. But a whole week had passed since her murder. Now that the team had her car registration details, their priority was to find that car before the killer had a chance to repair, repaint, rebirth or torch it.

As soon as they had identified her, investigators had visited the dead woman's last known address. It was a public housing studio flat in the central Singapore suburb of Eunos. She had shared it with an 82-year-old man who described her as "a friend". She had not paid him rent but she had bought food for him every day.

The officers took Choo's hairbrush and toothbrush, so that their forensic colleagues could back up her dental identification with a DNA match. The bristles of her toothbrush and hairbrush furnished enough cheek and scalp tissue cells to enable the extraction of a

DNA profile. That profile was then compared with DNA extracted from the bone marrow of the woman whose body was still lying in Dr Chui's mortuary. The two profiles matched.

In the meantime a routine police patrol had responded to the alert put out by Kwok's team. A yellow Chery QQ with a registration number matching the missing car had been spotted abandoned in a heavy vehicle parking lot in Jalan Kubor, near Sungei Road, about 20 km away from Bukit Batok Park.

Bloodstains were found on the centre of the steering wheel, on the driver's door, front passenger door, and the roof padding above the front passenger seat. DNA extracted from them matched Choo's. The stains suggested that she had either been attacked in her car or just before she got into it.

Who was Jennifer Choo?

But who was Jennifer Choo? And under what circumstances had she met her killer?

The life of this victim was anything but an open book. The Propnex communications manager later told a newspaper that she was a "loner" who avoided the various social activities organised at his office. Yet she had at least one friend. This woman had placed a small obituary notice for Choo in *The Straits Times*. It described her as "a kind woman" she could "always count on" and "a creature of habit". One of these habits was her daily visit to Geylang East Community Library (now known as Geylang East Public Library), where she went to use the Internet, always sitting in the same spot.

Choo also had a brother, whom police had contacted after they had confirmed her identity. And her family arranged a cremation for her. But, as is suggested by the fact that a Buddhist monk was commissioned to scatter her ashes in the waters off Changi, the dead woman had not been close to them.

With no network of close friends to fill them in on Choo's activities over the weeks before her death, the investigators' final information source would be her mobile phone.

The actual handset had not been found. But the police had put a trace on the number. They discovered that her phone had been still in use after October 16, the day that, by the forensic pathologist's estimate, she had been murdered.

There was always a chance that Choo had simply lost her phone and the person using it after her death was merely a thief. But it was more likely that the phone user was her killer.

Three numbers to follow

Three numbers stood out as having been called repeatedly in the few days since her death. The pre-paid SIM card associated with the first one belonged to a woman called Jelly. An Indonesian who had been working as a prostitute in Singapore, she was an "overstayer" on her visa (and her full name was never published or read out in court). But she was nowhere to be found.

The second number belonged to a woman called Zubaidah.

The third belonged to a man named Adros.

Zubaidah was easy to find. Interviewing her, the police learned that the man who had spoken to her on Choo's phone was called "Ali". He had promised Zubaidah a job as a cleaner with his company. He had then borrowed Zubaidah's own mobile phone and vanished without returning it.

Further enquiries yielded the fact that, between October 18 and 20, Zubaidah's stolen phone had also been used to call Adros. When the investigators found him, they were relieved to hear him confirm that he also knew Ali. In fact he had recently gone to the police to complain that Ali had cheated him with a bounced cheque.

Adros told the investigators that he had met Ali in jail, years previously. They had run into one another again recently and Ali had suggested the pair go into business. As proof of his financial *bona fides*, he had given Adros a cheque. In the meantime, however, he needed cash to pay some pressing bills for the new business. Could Adros help? First Ali needed S$1400, and then S$10,000. There was no need to worry, Ali reassured Adros. He would get paid when the cheque cleared.

Predictably the cheque bounced.

So Ali was the man using the dead woman's phone. He was probably her killer. But who was he?

Knowing the exact period that the two men had been in jail together meant that the investigators were able to assemble a book of mug shots of former inmates to show Adros, in the hope that he could point Ali out to them. Immigration authorities also provided a photo of Jelly to put in a parallel collection of mug shots. This Ali had a girlfriend, Adros had told police. The frequency of calls to her number suggested it might be the Indonesian woman Jelly.

The former prison buddy quickly found Ali in the book of mug shots. His name was Rosli bin Yassin and Jelly was, indeed, his girlfriend. Zubaidah was also able to identify Rosli as the Ali who had stolen her phone.

But where were Rosli and Jelly now? And what had caused Ali to morph from conman to killer?

The trail leads to Sentosa

On Friday October 31, Kelvin Kwok's team assembled for another briefing. The CID had received information, Kwok told the group, that the couple had been staying on Sentosa Island, a small beach resort only a short monorail ride away from the city centre.

Enquiries at the island's twenty-odd resorts and hotels had shown no Rosli bin Yassin in residence. If they were there, the couple were registered under false names. It was time for another "needle in a haystack"-style door-knocking exercise.

Half a dozen officers headed for the island and began working their way through the list of hotels. At each one, they showed reception staff photos of the couple. The investigators' luck changed at Siloso Beach Resort Sentosa, a palm tree-lined luxury eco-resort just a few metres away from the beachfront. A concierge nodded when she saw the pictures. The pair were guests. They were out at the time, but due back.

After a flurry of phone calls, all six officers converged on the establishment.

When their quarry returned, the police waited for them to retire to their room. Then they swooped. At that point the duo were being arrested for the fraud offences (known as "cheating" under local law) against Adros and Zubaidah. There was no evidence linking either Rosli or Jelly to the dead woman.

That would soon change.

Rosli was used to being questioned by police, and gave little away.

Jelly wasn't; before long she was tearfully confessing to having helped Rosli cheat Adros.

Asked what she knew about Choo, she dropped her boyfriend right in it. She said she had met Choo at the dead woman's *de facto* "office": the Geylang East Community Library.

"I don't know what happened after they left the library," she said.

Before they questioned Rosli again, the investigators examined footage from the CCTV cameras at the library's entrance and exit.

Kelvin Kwok knew from Jelly that Choo had left the library with Rosli on October 16, the day on which she had died. That day's

CCTV footage showed Choo leaving the library in the afternoon, with Rosli following later.

Physical evidence, so far, had been crucial to solving this case. The victim could not have been identified with any certainty without forensic dentistry and DNA.

The bloodstains that the crime scene officers had found on the steering wheel were proof that Jennifer Choo had been injured in the car. Meanwhile HSA forensic chemist Lim Chin Chin had established, through matching the paint and plastic fragments at the scene with Choo's car, that the car found abandoned in the Jalan Kubor car park was the same vehicle that had been driven away from Lorong Sesuai after it had crashed into a tree.

But the police had no forensic evidence to tie Rosli to the victim's body or the car.

In Singapore a murder conviction carries the death penalty. So Rosli was not going to make any admissions about having killed Choo.

Kelvin Kwok and his team were certain that he was the killer. They needed a human witness who could place Rosli at the crime scene.

Jelly's testimony would be vital

They had high hopes of Jelly. A cleanskin in comparison to Rosli, the Indonesian had already made full admissions about her role in her former boyfriend's dishonest schemes.

While she had worked as a prostitute and committed crimes of dishonesty, she drew the line at murder. Keen to avoid a murder charge herself, she ended up making a comprehensive statement implicating her former boyfriend.

She was the prosecution's chief witness at Rosli's murder trial, which opened in Singapore's High Court in October 2010.

By then she was an inmate of Changi Women's Prison, where she was serving a three-year sentence for the cheating and forgery offences she had committed with Rosli, along with her own immigration offences.

She told police that she had met Rosli in August 2008 in a Geylang coffee shop. In the two months that the pair had been together, Rosli had begun introducing her to people as his wife. Although he was a mechanic by trade he had initially claimed to be an immigration officer. At the time, however, he was unemployed.

Jelly testified that Rosli had introduced her to Choo on October 14 at the Geylang East Community Library, telling her that he and Choo were going into a business venture together. The exact nature of that business was never revealed. It seems most likely that it was related to two apartments that Jennifer Choo had advertised for sale in *The Straits Times* on that day.

On the morning of October 16, the couple returned to the library for another meeting with Choo. That afternoon, Rosli said he and Choo were going off to do some business together. He asked Jelly to wait for him.

Once again, the "business" they were doing was most probably related to the above-mentioned two apartments, which were located less than 2 km away from the part of Lorong Sesuai where Choo's body was found.

Two hours later, Rosli called and asked Jelly to meet him at a coffee shop on Sungei Road. This coffee shop was about 5 km away from the library but very near the car park where Choo's car would later be found abandoned.

Walking into the coffee shop, Jelly found Rosli looking sweaty, muddy, dishevelled, and stressed. He had a wound on his hand and he was carrying several items that were not his: a laptop, a brown handbag and a second mobile.

The handbag looked like Choo's. Rosli later transferred its contents into his pockets. He sold the laptop for S$300.

But Rosli was still short of money. Over the next few days he began using Choo's chequebook to help him solve that problem. Meeting up with Adros, he wrote out a cheque for S$500,000 and used it to talk his old prison buddy into lending him S$1400. Two days later, on October 20, Adros lent him S$10,000, with the money to be paid back when Rosli's cheque cleared.

The next day, flush with cash, Rosli and Jelly headed for Sentosa and booked into a room at the Siloso Beach Resort.

A few days later, Jelly told the police, Rosli picked up the newspaper but had to put it down again because his hands were trembling too much. The paper, she noted, was open at an article headlined "Who do these belong to?" and displaying photos of a woman's rings, necklace and watch.

Jelly recognised the items immediately and confronted Rosli. Initially he denied having had anything to do with Choo's disappearance. Eventually he admitted it, but claimed he had only acted in order to "protect" Jelly.

Choo, he told Jelly, had been an "immigration officer" and had been planning, along with a colleague, to abduct and kill her. Rosli had then become agitated, warning her to stop asking him about Choo. Jelly also claimed that Rosli had threatened to kill her if she tried to run away from the hotel.

Unsurprisingly, Rosli's defence lawyer Wong Siew Hong slammed Jelly's testimony as a "pack of lies". She had not found out about Choo's death at Sentosa, he alleged. Instead, he suggested, Jelly had accompanied Rosli and Choo to Bukit Batok Park. The barrister then accused her of remaining there during the assault and possibly also taking part in it. He also suggested that she had helped her boyfriend dispose of the dead woman's belongings.

The defence lawyer only managed to catch his quarry in one definite lie. Jelly had told the court she was 39, while her passport listed her year of birth as 1975, making her only 35. But the young woman did not wilt under the barrister's fierce cross-examination.

On the contrary, her steadfast testimony may very well have convinced Rosli that the judge would believe her. Jelly's version of events could be taken to suggest that he had planned to kill Choo. If the judge believed her, then Rosli would most certainly be found guilty of murder. In that case, his life would end with Singapore's chief executioner placing a noose around his neck.

Rosli's story changed

So Rosli changed his story. While he had killed Choo, he hadn't meant to, he said. Surely that would make things better for him. His account of Choo's death matched the forensic evidence – and most of Jelly's statement.

Rosli told the police that the fatal argument had been over the amount of money that he owed Choo. It had broken out in Choo's car in Lorong Sesuai, on the outskirts of Bukit Batok Park. Rosli had punched Choo on the head and face when they were in the car. This had caused the blood spatter later found on the centre of the vehicle's steering wheel. After he had hit her, she had jumped out of the car, brandishing her phone, calling him "a conman" and threatening to call the police on him.

Rosli had then grabbed her phone. Losing control, he had punched her on the head several times, inflicting the injuries that eventually caused her death. Panicking, he had then carried her body to the bottom of a slope, hiding it in the undergrowth.

Afterwards he had driven her car 15 km to the Jalan Kubor heavy vehicle parking lot where it was later found. He had then made his way to a nearby coffee shop, phoning Jelly and asking her to meet him there.

As a result of his confession the murder charge against him was reduced to "culpable homicide". This offence attracts a lesser penalty of 20 years' jail because it covers killings that occur as a result of a fight and are not pre-meditated. This lesser charge also applies when it can be argued that an accused person has "diminished responsibility" because of mental faculties that are substantially impaired.

Rosli, who had an IQ of only 69, well below the 90 that is the minimum to qualify as merely "average" had served time before. A "frequent flier" in Singapore's criminal justice system since the age of 31, he had notched up convictions for offences such as cheating, forgery, escaping from legal custody and theft.

Previously he had coped with the relatively short jail terms that these minor crimes had earned him. But things had changed for him by September 2011, when he faced the High Court to plead guilty to a culpable homicide charge and to charges of forgery, criminal breach of trust and cheating. By then he had been in detention for almost three years. He was cracking under the strain.

Waiting in the dock for his hearing to start, he was heard to say: "I want to die." Then, when the hearing started and a Malay interpreter began reading out his charges, he interrupted her.

"If my life is like this, then why should I stay alive?" he asked. "I want to tell the judge to let me die."

Justice Woo Bih Li disregarded that plea. He also ignored the arguments of the prosecution, who were demanding a sentence of 20 years' preventive detention. This is a kind of imprisonment intended for habitual offenders who are at least 30 years old and considered to be too recalcitrant for reformation. Instead, Justice Woo gave Rosli 12 years' preventive detention.

The prosecution then appealed, arguing that Rosli, by then 52, was a "menace to society" who should be "taken out of circulation for the longest time possible under the law to protect the public".

In March 2013 three Court of Appeal judges threw the book at Rosli, upgrading his sentence to 20 years. Jelly wasn't there to hear it. By then she had served her three-year jail term and had been repatriated back to her native Indonesia.

Case Two
THE CCTV CAMERA'S EYE SEES ALL

When a headless body was found floating in the Whampoa River, the forensic pathologist who was called to the scene told police that the victim was a "youngish" Indian woman. She had only been in the water a few hours and had been killed in the previous 24 hours, he said. But who was she? And who had killed her and dumped her body in the water? The many CCTV cameras in the area had done nothing to protect this woman, who may very well have been killed elsewhere. Had these cameras captured her killer as he carried her body towards the water?

Despite their city's reputation for cleanliness, Singaporeans have a history of dumping plastic bags, Styrofoam boxes, shopping trolleys and even broken rattan chairs into the Singapore River and its various tributaries. Given their city's legendarily low crime rate, relatively few citizens use the city's waterways to also dump bodies. But there have been a few cases. In 2005, two boxes containing the upper and lower torso of a woman were washed up on to the banks of the Kallang River (see *Death on Father's Day*). In 2011 the body of a man was found in a trolley bag in waters off Sentosa Island. Then, in 2013, at 7.25 am on Saturday December 12, a schoolboy was crossing the Whampoa River near McNair Road when he spotted a large, black, plastic-wrapped parcel floating in the murky green waters. Two feet protruded from it.

Police were on the scene within minutes, fencing off the area with crime scene tape and organising Singapore Civil Defence Force fire-fighters to retrieve the body. Meanwhile a forensic team began erecting a small, blue, crime scene tent by the roadside. It would give the dead body some protection from the curious stares of passers-by. It also allowed the on-call forensic pathologist some privacy while he unwrapped the body to do a preliminary examination.

Roy Lim, Deputy Superintendent of Police (DSP) and deputy head of the Criminal Investigation Department's Special Investigation Section, was the next to arrive, followed by Health Sciences Authority (HSA) forensic pathologist Dr George Paul. The forensic expert's observations about the time of death would dictate the initial direction of the investigation.

He told the detective that the body was a "youngish" Indian woman. Some *rigor mortis* – the process of stiffening that tends to set in three or four hours after death – was already affecting her limbs. Placing a gloved hand on the dead woman's back he pointed out some faint hypostasis. Also called "the darkening of death", this bluish purple or purple-red discolouration indicates the pooling of the blood in one spot, caused by gravity, that occurs after death. This suggested that the deceased had been lying on her back for a few hours.

The time of death was crucial

The forensic pathologist then considered the fact that the woman's body had been immersed in water: a situation that creates its own decomposition changes. Fat layers in the skin expand, causing visible deformation to a corpse within 24 hours. Here, however, there were no signs of such changes. This suggested that she had been in the water for only a few hours. There was also no evidence of other early signs of putrefaction, such as the greenish hue which may begin appearing on the skin of the abdomen on the second day after death.

Dr Paul's initial conclusions were that the unfortunate woman had been dead for about six to eight hours – and certainly for fewer than 24 hours. But until he had done a full post-mortem examination back in the HSA mortuary, he didn't want to speculate on the cause of death. At DSP Lim's request he took a blood sample at the scene, rather than wait until he was back in the autopsy room.

Whoever had killed this woman had cut off her head and hands to hide her identity. This was a clear indication that the killer was related or known to the dead woman. So the detective wanted her DNA profile as soon as possible.

The forensic pathologist's estimate of time of death was crucial. If this victim had been dead for less than a day and had been in the water for only a few hours, her killer had to have dumped her body into the water in the middle of the night.

It was now Saturday afternoon.

"Time is of the essence," Lim told his team. They didn't need to be reminded of the "48 hours" rule. A detective's chances of ever solving a murder are halved if the first good lead fails to materialise in the first 48 hours of an investigation.

Finding the body's head and hands would help solve the mystery of the dead woman's identity. Given that the water in the Whampoa River was very still, it seemed safe to assume that the body had been thrown into the water from somewhere close to where it was found. There was a strong chance that the killer had also dumped the murder weapon – and possibly also the woman's head and hands – in the vicinity.

Accordingly, Lim directed his team to search the immediate area around the river between McNair Road and St George's Road. Surely somebody had been awake in the small hours and had seen or heard something suspicious. He despatched other officers to question staff at local shops and riverside stalls, and to door knock residents of the riverside tower blocks overlooking the scene. The team also needed to retrieve all available CCTV footage covering these areas.

Could CCTV cameras find the killer?

Since May 2012 some 18,000 police cameras had been installed at more than 3000 Housing and Development Board (HDB) tower blocks and multi-storey car parks across Singapore. All the residential towers along the Whampoa River were monitored in that way. The aim, according to Singapore's Ministry of Home Affairs, was to improve the safety of residents and to prevent and solve crimes. These cameras had done nothing for the safety of the dead woman, whose body was, by then, lying in the mortuary at the HSA. But perhaps they would find her killer.

Police officers spent the weekend searching the riverbank area but found neither the murder weapon nor the missing head and hands. It was a gruesome possibility that the woman's missing body parts had been gathered up with the rubbish collected daily from the Whampoa River and its banks. If so, they would now be at the Tuas South Incineration Plant, the largest of four incineration plants in Singapore.

Roy Lim ordered a search of all the rubbish collected the day before from anywhere within a radius of 3 km from the spot where the body was found. Over the next few days, 30 police officers wearing face masks and protective gloves searched through five tonnes of rubbish at the incineration plant. They found nothing.

The officers assigned to check footage from CCTV cameras had more success. Hong Wen Primary School, located just a block back from the river, had several cameras. At 2.52 am on Saturday

December 12, cameras mounted on the school's front gate had caught two men struggling to wheel an obviously heavy suitcase along the street.

The two men and their suitcase

At 3.08 am, cameras on the school's side gate caught the duo again. This time they were carrying the suitcase on their shoulders and they were staggering under its weight. At 3.09 am, they were seen letting it fall to the ground.

The officer who had visited the school had taken a clip of it on her mobile phone to show her boss. DSP Lim played it, pausing it repeatedly. He couldn't see the men's faces well. They looked relatively young. But they were taller and stockier than the average Chinese Singaporean. And there was something about their style of dress, with shirts worn loose over their trousers, that made him think that they were not Chinese. He wondered if they might be Indian Singaporean? Or maybe more recently arrived from the subcontinent? And if they were not locals, what might their next move be? He would instruct the Immigration and Checkpoints Authority (ICA) to generate a list of all foreigners younger than sixty years who had left the country in the past eight hours.

Meanwhile other officers were back at CID headquarters, patiently viewing hours of footage from the more than 200 police cameras on HDB residential blocks in the neighbourhood. At 3.17 am a police camera on a housing tower in St George's Lane, on the other side of the river, caught the two potential suspects again. This camera looked back across the river to a spot where two men were standing in front of a garage door. By this time they no longer had the suitcase with them. And they appeared to be arguing.

This footage turned out to be especially important. Firstly it showed the two men standing in front of a standard-sized garage door. This allowed police to measure that door and work out their relative and respective heights. Secondly, it revealed the presence of a potential witness. An older man, wearing a striped sweater and carrying a plastic bag emblazoned with the words "Whampoa Mart", a supermarket on nearby McNair Road, was seen scrutinising the men as he walked past. Two officers headed down to the supermarket to review its CCTV footage. With luck they would get an even closer look at Mr Striped Sweater, note the time that he had left the checkout, and, ideally, get his name.

At the same time the investigators were trying to work out where the men with the suitcase had come from. Given they were on foot, it could not have been far.

Now that police had a CCTV image of the men, they could show it to the street stall operators, some of whom would still have been working in the small hours of that morning. A durian stall vendor on Balestier Road recognised the two men immediately. She had seen them the previous night, just across the road from her stall. In fact she'd noticed them struggling down Balestier Road before they doubled back, probably trying to find the quickest way down to the water.

Balestier Road was the team's next target. Their plan was to examine all available CCTV footage and find other eyewitnesses who had seen the two men and their suitcase. Lim and four officers, working in two teams, were already door-knocking their way along the street when Lim's phone rang.

A man who had just left Singapore

ICA had come up with the requested list of foreigners under 60 who had left Singapore on the morning of December 12 and were travelling without female companions. One name stood out. Early on December 12, just half an hour before the body was discovered, a 35-year-old Indian national had left the country, passing through Woodlands Checkpoint and crossing into Malaysia via the Causeway to Johor Bahru. His name was Harvinder Singh and he had been living in Singapore with his 33-year-old wife, Jasvinder Kaur. He was travelling alone.

A quick check of employment permits revealed that Jasvinder had a job at a beauty parlour. Its owner told Lim that Jasvinder had worked there until the previous week. On the previous Friday, December 11, she hadn't turned up for work. Her husband had called and said they were going back to India, and that Jasvinder wouldn't be returning to her job.

Fortunately for the investigators, the missing woman had left her water bottle at work. It still had water in it and was sitting just where its owner had put it on the previous Thursday night.

Its mouthpiece would almost certainly still be holding traces of Jasvinder's saliva, from which a DNA profile could be extracted. The bottle was bagged and sent to the HSA lab. The DNA profile it yielded would be compared to the DNA profile extracted from the blood sample that Dr Paul had drawn from the body found in the river.

While DSP Lim was at the beauty parlour, two of his officers were talking to staff at the credit company where Harvinder Singh had been working as a senior logistics co-ordinator. The man appeared to have very few friends in Singapore, his boss said. In fact there was only one: Gursharan Singh, a man he knew from his home town of Kurukshetra, around 170 km north of Delhi. Aged 27, he worked as a forklift driver.

At this point DSP Lim and his team had nothing but supposition to connect Harvinder Singh and his only known friend to the body in the river. But one person would be able to establish that link for them.

A witness

One witness had had the opportunity to get a close look at the two men caught on CCTV with the heavy suitcase – Mr Striped Sweater, the man with the Whampoa Mart shopping bag who had been captured on CCTV walking past the two men at 3.17 am.

Thanks to the supermarket's CCTV and purchasing records, the investigators were able to find him. This important witness could only confirm that he had seen the men arguing. He had no idea why.

But he had seen their faces. Moreover, because both Harvinder and Gursharan Singh were foreign workers, the police had been able to obtain their photos from immigration records. Gursharan's photo was also on file at his workplace.

When the witness was shown these photos, he confirmed they were the two men he had seen in the early hours of Saturday morning.

By Wednesday December 18 the DNA results were back: the DNA profile extracted from the lip of Jasvinder Kaur's water bottle matched the DNA profile extracted from the body found in the river.

That afternoon DSP Lim and his team swooped on Gursharan Singh, who agreed to go to CID headquarters to be interviewed. When questioned, he burst into sobs. Slowly, the story came out.

The second man tells his story

Gursharan had been at the Central Sikh Temple on Towner Road early on the morning of Friday December 11 when Harvinder arrived. Explaining that he was moving house to an apartment block nearby, he asked Gursharan for help. His wife Jasvinder was working late in the beauty parlour that day, he added, and wouldn't be able to assist him.

The pair then met at the temple at 11.30 that night and made their way to Harvinder's second storey apartment on Balestier Road.

There Gursharan waited in the first floor foyer while his friend finished packing. Half an hour later he heard a series of loud thuds as Harvinder dragged a suitcase down the stairs. The suitcase was so heavy it required the two of them to steer it.

After a few hundred metres of struggle, one wheel fell off and the bag hit the ground with a thud. Harvinder kept reassuring his friend that they didn't have far to go. His new house was close by. "Just near the canal," he said.

Gursharan wiped sweat from his forehead. They had only walked a kilometre but it felt three times as far with that suitcase.

Panting with effort, the two men hoisted the bag onto their shoulders and struggled their way through the humid December night. It was an impossibly cumbersome load to balance across two sets of shoulders. Within seconds, their burden was once again on the ground.

"What's in the bag?" Gursharan demanded, as he bent over and gasped to catch his breath again.

It was then that Harvinder broke down.

"I didn't do it on purpose," he wept. "You have to believe me, I didn't do it on purpose."

The killer's confession to his friend

The previous evening, Harvinder said, his wife had suddenly ended her phone call as he walked into their bedroom. She wouldn't tell him whom she'd been talking to. In fact she had insisted she'd just been listening to a message. But he'd heard her say, "I'll call you back."

"Give me the phone," he had demanded. She had refused and, after a struggle, he wrested it off her. The call she had terminated had been to a number in India. He had also noticed how the credit available on her pre-paid card had plunged within 24 hours. She had been talking to another man. He just knew it.

Furious, he punched her on the neck. She fell to the bed, unconscious, and he stormed out of the room. He returned later, after he had cooled down. But she was no longer unconscious. She was dead.

"Please help me," he begged Gursharan as they stood in the street, the suitcase at their feet. "Only you can help me. Help me carry the bag to the river."

Once they had reached the river, Gursharan left his friend and started walking back towards Balestier Road. He heard a splash but kept going, barely aware of where he was heading. All he could think about was the dead woman. How could Harvinder have done such a thing?

He was still close to the river when Harvinder caught up with him. He no longer had the bag with his wife's dead body in it.

"How could you kill her?" Gursharan demanded. At that moment a man in a striped shirt walked past, a plastic bag from Whampoa Mart on his arm. Pausing for a second, he stared at them.

The two men walked back to Harvinder's flat, where Gursharan noticed that the place was in disarray, with clothes scattered over a bare mattress and a powerful smell of perfume in the air. They then parted ways. Just over three hours later, at about 6.30 on the Saturday morning, Harvinder called to say he was heading for Malaysia. He was out of the country before the suitcase containing his wife's remains was spotted by a schoolboy.

Roy Lim listened attentively to Gursharan Singh's story. He wasn't yet ready to believe it or to accept that the forklift driver had already told police everything he knew about the murder.

On Thursday December 19, Gursharan was charged with Jasvinder Kaur's murder and remanded in custody for psychiatric assessment. It was exactly a week since her body had been found.

The wheels of justice turned more slowly after that. An Interpol red notice was issued for Harvinder's arrest but he appeared to have disappeared after the last sighting of him at Woodlands Checkpoint.

Finally in February 2015, the murder charge against Gursharan Singh was withdrawn, and replaced with "causing evidence of a murder offence to disappear" and "failing to report the offence to a police officer". In March Gursharan pleaded guilty to both charges. He was convicted and later sentenced to 30 months' jail.

The whole truth of what happened on the night of December 11 will never be known. Or, rather, not until Harvinder Singh is brought to justice.

The inquest raised more questions

The inquest into the death of Jasvinder Kaur, held in July 2015, raised as many questions as it answered. Coroner Marvin Bay found that 33-year-old Kaur had been murdered by her husband, Harvinder Singh, on December 11, 2013.

But the victim's head and hands were never recovered and forensic pathologist Dr George Paul was unable to supply a cause of death. In fact he could only tell investigators part of the story of what had happened to Jasvinder Kaur. She had been found between 15 and 20 hours after her death and had been placed on her back for between 5 and 8 hours after she died. He could also document eighteen external injuries, caused by two types of cutting implements and a blunt object.

But the police forensic team was unable to confirm where the victim's body had been dismembered. Nor could they recover the tools used. Moreover the crime scene specialists were surprised to find so few blood stains. In contrast to most killers, Harvinder Singh had carried out a meticulous clean-up of the murder scene.

As DSP Roy Lim told the court, hardly any traces of blood were found in the apartment or even in the toilet, which would have been the logical place to dismember the body. He agreed with the coroner's suggestion that the body might have been "bled out" before it was stuffed into the suitcase that was later dumped into Whampoa River.

"It seems to be very well organised for a crime of passion," the coroner concluded.

At the time of writing, Harvinder Singh remains one of 121 criminals on Interpol's "most wanted" list.

Case Three
LITTLE GIRL LOST

It was the case that, many said, finally helped Singaporeans rediscover their "kampong spirit" and start caring about the fate of a stranger. One morning in 2004, eight-year-old Huang Na left her home in the Pasir Panjang Wholesale Centre to walk to a local phone booth and call her mother in China. She never returned home. Within days of her disappearance, Singapore's Health Sciences Authority (HSA) forensic scientist Lim Chin Chin was already at the Pasir Panjang Wholesale Centre searching for evidence that might throw light on Huang Na's last movements. When the child's body was finally found, the scientist's evidence would be crucial to the case against the man accused of killing her.

Eight-year-old Huang Na was an unusually street-smart, independent and resourceful child. A Chinese national, she lived with her mother Huang Shuying in an upstairs flat in Singapore's vast and bustling Pasir Panjang Wholesale Centre.

The girl was in Singapore, the local newspapers would later report, because her mother was a "study mama" – the term used to describe Chinese nationals who brought their children to Singapore to secure them a brighter academic future than available back home.

It was certainly true that Huang Shuying's job at a Pasir Panjang vegetable stall could earn her much more than equivalent work at home in Putian, in the eastern mainland Chinese province of Fujian.

In fact the money in Singapore was so attractive that Huang Shuying had left her baby daughter behind to be cared for by relatives.

The "study" part of the arrangement was also working well. Huang Na had been doing well in the Primary Two class at nearby Jin Tai Primary School, winning a prize for her schoolwork. She had even told her mother she wanted to become a doctor when she grew up.

It was unclear when the child did her homework. But the way she spent the rest of her time was well documented. She was often seen wandering around the vast wholesale centre on her own, day and night, chatting to her "aunties" and "uncles" among the different fruit and vegetable stallholders. And she had her routines, spending afternoons after school with the proprietors of a mini mart on the floor below her mother's flat. Sometimes she dined alone at a nearby hawker centre. She would then return home to a shared flat where their bedroom was so tiny that it could hold only one single bed. Mother and daughter slept in it together.

Of course such detailed information about an otherwise unknown eight-year-old is only on public record because something unspeakably awful happened to her.

Huang Na vanishes

On October 10, 2004, Huang Na was being looked after by her mother's flatmate Li Xiu Qin. Her mother had flown home to visit Huang Na's baby half-sister, then eleven months old. She was due back that night. But she had been away almost a fortnight and Huang Na was missing her terribly.

It was a Sunday morning and, without school to distract her, Huang Na could think of nothing else. She wanted to hear her mother's voice. And she also needed to remind her about the two presents she'd asked for: a computerised English dictionary and a pair of sandals.

Shortly before 1 pm Huang Na headed off to the phone booth at a nearby food court – a walk of less than 500 m. She never returned.

Li Xiu Qin did not panic when the young girl didn't come home immediately. She assumed that Huang Na had stopped to chat with one of her many "aunties" in the market.

But by 2.30 pm Li had grown concerned. She began searching for the girl, starting with the market area. Finding no trace of the child, she then walked to Jin Tai Primary School, 15 minutes away by foot – just in case Huang Na had decided to go there.

Increasingly frantic, she returned home and told the three other people who shared the flat that Huang Na was missing. The four adults spent the rest of the day searching the market area: stopping any stallholders they saw, asking them if they had seen the girl.

Only one man had seen her: Took Leng How, a 22-year-old vegetable packer who worked with Huang Na's mother. But he had seen the eight-year-old at 1 pm. And it was now 9 pm.

At ten that night, Li called the police.

The story of the little girl's disappearance became a national obsession in Singapore over the ensuing three weeks.

Her mother returns

Rushing back to Singapore, Huang Shuying began searching the island personally. She showed pictures of her daughter to shoppers and passers-by in Race Course Road in the island's Little India district and in Geylang, close to the Central Business District area. She visited the tiny resort island of Sentosa, where she had once taken Huang Na. She climbed the heavily wooded slopes of Bukit Timah Hill. She even went to Mount Faber, after one of her relatives had a dream about her daughter being held on a mountain.

Huang Shuying knew that her daughter had made it as far as the food court because she had taken her call. In fact she'd had to tell her daughter that there was a problem with her flight and she wouldn't be coming back that night. Her daughter had been OK with that. A coffee shop worker had seen her at the food court, walking barefoot and wearing shorts and a denim jacket. Then – nothing.

An army of volunteers joined the weeping mother in her vigil, handing out flyers bearing Huang Na's photo. These had been printed by the owner of a recycling company who had also set up a website on unsolved crimes in Singapore. A cab company mobilised the drivers of its 17,000 taxis to look out for Huang Na. It also announced a plan to distribute posters. Meanwhile parents across Singapore looked on anxiously and kept an even closer eye on their own children.

The media covered the search in exhaustive detail, pumping Pasir Panjang stallholders for minor details about the missing girl's daily life. The newspapers also editorialised on the meaning of the outpouring of feeling for Huang Na. They interpreted it as an expression of "kampong spirit": a spirit of community and caring for one another that is generally mourned as having disappeared in modern Singapore.

Perhaps, *The Sunday Times* suggested, the local reaction to the disappearance was "uncovering for Singaporeans a side of their psyche which a people hardened by materialism and competition for space have kept repressed. This is the side which is demonstrative, spontaneous, kindly, ready to reach out to help and to comfort".

Sadly, that piece was published on October 31, the day the news broke that the child's body had been found. Volunteers stopped searching to gather, weeping, at prayer sessions.

Over at the HSA's Forensic Chemistry and Physics Lab, the scientists were doing their best to ignore the blanket media coverage of Huang Na's disappearance. Their Outram Road headquarters was less than 7 km from the Pasir Panjang centre. If the story ended with the discovery of Huang Na's body, they would be the ones to examine the child's clothing and any material gathered at the crime scene and to testify about it in any court case that followed.

Contrary to the impression given by TV shows such as CSI, government forensic scientists are not members of the police or prosecution team. Certainly, they are called in by the police and the evidence they collect will be presented by the prosecution. But their first duty is to the evidence. It is their job to communicate what that evidence is telling them – a process that is easier with a mind uncluttered by media reports.

The investigation begins

The daily news reports that the scientists were ignoring were offering a detailed and, mostly, accurate summary of the police investigation.

The detectives' initial focus was on the area of the wholesale centre where the child had disappeared. They soon established that she had last been seen alive in the company of Malaysian-born Took Leng How.

The vegetable packer was the man that Li Xiu Qin and her flatmates had spoken to at 9 pm on the night of the girl's disappearance. He was also a former flatmate of Huang Na's mother.

Despite their age difference, the 22-year-old had been described by some witnesses as a regular playmate of Huang Na's. This comment is less surprising when you note that his IQ was later revealed to be 76. This meant that his intelligence was almost low enough for him to be regarded as intellectually disabled.

The police had first spoken to Took on October 19. He had told them that he had seen Huang Na immediately after she had made the phone call to her mother. He had told the girl to go home, he said. He even offered to show police the exact spot where he had last spoken to her. By the following day, however, his story had changed, with him telling police he had actually witnessed the child being abducted.

She had been kidnapped by another trader at the centre, he said – someone who wanted to "teach (the girl's mother) a lesson".

Took claimed that he would be able to arrange for the girl to be released. But the number he needed to call was in one of his phones. One phone was at his flat; the other was at his workplace. He also agreed to a police request that he take a lie-detector test the following morning.

Four officers from the Singapore Police Criminal Investigation Department's (CID's) Special Investigation Section accompanied the packer to his flat and then to Pasir Panjang to collect the phones.

The suspect vanishes

Took offered to take the test at the CID headquarters that very same night. On the way there he told the officers he was hungry and they stopped at a 24-hour restaurant in Tanjong Pagar Railway Station. Halfway through his meal of *roti prata* and chicken curry, he excused himself to visit the establishment's toilet.

The man may have had a low IQ. Yet he was cunning. He walked out of the back door – and disappeared. His escape from Singapore displayed even more cunning – and a great deal of *sangfroid*. During his interrogation at police headquarters he had been given a visitor pass which displayed the CID emblem. He kept it on as he coolly walked through the Singapore Customs Checkpoint on the Causeway into Malaysia. Clearly he had been hoping that the customs officer on duty would think he was a police officer. And the ruse had worked.

Initial media reports on the subject of his escape had not included these embarrassing details. Instead they quoted the police as saying there had been insufficient grounds to detain him, but that his sudden disappearance had made him a suspect.

Meanwhile, within days of Huang Na's disappearance, a team of forensic scientists was already at the Pasir Panjang Wholesale Centre.

The people of Singapore were still hoping against hope that the girl would turn up safe. They were unaware that forensic officers were already looking for evidence that would be helpful if police ended up finding her body. But it was important for the forensic investigators to move quickly. Any trace evidence or biological material had to be stored and protected from deterioration.

The missing girl had last been seen with Took. So his work area had to be the obvious starting point for the forensic team. Yet there were frustratingly few other investigative leads. There was Huang Na's estimated time of disappearance. There was the report that she was wearing a denim jacket on the day she disappeared (fibres from it might be collected). And there was the fact that, according to a witness, Took had bought some mangoes close to the time of the girl's disappearance.

The knowledge of the mangoes would be useful if Huang Na were to be found dead. The presence of mango remnants in her stomach contents might suggest a link with the accused.

The investigators' immediate concern was to locate the "primary scene" – the place where the crime might have actually happened. The storeroom in Block 15 of the centre was considered a possibility. This was where Took worked. It was also where the first police on the scene had noticed what looked like bloodstains.

The investigators searched the storeroom and collected fibres from a table in the office that adjoined it. They swabbed a faint smear on the wall, collected strands of hair and swabbed stains from the carpet. Preliminary tests confirmed they were blood and urine.

On October 22, just 12 days after Huang Na's disappearance, the newspapers named Took as someone police were looking for. The manhunt that ensued soon spread to Penang – his hometown. On Saturday October 30, after more than a week on the run, Took surrendered to police.

His recapture triggered the next stage of the forensic science operation.

Took is recaptured

After he was handed over to Singapore police on that Saturday night, Took told the detectives that he had not killed Huang Na. Instead, he said, she had fallen and gone into a kind of spasm while the pair of them were playing a game of hide-and-seek in the dark. This game, he told police, involved the girl's ankles being tied together.

They often played games like this, he told the officers. He would tie up Huang Na's hands or legs and she would try to untie herself. But this time something went wrong.

He had turned the lights off and left the girl alone so she could hide in his office, he said. After a short time he returned, and began thumping on the table and calling her name to let her know he was back and ready to start looking for her. Then he heard an odd thud. Switching on the light, he saw Huang Na lying on the floor.

"Something was amiss," he told the police. "She seemed to have vomited blood because blood was trickling out from the right corner of her mouth."

"She seemed to be going into a spasm. Her eyes were wide open and there was urine all over the floor. I immediately went over to call her name but she did not reply and she was still having her spasm. I did not know what to do. I wanted to untie her ankles but I did not know how to undo the knots. I sat on the chair in a daze and looked at her…"

He had then, he said, "chopped" the back of her neck to try and wake her up.

When the girl didn't stir, Took appeared to have panicked, although he made so many rambling statements it was hard to know exactly what he was thinking.

At one point, he told his interrogators, he had been at a loss over what to do.

"My mind was totally blank. I did not know why but I put both my hands round her neck and pressed it. I pressed it momentarily with my eyes closed… After some time, I relaxed my hands. I opened my eyes and looked at her. This time I noticed her face was greyish white although her eyes were still open."

The girl then started hiccupping, Took said. "This went on for very long and it scared me."

It was then, he told police, that he stamped on her body. He stripped her and molested her with his fingers, so as to give the impression that she had been raped.

Later he packed her naked body into a cardboard box. He then loaded it on to his motorbike and drove to Telok Blangah Hill Park. Its summit features a series of semi-circular terraces that offer splendid views over Singapore and to the island of Sentosa. But Took hadn't been looking at the view as he hurled the box over the edge. His eyes had followed the box as it tumbled downwards, finally landing in a heavily wooded area below the road.

Police find the body

The morning after that interview, police were swarming over the slopes of the park. Their guide was a map Took had drawn. After half an hour of searching they found the box, 30 m below the spot where Took said he had been standing.

Sealing the box in a plastic bag, they delivered it to Block Nine of the Singapore General Hospital. Just down the road from the HSA headquarters, this building houses the Forensic Medicine Division's mortuary.

It was here that Huang Shuying made a preliminary visual identification of her daughter's body. She recognised her little girl's front teeth. One was slightly larger and set at an angle to its neighbour.

Scientific certainty was later provided by forensic dentist Dr Tan Peng Hui, who had noted that the dental development on the body appeared to be that of a child aged about eight. He had then taken an X-ray of the dead girl's jaw and compared it to dental records provided by Huang Na's school.

Both records displayed the same two fillings, the same decayed tooth, and the same 12 missing or extracted teeth. Huang Shuying also gave a blood sample, so that her DNA could be compared with a sample from the dead body.

Dr Paul Chui, a forensic pathologist and director of HSA's Centre for Forensic Medicine, performed the autopsy. He began by carefully unknotting and unwrapping each of the nine plastic bags that had encased Huang Na's body. He noted, as he did so, that they had contributed to the "remarkable state of preservation" of the body.

These bags were then given to forensic officers who had already collected the cardboard and other materials that the accused had used to pack up Huang Na's body. They had to be compared with the packing materials that had been observed at Took's workplace.

The hunt for physical evidence

The forensic officers' earlier visit to the storeroom had been a quest for evidence that might offer clues to the fate of a missing child. Now that the scientists knew Huang Na's fate, they began looking for evidence that would either support or contradict the accused's account of sealing the unfortunate child's body in one of the cardboard boxes.

The scientists were doing their work well in advance of the trial – which did not take place for another eight months. They couldn't assume that Took's account of events would feature in the evidence. The interests of justice were best served by the scientists collecting physical evidence that would – by itself – provide an articulate "silent witness" account of the demise of Huang Na.

The evidence collected by HSA forensic scientist Lim Chin Chin and her team did just that. It established a series of links between the suspect and the deceased, the murder scene and the place where the body was found.

Using forensic adhesive tape, the scientists began by collecting fibres from the office table, from a roll of adhesive tape, and from a pair of scissors and a box-cutter found in the storeroom.

Microscopic examination showed them to be denim fibres. They matched the denim in a skirt of Huang Na's – the very skirt she had been wearing when she disappeared.

DNA testing of a faint smear of blood on the wall, of a strand of hair, and of bloodstains from the office carpet produced Huang Na's DNA profile. Several fluorescing prints resembling a child's fingerprints were found on the underside of the tabletop. These prints were most likely to have been deposited after the girl had consumed mango, as mango juice exhibits florescence under special lighting.

Meanwhile the forensic team's examination of the plastic bags and tape used to wrap the dead child's body provided conclusive links to Took.

First Lim Chin Chin examined the bags in which the body had been wrapped. She noted that they were similar in class characteristics, polarised light patterns and heat-seal marks to an unused plastic bag found in the shop where Took worked.

CCTV cameras revealed that he had visited these premises late on the afternoon of October 10.

The bags, the scientist noted, were most likely to have been produced by the same machine as the bag in the shop because each machine leaves a distinctive pattern on the plastic sheet during the manufacturing process. Each heat seal, which fastens one end of the plastic bag, is unique to the machine as well.

The strips of adhesive tape used to close the carton also had a story to tell. The shape of the ending of the last strip of tape was an exact match to a roll of tape found in the storeroom. The free end of that tape also bore a fingerprint: Took's.

The carton in which the girl's body had been placed was similar to the ones found in Took's workplace. The construction of the knots used on the bags was like those usually tied by Took. The way that one bag was placed into another suggested the systematic approach of a man who was, like Took, a professional packer.

The autopsy

Meanwhile, as part of the autopsy, Dr Chui collected the child's stomach contents and sent them for testing. It is often useful to know a victim's last meal because it may throw *some* light on the time of death. Contrary to suggestions made in shows such as CSI, real-life forensic pathologists regard as arrant nonsense any estimate of time of death calculated on the basis of stomach contents. If stomach contents match independently verified information about a deceased's last meal, they can help define the "window" for the time of death. But that is it. Any statement about time of death that is based on the state of an individual's stomach contents – or the absence of them – is, at best, a "guesstimate".

Given that the accused had bought mangoes just before Huang Na disappeared, the forensic team was especially interested in this sample of partially digested food and gastric acids. As expected, it was found to contain mango residue, providing yet another link with Took. This later added weight to the prosecution's theory that he had used the mangoes as bait to lure the child into the storeroom.

Dr Chui certified the child's cause of death as acute airway occlusion or blockage. It was his opinion that this could have been caused by Took smothering her by covering her mouth and nose with his hand.

The expert identified five injuries on the girl's face, just near her mouth. All of them could be regarded as consistent with the forcible covering of the mouth and nose with a hand. This process, as he would later testify in court, was enough to obstruct the air passages of the nose and mouth, and cause death.

Dr Chui noted injuries to the scalp, caused either by the head banging against some flat hard object or something heavy hitting the head. He said that someone kicking the deceased's head or stomping on it could also have caused these injuries. And there were injuries to the deceased's right arm and left thigh. It was impossible to say, from his examination, whether or not the child had been sexually assaulted. But, as he would explain in the trial, lack of physical evidence on the body at the time of autopsy did not automatically mean that no sexual assault had taken place.

Prosecutors always hope that a forensic pathologist's report will provide clear physical evidence to support their version of how a victim's death has occurred. In this case, they didn't believe Took's story that there had been some kind of accident.

Certainly Dr Chui's findings could be taken as support for their belief that Took had killed the child so she could not report him for having sexually assaulted her. This was not a case, they believed, of him panicking after the child had had some kind of accident.

During the trial, which opened on July 11, 2005, the prosecution alleged that Took had used an offer of mangoes and a game of hide-and-seek to lure Huang Na into the storeroom where she was sexually assaulted and smothered. As her body went limp, Took had stamped on her and kicked her, before wrapping her in nine layers of plastic bags and stuffing her body into a cardboard box.

Dr Chui's findings, along with Took's chilling re-enactment of the crime, made the prosecution case look very strong indeed.

The defence lawyer on the attack

But when Took's defence lawyer, the late Subhas Anandan, started cross-examining the forensic pathologist, he did an excellent job of unearthing areas where Dr Chui's opinions could also be used to support the defence case that Huang Na had died, in some way, accidentally.

On cross-examination by the defence counsel, Dr Chui agreed that it was possible that the "airway occlusion" that killed Huang Na could have happened as a result of suffocation – if for example the child had been put into a plastic bag while she was still alive. He also agreed that it could have happened if the child had choked on her own blood or vomit.

The defence had raised the possibility that Huang Na had suffered some sort of fit or seizure. Dr Chui said that children usually did not develop fits without any medical or family history. He also thought it was unlikely that the girl's bumping of her head against a table could have triggered an onset of fits. Yet he had to agree that he could not detect whether or not there had been bleeding in the child's brain because decomposition had caused it to liquefy.

The expert accepted that Took's description in his statement, of spasms, urinating and hiccupping, actually matched the symptoms of a seizure. He conceded that the bruise on the girl's tongue (which the autopsy revealed) could have been caused by the deceased biting her own tongue during a fit.

He also agreed that it was possible that the victim's tongue could have slipped backwards due to a seizure, causing airway obstruction.

But just because other explanations were "possible" didn't make them fact.

The re-enactment

Meanwhile any uncertainty about Took's actions on the day of October 10, 2004, was banished by the screening of the video of the accused man re-enacting his role in Huang Na's death.

In this chilling video, shot by police after his arrest, the man was seen showing police how he had wrapped the child's body in a series of nine plastic bags.

Using a dummy of a child, he was seen showing police how he pressed his fingers on Huang Na's neck. He also demonstrated how he "chopped" the girl on the back of the neck three times. Finally he was shown stamping on the dummy's head, just as he had told the police he'd done to his former playmate. As he did it, he was heard to say, in Mandarin: "Just like that, just like that." Finally he was shown demonstrating how he had tied Huang Na's feet with raffia.

Certainly, as his own defence lawyer Subhas Anandan pointed out in his memoir *The Best I Could*, this violent demonstration did a lot of harm to his "not guilty" plea.

Would he have taken part in such a video if he were innocent?

Subhas was convinced that his client was mentally retarded and therefore highly vulnerable to police suggestions.

"When we asked him," the lawyer wrote, "he accused the police of persuading him to do it. Ah Took also said that he was asked to do specific things for the recording but couldn't remember if he really did them to Huang Na. (Of course his actions on the video matched his initial statement to police.)

"Ah Took himself felt that if he cooperated and did what the police told him to do, they would certainly help reduce his charge."

So why didn't the accused man simply take the stand and explain that, for example, the dead girl had suffocated during a seizure?

According to Subhas, his client was in no state to be able to give coherent evidence. Two months after his arrest, he had changed the story he gave to police. He had had nothing to do with the death of Huang Na, he told the psychiatrist who was assessing him for the defence. Instead "three Chinese men" had entered the storeroom. They were the ones, he said, who had tied the deceased up and strangled her.

By this point, the defence lawyer wrote, his client was making little sense.

"From the instructions he gave us, we could not make head or tail of what he was saying. He was full of delusions by then."

The psychiatrists' debate

Took's mental state was the subject of much argument during the trial. It was Subhas' argument that his client was suffering from schizophrenia at the time of the offence (and afterwards) and that this qualified him for the defence of diminished responsibility.

He called Dr R Nagulendran, a psychiatrist in private practice, to explain.

Took, the psychiatrist told the court, displayed three key symptoms of schizophrenia. The first was "grossly disorganised or catatonic behaviour". The "irrational, motiveless and unplanned" murder of Huang Na was a symptom of this. The second symptom was "emotional flattening" where a patient's moods were not a good fit for the situation he was in. As an example of this, Dr Nagulendran cited Took's failure to display remorse or regret for having killed a little girl who was close to him. The psychiatrist also cited a third symptom: the "delusions" that Took was harbouring in his account of the "three Chinese men" who supposedly killed Huang Na. (The prosecutor preferred to give this story a simpler label. He called it "lies".)

The prosecution called Dr G Sathyadevan, a senior consultant psychiatrist at the Institute of Mental Health, to rebut the defence's psychiatrist. Dr Sathyadevan argued that, in order to decide if Took was suffering from schizophrenia, it was important to analyse his conduct before, at the time of, and after the alleged offence.

The specialist said he had never seen a case where the patient became mentally ill suddenly at the time of the offence: the patient would normally display some signs of disturbance, such as social or occupational dysfunction, beforehand.

He also argued that there was no basis to conclude that the accused's acts on October 10, 2004, were "irrational, motiveless and inexplicable". On the contrary, the psychiatrist noted Took's ability to efficiently dispose of his victim's body (and to plan his escape to Malaysia) as inconsistent with the condition of schizophrenia, where the patient's state of mind would be disorganised.

The crime scene evidence that Lim Chin Chin presented was the only prosecution evidence that the defence did not dispute.

Without it, Subhas Anandan might have had much more room to move in contesting the state's case.

As it was, he could contest the notion that Took had been responsible for Huang Na's death. He could argue that the man was mentally ill. But he could not dispute the fact that his client had coolly and methodically packed up and disposed of the body of a young girl who used to call him "uncle".

HSA's efficient crime scene work showcased the work of a man who was nearly as well organised as the people investigating him.

In fact Judge Lai Kew Chai made a point of commenting on Took's planning abilities in his judgement.

Specifically, he drew attention to Took's awareness of closed circuit TV cameras at his workplace. He noted the fact that Took used the rubbish dump in Block 16 to dispose of his victim's clothing, because there were no cameras covering that area. In Block 15, where he worked, cameras overlooked the rubbish area.

The judge used this example to indicate that he did not accept the defence argument that Took was suffering from schizophrenia at the time of the crime and could therefore use the defence of diminished responsibility.

"His conduct after the killing was clearly the product of a cool and calculated mind," he said.

On August 26, 2005, Judge Lai found Took guilty of the murder of Huang Na and sentenced him to death.

Took then appealed.

The Court of Appeal upheld his sentence on January 25, 2006. But it was a rare split decision.

The issue behind this very unusual case of divided judicial opinion was the interpretation of the forensic medical evidence.

Chief Justice Yong Pung How and Justice Chao Hick Tin both upheld the conviction, but Justice Kan Ting Chiu disagreed, arguing that the prosecution had failed to prove their case beyond reasonable doubt.

While the three appeal judges had agreed that Took Leng How had not been suffering from any mental disorder, they disagreed on the conclusions that could be drawn from the forensic evidence about the cause of Huang Na's death.

The Chief Justice and Justice Chao accepted Dr Chui's finding that Huang Na had suffocated, most probably as a result of Took pressing his hand over her mouth and nose.

Justice Kan, on the other hand, was of the view that there was not enough conclusive evidence.

"The absence of injuries to the nose, when bruises to other regions were present, raised a doubt whether there was smothering of the nose ... It was a serious doubt the Prosecution had to remove if it were to prove its case, and the Prosecution had not done that," he wrote. He said that there was "nothing inherently unbelievable" in the convicted man's description of the supposed "seizure" that Huang Na suffered.

Justice Chao disagreed, describing the idea that Huang Na died from a seizure as "at best, a possibility that was unsupported by any tangible evidence or basis".

It was two judges against one. The death sentence stood.

On October 23, 2006, it was announced that Took's plea for clemency to Singapore President S R Nathan had failed.

Took was taken to the gallows on November 3, 2006.

Lawyer Subhas Anandan died in January 2015. He went to his grave believing that his former client had been mentally ill. The chapter in his memoir devoted to this case is entitled, "The man who should not have been hanged".

Case Four
DEATH ON FATHER'S DAY

When Eu Lim Hoklai saw another man leaving Yu Hong Jin's flat at seven in the morning, it was the last straw. He told his mistress he was finished with her and would pass on his half-share in her massage parlour to someone else. But Yu Hong Jin told Eu he wasn't going anywhere before he paid her S$30,000 as "compensation for ending our relationship". The pair arranged a meeting to sort out their break-up. An hour later Yu Hong Jin was found dead on a bed in her massage parlour. Eu Lim Hoklai was lying on the floor beside her, bleeding from a series of wounds to the stomach. Had he killed her in self-defence after she attacked him? Or had he gone to their meeting with murder on his mind? Only the forensic evidence could answer this question.

According to his three daughters, Eu Lim Hoklai was a kind, generous and gentle man who never raised his voice, let alone his fists, to his daughters – even when chastising them for bad behaviour.

The 52-year-old seafood stall owner was equally kind, generous and tolerant towards 29-year-old Yu Hong Jin, a masseuse from China who had been his mistress for more than a year.

Given that Eu was also a married man, this was a situation replete with potential problems. His wife of 28 years, Ng Mooi Huang, was the mother of their three daughters, the eldest of whom was married and living with her husband in their own flat. His wife was also his partner in the family seafood business, a *tse char* stall, to use the Hokkien word for a food stall offering a selection of cooked meals. A successful enterprise that had been running for 22 years, it made the couple a monthly profit of between S$3000 and S$4000, from which they drew a combined salary of S$2200.

Unbeknownst to Ng, her husband's mistress had stepped into his life one morning in March 2005. Eu had just been to his barber, whose shop in the Ang Mo Kio district was a few doors away from a massage parlour called Man Tian Ti. As he was walking past, Yu Hong Jin had stepped out and offered him a massage. He accepted. And their relationship began.

A "study mama"

A "study mama", Yu had come with her son to Singapore in 2002, leaving her ex-husband and family behind so that her son could have the benefit of a Singapore education. As one of the island nation's 7000-odd "*pei du* mamas" or "study mamas" – women who get a special visa to come to Singapore so they can enrol their child in a school – she became part of a minority that was the object of a great deal of stereotyping and moralising in the local press. One newspaper article of the time may have played a role in this process by describing study mamas as "typecast as having questionable morals, including stealing the husbands of Singapore women".

It certainly seems to be the case that some "study mamas" worked as massage therapists, to make ends meet. This should have been no surprise, or cause for moral judgement. Not only were they not eligible for work permits until they had been in Singapore for a year, but there were restrictions on the work they were allowed to do. Given that the purpose of their stay – and visa – was to look after their children, they were barred from night work in bars and clubs.

73

Like many "study mamas", Yu was short of money. Her new boyfriend was kind and supportive and always lent a sympathetic ear to her problems. He drove a Mercedes Benz car and had begun providing her with significant financial support. She may very well have seen him as a sugar daddy.

He was certainly starting to behave like one. In March 2006, when she decided to start a new massage parlour in Ang Mo Kio, Eu put S$8500 into her new business. She named it Feng Ye Beauty and Healthcare Centre.

"Whenever she was short of money, I would give her whatever amount of money she asked for," Eu would later say. When she wanted to visit her family back in the Chinese city of Fuqing, he bought her the air tickets.

His generosity also extended to paying the rent on her flat, although he was never permitted to stay there. It wasn't that she was sheltering her son from her love life. Her ten-year-old was actually living elsewhere with a relative to whom his mother was paying $800 a month for upkeep and tutoring. As would later become clear, she had her own reasons for keeping Eu away from her flat.

Yu's business

Once Yu Hong Jin had started her own business, the couple began seeing each other more often. Eu went to the Ang Mo Kio market every morning to buy seafood for his family food stall – a journey that took him within a few blocks of Feng Ye.

Every second day, Eu would drop by the massage parlour, parking his Mercedes Benz outside before helping his mistress open up the shop. As well as sweeping the shop and doing housekeeping chores for her, he would buy her breakfast and pay for her shopping. He would then head for the family business in Tampines, twenty minutes' drive away.

Their connection was close, with Yu Hong Jin sharing her personal and business worries with her older lover. But the relationship itself remained secret from Eu's wife and daughters.

It is obvious why. His wife in particular would have been unimpressed by the fact that the money she was earning was ending up in the pockets of her husband's mistress.

Eu wasn't a calculating man. He had not been educated past Primary 3 and, as would later be revealed, he had a lower than average IQ. He may have been ill-equipped to tell the difference between a woman who truly loved him and a woman who saw him as a walking ATM.

Another man in her life

At seven in the morning on June 14, 2006, Eu saw his lover leaving her apartment with another man in tow. When he confronted Yu Hong Jin about this, she denied it, although the man had parked his blue lorry in her apartment block's car park.

During the resulting argument, she continued to insist that she hadn't slept with the man. In fact she got so angry that she slapped Eu and then punched him on the head. He did not retaliate, although this wasn't the first time that she'd hit him. Previously she had lashed out at him when he had tried to talk her out of visiting the local karaoke lounge and getting drunk.

This time, something snapped for Eu. He wasn't going to play second fiddle to another man. He was leaving, he told his mistress. And he was taking his S$8500 stake in her massage parlour with him. He would simply transfer it to someone else. Furthermore, she owed him S$5000 and he wanted it back.

Yu Hong Jin wasn't having any of that. She wasn't going to allow their relationship to end that way. If he were serious about leaving, he would be paying her some compensation for the privilege. And if he didn't want to pay up, then his family would be learning all about what sort of a husband and father he really was.

The argument continued

Their argument lasted most of that Wednesday morning. They rehashed it the next day. And the next.

Eu continued to beg his lover to break up with the man she'd spent the night with. Meanwhile she moved from denying everything to telling him he had no right to interfere with her freedom. She wasn't going to be tied down.

Eu ended up giving in on that point. This was reasonable, given that he himself had another woman: his wife. But the pair kept arguing and Yu Hong Jin "continued to show a long face", as Eu put it, whenever he visited her in her shop. She also kept demanding money: S$30,000 "compensation for ending our relationship".

That Saturday morning, Eu took both Yu Hong Jin and her son to the market, as was their routine. As they walked, she asked him to meet her at her shop the following morning at about 10 am "to settle the matter once and for all". Keen to sort things out, he agreed. They'd only been arguing for a few days but the situation was getting to him. At night he'd been barely sleeping. By day he could think of little else.

How was he going to get out of this with his marriage – and the family finances – intact? He didn't have that sort of money. He was also terrified that Yu would tell his wife. He had to sort something out.

Unsurprisingly, he had been unable to hide his anxiety and upset from his two daughters living at home. He had to tell them something. So he came up with the best sort of lie – something that was partially true.

Eu confessed to his daughters that he had bought a share in a massage parlour business and that he was troubled because his partner owed him money. He even drove them past Feng Ye and showed them the rented flat where Yu lived. Of course he referred to her as his "business partner", not his mistress.

Just one more restless night to get through and it would be Sunday. Then Eu's heart sank as he remembered that Sunday was June 18. Father's Day. His daughters always liked to make a fuss of him on that day. How on earth was he going to get away from them to sort things out with Yu?

"Bad" fish: an excuse to go out alone

His daughters, unknowingly, presented him with an escape. That morning they offered to do his daily trip to the market. They wanted to treat their father to the novelty of a sleep-in before they took him out for a family dim sum lunch. It would be a double celebration: Father's Day and an early celebration for his 53rd birthday, the following Wednesday June 21.

The fish they brought home from the market was perfectly fine. But as they handed it over, Eu made a point of inspecting it closely.

Wrinkling his nose, he frowned. Some of this wasn't the best his fishmonger could do, he told them. He would take it back, and get the man to exchange it.

His daughters watched him drive off in the direction of the market. In fact he was driving straight to the massage parlour. He had told the girls that, after exchanging the fish, he would collect their older sister from the flat she shared with her husband, and bring her home. Then they would all go to the restaurant together.

He never made it.

A call for help

Shortly before 11 am, Eu's middle daughter Eu Sui Lin had been trying to call her father, but the phone repeatedly rang out. At 10.56 am, he called back. "Rescue me, please. Come quickly," he gasped. He managed to tell her he was at Feng Ye. Then he hung up.

The girl remembered the massage parlour her father had shown her a few days earlier. Hailing a cab, she headed for Ang Mo Kio. But when she got to Feng Ye, the front door was locked and she could see no other way to get in.

Panic-striken, she rushed into the next-door shop, a hairdressing salon, to ask if there might be a connecting door between the two businesses. There wasn't. So she called the police.

By then it was 11.14 am. A few minutes later, her mother and younger sister arrived.

Desperate to get into the massage parlour, Ng Mooi Huang sought help from a couple who lived upstairs. They let her into the building via a back door, and she made her way into the massage parlour.

The establishment had three curtained massage cubicles. The first two were empty. Tearing aside the curtains of the third, the worried wife found herself staring at the body of a woman lying on her back on a massage table. She was fully clothed, but there was a knife in her hand. She looked dead.

Hearing moans, Ng looked down to see her husband lying on the carpeted floor. His clothes were bloodied, but he was still alive.

The sound of sirens sent her rushing to the front door, which she opened to admit the police and her two daughters. In the meantime paramedics had also arrived. Examining Yu Hong Jin, they pronounced her dead at 11.41 am.

Eu, on the other hand, was still semi-conscious, despite nine deep stab wounds in his abdomen. Minutes later he was on his way to Tan Tock Seng Hospital.

He was soon in an operating theatre, where surgeons began stitching up the nine wounds in his abdomen. He had been extraordinarily lucky. The knife found clutched in the dead woman's hand had penetrated his abdominal cavity in four places. Yet he had sustained no injuries to any of his internal organs: a fact that medical staff established by, literally, "opening him up" to check. He was left with a long line of stitches down his middle after an operation that most doctors might describe as unnecessary surgery. The usual practice is to do a scan. If no internal bleeding is detected, surgeons will simply close the wounds and continue to monitor them.

Eu was well enough for police to interview him in his hospital bed the next morning.

"She attacked me," Eu said

In that first interview he told police that he had gone to meet Yu to "sort things out" but their discussion had rapidly descended into a screaming match. When he arrived, she had asked him if he had brought the S$30,000 "separation fee" he owed her. If he didn't pay, she threatened, she would tell his wife all about their relationship.

Eu told her he didn't care. She could tell his wife whatever she wanted. He had no money to give her, but he would not pursue her for the return of the S$8500 he had put into her massage parlour business. And he would not be coming back to the massage parlour again.

When he turned to leave, he told police, he felt her hand snake around him from behind, lifting the front of his T-shirt. He then felt a sharp, intense pain as she stabbed him in the stomach.

He fought back, grabbing his former lover's neck, and pushing her against the wall as he tried to wrest the knife from her grip. As they struggled, he heard her scream in pain. He assumed at that point that the knife, by then slippery with blood, had also stabbed her. He didn't know if it was just a superficial cut or a deep wound. He then used his right hand to grab her neck from behind and push her on to the massage bed.

"I heard her make a noise as if she wanted to talk or say something," Eu told the police.

"Her legs were kicking my right leg. I then used more strength on her neck with both my hands as she was kicking me. I wanted to make her unconscious as I was also in pain."

Desperate to render his lover unconscious so she would stop stabbing him, he wrapped both his hands around her neck. As he did so, he felt more sharp stabbing pains in his stomach as Yu continued to wield her knife. Blood began drenching his clothes.

Throughout the struggle he could hear his mobile phone ring repeatedly. He could see it was his daughter. Later, freeing his left hand for a second, he needed only to jab at the phone with his finger to make it call back. Gasping out his "rescue me" message, he threw the phone on to the massage bed. Then he returned to squeezing his former lover's neck with both hands.

At that point his memory of the morning became hazy. He said his stomach was in agony. He was sure this meant that he was dying. Of course he wasn't. It was his mistress who was dying. He was merely passing out from the pain.

Later he remembered coming to, with someone (probably a paramedic) slapping his face and calling him "uncle". By that time, his former lover was dead.

Early in the afternoon, Eu gave another statement in which he clarified what had happened. Hong Jin, he emphasised, had started the fatal fight.

"She was trying to stab me with a knife first. She stabbed me a few times. I squeezed her neck trying to stop her from stabbing me further. I was unable to snatch the knife away from her. I did not intend to kill her. That's all."

But was it?

His family certainly believed him. His youngest brother, his three daughters and his son-in-law had been at the hospital all day but were not allowed into his room while he was being questioned by police.

Charged with murder

At 3 pm a special bedside hearing was convened and Eu was formally charged with the murder of his mistress. Only a Hokkien-English translator and his lawyer, high-profile local criminal lawyer Subhas Anandan, were allowed into the room.

There was no doubt that Eu had caused his mistress's death. But had events really unfolded in the way that he described?

Eu's youngest brother, 42-year-old Eu Hock Chye, considered his older brother incapable of murder. And, as he told a reporter, the rest of the family agreed.

"He is such a gentle person that he doesn't even scold his children," he said. "He dropped out of school at a very young age so he could work to support the family. He even put me through school."

Eight days later, when Eu made his first court appearance, his brother and daughters were there again to offer moral support.

Once again his sibling spoke to reporters, emphasising that Eu had the full support of his family, including his wife. Apparently she did not believe her husband had been having an affair and was paying for his lawyer.

A 10-year-old chooses his mother's burial clothes

In the meantime, Yu Hong Jin was quietly laid to rest. Responsibility for her funeral arrangements had to be taken by her ten-year-old son, who had chosen both her coffin and her final outfit. The pink tank top and cardigan, white lace-trimmed shorts and pink high heels that he selected were an outfit she had set aside for "a special occasion".

The woman's wake was an especially sad affair. Delayed a few days until her ex-husband and brother could get passports to make the trip, it was held at a car park next to the Ang Mo Kio apartment block where she had rented a room. The only mourners were her ex-husband, brother and sister-in law.

None of her friends or work colleagues turned up, possibly scared away by the crackdown on mainland Chinese massage parlour workers that was launched in the wake of publicity about the murder. In one week, 29 parlours had been forced to close down and 37 were found to have hired foreign workers illegally. Police arrested 77 foreigners, including Chinese, Malaysians and Thais for immigration or employment offences, while 18 "study mamas" lost their jobs.

The trial

Almost a year passed before Singapore's public prosecutor was ready to formally order Eu to stand trial.

Emotions ran high during that preliminary hearing, in which the prosecution laid out the bones of its case, listing the 35 witnesses it would call. Eu's wife and three daughters, by then aged 17, 23 and 28, were included.

Eu was in obvious distress, calling out the words "I did not kill her" in his native Hokkien dialect when the charges were read out. When his wife walked into the courtroom to confirm her police statement, Eu began sobbing. He continued to weep as his daughters were called to enter the courtroom. Trying hard to control their own emotions, they all avoided looking at him, until his youngest daughter broke down.

When the hearing ended and the presiding magistrate allowed Eu's family members to approach the dock and talk to him, his daughters rushed over to embrace him. His wife did not join them.

The job of the court would be to establish exactly what had happened. If Eu were telling the truth, then he could be judged guilty only of "culpable homicide". This meant that Yu Hong Jin's death was not the result of a planned assault by him but had occurred as the result of a sudden fight, or of him defending himself. In that case he would escape with his life, although he would receive a jail sentence of at least ten years.

But if he were lying, and, as the prosecution was suggesting, he had strangled his mistress in cold blood because he was jealous of her new lover and afraid that she would expose their affair to his family, then he would hang.

It was clear, even at that preliminary hearing, that the prosecution would be relying on forensic science evidence to prove its case against Eu. Its star witness would be Health Sciences Authority (HSA) senior forensic scientist Lim Chin Chin. Lim had a masters degree in chemistry and a big reputation as a crime scene reconstruction expert.

In the meantime Eu's defence lawyers, Subhas Anandan and his colleague (and nephew) Sunil Sudheesan had commissioned an independent forensic expert. They hoped he would be able to provide a different interpretation of the crime scene.

When the trial finally opened on January 21, 2008, its first two days were spent hearing thirty different witnesses fill in the details of the alleged murder and the affair that preceded it. Eu would testify later. But the statement that he had made to police from his hospital bed was also admitted as evidence.

First the court heard Eu's wife and daughters give their accounts of the fateful morning of Father's Day. These four, along with three of Eu's employees at the seafood stall, all testified that they had never seen the knife that had been used to stab both Eu and his former mistress. Interestingly, Eu had said it was one of his. He said he had given it to his mistress weeks earlier because the knives in her kitchen were no good. Meanwhile the hairdresser from the shop next door told the court that she hadn't heard any commotion in the massage parlour that day.

All this testimony was mere prologue. The main act was going to be a battle of the forensic experts, with the verdict – and Eu's life – hinging on the opinion that Judge Kan Ting Chiu found most credible.

The prosecution's forensic scientists testify

The prosecution had assembled an array of forensic scientists to support their argument that Eu had been lying when he told police that Yu Hong Jin had stabbed him first and that he had acted in self-defence. The prosecution's argument would be that events had unfolded in the reverse order. Eu, they would say, had strangled his lover in a jealous rage. He had then stabbed her and "arranged" the scene by stabbing himself and placing the knife in the dead woman's hand. After that he had passed out from the pain of his self-inflicted injuries.

The defence's expert, of course, would be presenting evidence that suggested Eu had been telling the truth.

Frustratingly for the Singapore public, which was agog at the case, the hearing was then adjourned. Everyone would have to wait two whole months to hear the first of the forensic scientists give evidence.

The first scientist to testify was HSA's senior consultant forensic pathologist, Dr Wee Keng Poh. It was his job to examine a victim's body to establish the cause and manner of death. In this case, given that there were two clashing narratives about the death, his evidence was going to be especially important.

As is the best practice in forensic pathology, he had visited the massage parlour to inspect Yu Hong Jin's body *in situ* before carrying out the autopsy back at the mortuary of HSA's Forensic Medicine Division.

In the report he wrote after the autopsy, Wee had certified the cause of Yu Hong Jin's death as "acute haemorrhage due to stab wounds (in the) abdomen and asphyxia due to manual strangulation". He had explained that the woman had "died as a result of two different modes of injuries – that of being stabbed in the abdomen and strangulated (compression of the neck) by the assailant's hands".

Testifying in court, he elaborated on those findings, explaining that, in his view, the deceased would have died from the stab wounds in her abdomen within one to two hours. Meanwhile it would only have taken between three and five minutes of strangulation to cause her death.

Wee's view was that the strangulation had occurred before the stabbing: a direct contradiction of Eu's account.

He concluded this, he explained, because there were "very marked changes" around Yu's face and internal neck structures, because she had minimal defensive injuries and because there was minimal blood spillage outside her abdomen.

Eu's story had been that he and Yu Hong Jin had been standing as they struggled for possession of the knife. The weapon had then penetrated his mistress's abdomen as he was struggling to disarm her.

Wee disputed this version of events. After looking at a photograph of the deceased, showing mucus flowing from her mouth, the forensic pathologist concluded that the deceased was strangled in an upright position – and not lying down, the position in which she was found. He also believed it was "very likely" that Eu's mistress had been lying on her back when she was stabbed in the abdomen.

Wee based his theory on the fact that about 400 cc of blood (about one and one-third cups) was found in the victim's peritoneal cavity: the space in the abdomen bound by a thin membrane that contains the intestines, the stomach and the liver. If she had been stabbed while she was standing up, he believed, there would have been more blood outside the body than the relatively minimal amount found smudged on the wall of the cubicle.

Did this evidence damage Eu? His defence lawyers did not seem unduly worried by it.

The crucial point they took from Wee's testimony was that he had agreed that there was, in fact, a struggle between their client and his mistress and that the stab wounds on the dead woman could have been caused in that struggle.

The prosecution, after all, would have preferred a report that suggested that Eu had murdered his former mistress in cold blood. Wee had not given them that.

Furthermore, as the defence lawyers would remind the judge in their closing submissions, "Dr Wee had agreed that the lack of defensive injuries did not mean that there was no struggle." In fact, in this particular case, there were injuries that could be classified as "defensive" on both Eu and his dead mistress: the scratches on his face and the cut on her finger.

During cross-examination, defence lawyer Subhas Anandan had also asked if the deceased's stab wounds could possibly have been self-inflicted. He had been delighted to hear Wee answer that it was, in theory, possible.

Of course Subhas did not believe that Yu Hong Jin had stabbed herself. But it was the prosecution's theory that, after stabbing and strangling his mistress in cold blood, Eu had stabbed his own body, in order to fake evidence for his story that she had attacked him. The lawyer was merely scoring a point in advance. If it was "possible" but "fanciful" that Yu Hong Jin had stabbed herself, then it was also possible, but equally fanciful, that Eu could have stabbed himself.

The prosecution's next witness, HSA forensic pathologist Dr Paul Chui, another senior consultant forensic pathologist, had been called to Tan Tock Seng Hospital on the afternoon of Sunday June 25 after Eu had been rushed to the hospital by ambulance.

By then Eu was already being treated by doctors who had noted that he had nine stab wounds in his abdomen. The doctors had also recorded the fact that four of these wounds were very deep. So deep that they had penetrated the three layers of muscle that comprise the 5-7cm thick abdominal wall and entered the peritoneal cavity. But the wounds were not so deep as to damage any major organs.

Might Eu's injuries have been self-inflicted?

Chui was asked to examine these injuries to determine whether the man's injuries could have been self-inflicted.

He was also asked to look for defensive injuries, which were minimal: a fact that the prosecution would make much of. The forensic pathologist documented two dried scratch abrasions, each between 1 cm and 1.5 cm long, on Eu's right cheek. Both were possible fingernail scratches. There were also two tiny scratches, 3-4 mm each, on his left thumb.

The abdominal wounds, he noted, were serious and consistent with having been caused by the knife that the dead woman had been found clutching. This knife, the only knife involved, was examined for DNA. The DNA of both the accused and the deceased were found on its handle. The DNA of the accused was also found on its blade.

The fact that Eu's DNA was on the knife handle was consistent with his insistence that he had wrestled with his mistress over it, thereby stabbing her. But, after her death, might he also have used this knife on himself?

Significantly Chui had not committed himself to either the prosecution or the defence position in his written report. He had merely stated that, in his opinion, the position and nature of the abdominal wounds "(did) not preclude self-infliction" as their cause. That didn't mean much. It would be difficult to imagine a stomach wound that could not be described in this way.

Nevertheless his testimony gave some support to the defence view that Eu's injuries were far too serious to be self-inflicted.

In the witness box, Chui described the stab wounds as "rare" and "exceptional" and said Eu was "lucky" not to have sustained any organ damage. He explained that 75 per cent of stab wounds to the abdomen end up penetrating the abdominal cavity. And of those that pierce the abdominal cavity, 75 per cent damage an organ.

At this point, defence lawyer Subhas Anandan stepped in to ask the obvious question. How could Eu, who had a below-average IQ, have risked stabbing himself so deeply when the danger of hitting major organs was so high?

Eu's low IQ key to his defence

Eu's low intelligence and Primary 3 education would continue to be a key plank in his defence. Take his first account of the events of Sunday, given to police when he was still recovering from surgery and was drowsy and drug-affected. It would have to be considered remarkable – or impossible – that he would be able, especially in this state and with his low intelligence and lack of medical knowledge, to give an account of events that was totally false but still consistent with the medical evidence.

How, if he had made up that first account in a drugged state, would he be able to reproduce it during several interviews? And then, two years later, when he would spend three days on the witness stand during his trial, how would he be able to repeat it without getting mixed up. Did he really have the brains to fabricate additional evidence that was not in his original police statements but was still consistent with the forensic evidence?

The next prosecution expert to take the stand was local star forensic scientist Lim Chin Chin. Her crime scene analysis contradicted Eu's account in almost every detail.

Like her HSA colleague Dr Wee Keng Poh, Lim said that her findings suggested that the dead woman had been lying down when (and after) she was stabbed (as opposed to standing up, as Eu had said).

Firstly, the bloodstains on the front of her camisole were localised, and corresponded exactly to the stab wounds on her body. There were no downward vertical stains, as you might expect if she had been standing up. There were also no "secondary transfers" from the bloodstains on her camisole to her blouse. This suggested that the position of her clothing, with her blouse pushed up higher than the camisole, remained unchanged. Unlikely, in the case of a struggle, you would think.

Lim Chin Chin drew attention to the lack of defensive injuries on the dead woman, except for a single superficial cut on her right third finger. This suggested that she put up little or no struggle when she was stabbed. Lim hypothesised that the woman could have been caught by surprise and quickly overwhelmed during the stabbing. Or she could have been in a weak state and unable to resist. (In Eu Lim Hoklai's version of events, it was of course he who was surprised by his ex-lover attacking him.)

The scientist also drew attention to the fact that the dead woman was found holding the knife in an unusual, awkward way. To her, this suggested that Eu had placed it there.

"Her thumb was not curled around the handle in the opposite direction as the four flexed fingers (which is the usual way a knife is held)," she said. "Instead the victim's thumb and fingers were on the same side of the handle."

It was also her view that some, if not all, of Eu's wounds were self-inflicted. The fact that the nine wounds were all clustered within his right flank and the left front abdominal region suggested this, she said. As did the absence of slash wounds on his abdomen and the lack of defence injuries on his forearms.

Before Eu Lim Hoklai's defence lawyers could call their expert forensic witness to refute any of this damning-sounding evidence, the accused man himself was summoned to the witness box.

A bizarre re-enactment

His appearance signalled the courtroom's temporary transformation into a theatre, as the accused was invited to perform a re-enactment of the crime.

During this interlude, a model of the massage parlour cubicle, complete with a massage bed, was set up in the courtroom. Eu went through his actions on the morning of Sunday June 18, with a dummy playing the role of Yu Hong Jin.

Deputy Public Prosecutor Winston Cheng prompted Eu to demonstrate how, after Yu had stabbed him, he had spun around and pushed his mistress against a wall. Eu then showed the court how he had gripped the woman's neck with one hand while grabbing her right hand, which was wielding the knife, with the other.

He also showed the court how he had shoved Yu after she had lifted his T-shirt and stabbed him in the abdomen. Holding the dummy's neck with his right hand, he demonstrated how he had used his left hand to raise his T-shirt and see the damage the knife had done to his stomach. He said it was then that his lover had stabbed him again, with four quick plunges of the knife into his stomach. He had then begun strangling her until he ended up pushing her back on the bed. He had continued to squeeze her neck until she stopped struggling. He had subsequently blacked out.

DPP Cheng then suggested to Eu that this version of events was a fabrication, concocted to explain the absence of cuts to his T-shirt. But Eu vehemently denied it. In fact the prosecutor was wrong when he said the T-shirt was undamaged. There were four small cuts on it.

These cuts might, as the defence's expert would later suggest, have represented stabbing attempts. Lim acknowledged this possibility, although she also suggested they might have been caused by medical staff treating him. The staff were never questioned, however, so the cause of these cuts was never confirmed.

The defence's Australian expert witness

The final witness was the defence's expert, Australian forensic pathologist Dr Johan Duflou. Now in private practice, he was then the chief forensic pathologist in the New South Wales government's Department of Forensic Medicine. He continues to be an Associate Professor at the University of New South Wales.

Duflou's evidence was a welcome return to a more sober analysis of the case. The Australian forensic pathologist agreed with the prosecution's first forensic expert Dr Wee Keng Poh that Yu Hong Jin had died from "acute haemorrhage due to stab wounds in the abdomen and asphyxia due to manual strangulation". He agreed with Wee's colleague Dr Paul Chui that the accused man's wounds were consistent with having been caused by the knife. He also agreed that it was a theoretical possibility that the wounds were self-inflicted.

Like all good real-life forensic scientists, Duflou never displays the instant certainty of a television series scientist when he is asked such leading questions as "Did this weapon cause this wound?" It's a characteristic that has infuriated homicide detectives, prosecutors and defence lawyers in equal numbers over Duflou's 25-year career.

"I am the exact opposite of CSI," the forensic pathologist says. "I spend my life saying 'Hmm. I don't know' or 'Possibly' or 'Maybe' or 'I am not really sure'."

Duflou's evidence in the Eu Lim Hoklai case was characterised by his usual caution.

Eu was not lying, the Australian expert said

On the key question of "Were Eu's wounds self-inflicted" he acknowledged that self-infliction remained a theoretical possibility. But, as he put it in his report, it was, in his opinion, "a preferred likelihood" that the abdominal stab wounds were not self-inflicted and that Eu Lim Hoklai's account of events was not the pack of lies that the prosecution were alleging.

When it was his turn to enter the witness box, he expanded on this opinion.

In the first place, he said, there were none of the "hesitation marks" which are a classic sign of the self-inflicted wound. These are shallow superficial incisions made in a person's initial and unwilling attempts to wound him or herself.

Secondly, self-inflicted injuries tend to be tightly grouped, while the nine stab wounds that Eu sustained were all over his abdomen.

Thirdly, he told the court, self-inflicted wounds were usually found on the wrist or neck, not the abdomen. At this juncture Justice Kan Ting Chiu interrupted to make the point that this preference may not apply across all cultures. Duflou agreed with that.

Fourthly, he said, one hallmark of self-inflicted injuries was that they tend to be superficial. But four of Eu's wounds had been so deep as to penetrate the abdominal wall, which can be between 5 cm and 7 cm thick.

Duflou noted that the parts of Eu's clothes covering the injuries had not been damaged. But clothes move during struggles and Eu had testified that his lover had lifted the front of his T-shirt before stabbing him. He repeated his view that it was unlikely that Eu had inflicted nine such stab wounds on himself.

The forensic pathologist also queried Lim Chin Chin's analysis of the crime scene. He disputed her conclusion that there was no struggle and challenged her interpretation of the unusual position in which the dead woman's hand was holding the knife.

In his view there were three equally plausible explanations why the dead woman's hand might have been holding the knife in that overhand way.

She may have changed her grip on the weapon during the process of dying. She might have held the weapon with her thumb against the top of the handle because it allowed her a better grip and prevented her from cutting herself; or Eu had put the weapon in her hand shortly after her death.

Ms Lim, he said, had gone straight to the third option without considering the first two.

"With the issue of the knife in her hand, they were making the assumption that the knife was in her hand all the way through," he explained later. "And hands move. Add all these things together and it became harder and harder to stay with the prosecution's hypothesis."

Duflou agreed with the Singapore analyst that the death scene was relatively undisturbed. He noted that the disarray in the room was minor, compared to the many homicide scenes he had attended.

But he pointed out that the room was small and had very few loose objects in it, while the massage table was unlikely to move significantly during a struggle, even a violent one. He also pointed to the significant blood smearing on the clothes and bodies of both the deceased and the accused.

"There had obviously been a violent interaction between the two persons," he said.

Absence of bloodstains

Most importantly, as a forensic pathologist (and therefore also a medical doctor) he had a different view of the lack of impact spatters on the accused's and deceased's clothing. As he pointed out in his report, absence of bloodstains was not conclusive evidence of the absence of a violent struggle.

Why? Because abdominal wounds do not necessarily bleed dramatically once they have been sustained. It is possible to have stab wounds to the abdomen that bleed very little. The blood also needs to soak into clothing first.

In conclusion, Duflou noted that Lim Chin Chin's report on the case provided "a possible reconstruction of the events". But it was not the only one. In his view, he wrote, the injuries to both people involved and the evidence at the scene were also consistent with Eu Lim Hoklai's account of events. In other words, it was equally possible that the accused was telling the truth.

It was then left to the judge to weigh all the evidence and come to his conclusion.

The verdict

Almost a year later, when Justice Kan Ting Chiu brought down his sentence, it was clear that he had weighed the evidence. But he had not done it in quite the way that most observers of the trial expected.

In the first place, the judge appeared to have given huge weight to the evidence given by a witness whom almost everyone else had pretty much ignored.

That witness was Wong Choon Me, the owner of the hairdressing shop next door to the massage parlour and a potential "ear-witness".

The two shops were separated by only a wall comprising a series of aluminium doors with glass panels. This was an ineffective sound barrier that usually allowed Ms Wong to hear if voices were raised in the massage parlour.

The accused had clarified that there was essentially one scream followed by a series of muffled noises. But on the morning of Yu Hong Jin's death, Wong told the court, she had heard no sounds of a struggle or a fight from the next-door shop. For this reason, her appearance was not a highlight of the trial and many of the newspapers covering the trial did not even report her testimony.

Meanwhile the defence team, considering her testimony relatively unimportant, had refuted its significance. The lawyers simply argued, in their final submission, that Wong's failure to hear a scream was "not conclusive".

Their main point was that Wong herself had agreed that it was possible, since she was concentrating on cutting the hair of a client, that she did not hear the scream. Accordingly, her failure to hear a scream didn't mean that there wasn't one.

Justice Kan Ting Chiu saw it differently.

To him, Wong's failure to hear anything was an indication that there had been no struggle.

"Ms Wong was an independent witness," he wrote in his judgement. "It was not disputed that she was in her hairdressing salon at the material time, and there was no suggestion that she had any reason to give false evidence against the accused. Against that background, and having observed her when she gave evidence, I accept her as an honest and reliable witness. Her evidence raised a serious doubt over the accused's description of the events."

The judge's approach to the forensic evidence

The judge's approach to the forensic evidence was even more odd. In the first place he made it clear that he was going to effectively disregard Duflou's evidence because the scientist had done his report without being shown Eu's statements to the police, in which he had been grilled in detail about the mechanics of his fight with his mistress. Instead, the forensic pathologist had been given Eu's interview with a psychiatrist, in which he gave a less-detailed account of events on that fatal Father's Day.

In fact, as he explained later, Duflou would have been happy to have been given even less background information.

Like all modern forensic scientists, Duflou is keenly aware of the issue of potential "cognitive bias". Forensic scientists now argue that they should know as little as possible about the context of the injuries or evidence that they are examining. They prefer to let the evidence, rather than extraneous background information, do the talking.

The judge, it seems, was not aware of this way of thinking.

But he had still been very interested in the details of the altercation.

During the trial, he had actively expressed scepticism towards Eu's account of events. He had even interrupted the accused while he was in the witness box explaining that he had killed his lover in self-defence. This happened when Eu was telling the court that his mistress was standing behind him when she stabbed him in the stomach.

Justice Kan had broken in to say that that was hard to believe.

"It would be so much simpler for her to stab you in your back instead of reaching over to pull up your T-shirt and then stab you on the front right side of the abdomen," he had said.

In his judgement, Justice Kan also dealt with the re-enactment of the attack, pointing out that when Eu demonstrated how he had grabbed the deceased's wrist, the knife was pointing towards the floor, not the deceased's abdomen at any point.

"It was thus unlikely that the deceased could have accidentally stabbed herself as the accused claimed," he wrote in the judgement.

The judge had also emphasized that the evidence of two forensic scientists contradicted the accused's account, which had the stabbing taking place with the couple both standing and the strangulation happening with Eu's mistress lying on the massage bed.

While both the prosecution and the defence were interested in this, they didn't see it as crucial. For both sets of lawyers, the key issue in the trial was Eu's wounds. Were they self-inflicted? Or not?

The crucial issue: Were the wounds self-inflicted?

Had Eu, as the prosecution was saying, strangled and stabbed his ex-lover in cold blood and then re-arranged the scene, using the knife to stab himself before placing it in his mistress's lifeless hand? Or had events unfolded the way the accused man himself had described them?

The judge had failed to make a finding on this all-important issue. This was, at the least, surprising.

It was also strange that he had rejected any possibility that Eu had been acting in self defence, had been in a "sudden fight", or had been responding to provocation. He had, after all, failed to rule out the possibility that at least some of Eu's wounds had been inflicted by the deceased. In that case, Eu's stabbing by his mistress would have provided grounds for one of the above "self-defence", "provocation" or "sudden fight" defences.

One thing was certain. With these defences excluded, the only option left was to convict Eu of cold-blooded, pre-meditated murder.

On the morning of June 30, 2009, the sounds of sobbing filled the courtroom as Justice Kan read out his judgement and death sentence. Eu's mother wept loudly, and Eu himself broke down. His lawyers, on the other hand, while disappointed, had already noted the many surprising aspects of the judgement. They were confident of having both grounds for appeal and a good chance of achieving a different result from an appeal hearing.

Appeal against the death sentence

As the defence lawyers had hoped and expected, they were granted leave to appeal. At the hearing, held in September 2010, they presented a revised assessment of the evidence of the hairdresser Wong.

It had not been established, the defenders argued, that the woman was even in her shop when the fatal altercation between Eu and his mistress took place.

Eu had stated that he had left home for the massage parlour "some time after 9 am, close to 10 am". In the statement he gave to the police on June 19, 2006 – just the day after the alleged crime – he had said that he arrived at 10 am. It was therefore very plausible that the noisy row between Eu and his mistress had taken place even before Ms Wong arrived at her hairdressing salon, which was, according to her testimony, at 10.15 am.

When the three appeal judges brought down their decision in April 2011, they criticised Justice Kan for placing "undue reliance" on a witness whose presence in her shop at the time had not even been satisfactorily established.

More importantly, they were also very critical of his approach to the forensic evidence.

Justice Rajah, who delivered the three judges' joint judgement, said that Justice Kan should have made a definitive finding on whether Eu's wounds were self-inflicted and whether a violent struggle had taken place.

A finding on how the accused's wounds were sustained, he said, was essential to a proper evaluation of the defences available to the accused. Justice Kan's failure to do so was "an error" which made the conviction unsafe.

The appeal judges were also critical of the reliability of Lim Chin Chin's testimony on various points.

"Ms Lim often gave her opinion on areas unrelated to her area of expertise as if it carried the weight of an expert opinion," they said. "She also infused her reconstruction report with suppositions that, in the end, she had to admit, amounted to pure conjecture."

In several instances, on the other hand, the appeal judges quoted Professor Duflou's opinions with approval.

In particular they drew attention to his evidence, accepted by the prosecution, that the petechial haemorrhaging on the deceased's face indicated that, at least part of the time, "there was release of the compression of the neck and then probably episodes of reapplication again". This meant that the pressure of strangulation was intermittent and not continuous and was consistent with a struggle taking place.

They also drew attention to Duflou's evidence about the relative absence of blood spatter on the clothing of both Eu and Yu Hong Jin. Lim Chin Chin had cited this absence as an indication that Eu had been lying when he said he had struggled with his mistress.

But Duflou had testified that it was "entirely reasonable" for stomach wounds to bleed only in a limited and delayed fashion, meaning that blood would not be dripping down from then.

He had told the court that large amounts of blood did not necessarily flow out externally from a stomach wound, particularly where there was no injured internal organ to produce most of that blood. He had also testified that none of the wounds sustained by the accused would have been immediately incapacitating. In fact, he said, it would have been entirely possible for the accused to have performed a range of activities (such as continuing to struggle with the deceased) "like an uninjured person, without having been aware of his having sustained some or all of the stab wounds".

The appeal judges were openly critical of the prosecution's case, describing the prosecution theory that the crime scene was staged as "rife with improbabilities".

It had been established, the judges said, that there had been a struggle during which both protagonists were injured. Certainly it was not clear how that struggle had begun and who struck the first blow. But if there was doubt, then the benefit of that doubt had to go to Eu.

Meanwhile, they wrote, the prosecution had not been able to satisfactorily explain why this was a premeditated murder in cold blood.

"It was, on its face, highly unlikely that an accused who was due back home for a special family outing went to the massage parlour with murder on his mind.… There was no suggestion made that the accused was prone to lash out physically."

The judges then quoted Eu's evidence of the dead woman's previous violence towards him.

"He testified that in response to his advising her not to drink so much, she had previously slapped and punched his head and that just a few days before the incident on June 18, 2006, she had slapped and punched his head again when they argued over her alleged affair. Both times, he did not retaliate.

"Even assuming, therefore, that he had initiated the fatal chain of violent actions on June 18, 2006, it would be reasonable to believe that for him to have done so there must have been some very grave provocation or assault on his person that went beyond slapping or punching on the part of the deceased.

"With the facts above compounded by the lack of clarity and the worrying gaps in the prosecution's case as to what actually transpired, it would be unsafe to conclude that this was a case of murder in cold blood. Rather it appears to have been a death caused in the heat of the moment, either upon a sudden fight or grave and sudden provocation and we find so. The accused is only guilty of having committed culpable homicide not amounting to murder."

The murder conviction set aside

With that, the three judges set aside Eu's conviction for murder, instead finding him guilty of culpable homicide not amounting to murder. They then sent the case back to the original judge for resentencing.

The following month, Justice Kan resisted the urgings of prosecutors who were asking for a life sentence. Instead, he jailed Eu for ten years, backdated to 2006 when he was first arrested. If he were granted the usual one-third remission for good behaviour, he would be due for release by 2012.

Eu's 86-year-old mother was, as usual, in the court. After the hearing she sobbed as she embraced lawyer Subhas Anandan.

"You saved my child," she said in Hokkien.

Eu's daughters at the court

Eu's three daughters were also there, and were later interviewed by a reporter from Singapore's *New Paper*, telling her they had forgiven him.

"I don't care about the past," his eldest daughter said. "We just want him to come home soon. It has already been five years and we miss him very much."

His second daughter also said she missed having their father around.

"The flat feels empty without him. We have lost so many years with him. We hope to give him a good life when he comes out of prison."

Eu's wife was not present. While she had testified at her husband's trial, she had stayed away on subsequent court days.

With her husband in prison, Ng Mooi Huang had been left to manage the family seafood stall on her own. She had to do this while doing her best to ignore the stares of passers-by who, she knew, were gossiping about her plight.

Earlier she had told a reporter from the Chinese afternoon paper *Lianhe Wanbao* that she was still hurting from the sting of the betrayal.

"As long as you are a woman, you would not be able to forgive him," she said.

Reflecting on the case, defence lawyer Sunil Sudheesan spoke of the evidence of forensic pathologist Johan Duflou as the key to winning the appeal in this case and saving Eu from the hangman's noose.

"Winning" is a word that the forensic pathologist expects lawyers to use. But he hates to hear it in the mouth of an expert witness.

An "opinion" witness

"One thing that makes me really angry is hearing a forensic expert say 'I've never lost a case'," Duflou says.

"You go there to advocate your view, not a side. You have to sell your view to the court. You are an opinion witness."

The issue of the death penalty meant that Duflou had to think twice about taking this case. As a staunch opponent of capital punishment, he was concerned about maintaining his impartiality.

It was impossible to stop the question "Can I help this man get off the death penalty?" from popping up in his thoughts.

"That was a dilemma because, emotionally, I wanted to do that and that is not my role as an expert witness."

Fortunately, once he saw the evidence his worries disappeared. He could see serious flaws in the prosecution's case. In his usual way, he was not taking sides. Instead he was just looking at the facts. Certainly, he could not discount the possibility that Eu's wounds were self-inflicted (although he preferred the opposite view). Most importantly, he had found it "entirely possible that the stabbing had taken place as described by Eu".

He had also been bothered by the blood spatter evidence relied on by the prosecution in this case. For him, it typified the faults of much of the blood spatter evidence he hears in court, in that it was given from a "blood spatter physics perspective" without equal understanding of the human body and the way it moves and responds.

"Overly certain" blood spatter experts worry Duflou, who is critical of the tendency to treat the behaviour of human bodies in action as if they were as mappable and predictable as objects in a carefully constructed physics experiment.

"Blood spatter experts don't know any pathology," he says. "Their understanding of the mechanisms of injury is rudimentary at best. The expertise of forensic pathologists is based on that understanding.

"My approach to bloodstains is quite different from the pure physics of bloodstains. One person at a recent conference pointed out that bloodstain analysis is based on trigonometry essentially –

and most of it works on the basis that droplets of blood travel in straight lines. Let's imagine that you project a bloodstain on to a surface – it's not going to continue to go in a straight line for any period of time. You have a parabola, not a straight line pattern."

It was his view that, in this case, HSA expert Lim Chin Chin had "fallen into the prosecutorial trap".

"You start off with the assumption that the person has done it; and you show that the physical evidence supports that assumption. I am a great believer that, regardless of who calls (you), you start off with the opposite view."

Case Five
THE BODY PARTS IN THE KALLANG RIVER

When two boxes containing segments of a headless female body were found in Singapore's Kallang River, Deputy Superintendent of Police (DSP) Roy Lim could not rule out the possibility that the victim had been murdered thousands of kilometres away. The boxes could have been heaved off the deck of one of the hundreds of ships that sail into the busy port of Singapore every day. With the head still missing, forensic scientists were limited in what they could tell police. Miraculously, they were able to take the mystery woman's fingerprints and Criminal Investigation Department officers began searching government databases for a match. After only six hours from the discovery of the body, they had a breakthrough.

The tree-lined waterside jogging track at Singapore's Kallang Riverside Park is a tranquil, beautiful place. Dragon boat teams and kayakers skim silently along the water, past walkers dawdling in the shade of palm trees.

But on Thursday June 16, 2005, the regular lunchtime joggers arrived at the park to find crime scene tape barring their way.

At 9.15 that morning, a park cleaner had made a horrific find. He had been making his way along the riverbank collecting the usual take-away food-related detritus when he spotted something unusually large. It was a waterlogged brown cardboard box, sealed with masking tape. As he attempted to move it, it fell apart, disgorging its contents. Inside was a greenish translucent plastic bag containing the lower half of a female body, neatly severed at the pelvis and knee joints.

Aghast, he called the police. A short time later a second package of remains was found. About 200 m downstream, a red and white cardboard box had beached itself on the opposite bank. Inside it was a second pale green translucent plastic bag. This one contained the upper half of a woman's body, with arms and hands. The head was missing.

By afternoon Police Coast Guard boats were patrolling up and down the river. Meanwhile thirty Special Operations police officers were searching the riverbanks and combing through the adjacent greenery.

Where had the crime happened?

After darkness fell, the police set up floodlights so their dogged land and water search could continue into the night. They were desperate to find the unfortunate victim's head. Without it, she was going to be difficult to identify. And without an identity, the investigators had no path that might lead to her killer.

The setting of a crime often offers clues to its perpetrator. But with a public location such as this, the police could not even assume that the victim had been killed nearby. Yes, the crime may well have happened in Singapore. But the investigators also had to consider that they were standing on the bank of a river that flows into the sea off one of the world's busiest ports. Might this woman have been murdered and dismembered on a ship? Could the boxes containing her body parts have been dumped overboard and left to drift to shore? It was possible.

All that could be said with any certainty, at this point, was that the boxes containing the body parts had been in the river. When the tide had receded at about 8 am it had beached them on the bank.

The Kallang River is Singapore's longest river. It extends from the Lower Peirce Reservoir in the Upper Thomson area, runs through a canal in Bishan in the northernmost part of central Singapore, and flows past the riverside park and into the Kallang Basin. Eventually it empties into Marina Bay and then the sea.

After a survey of the currents, Deputy Superintendent of Police (DSP) Roy Lim could not rule out the possibility that the boxes had been heaved off the deck of one of the hundreds of ships that sail into the busy port of Singapore every day. The currents might have then carried them into the Kallang Basin and up river. The Singapore Coast Guard was asked to provide a list of ships that had been in the area that day.

The material in which a dead body has been wrapped will often present an investigator with valuable clues. Here, the remnants of Chinese newspaper used to wrap the body parts were common enough, as were the bags themselves. And the first cardboard box was too waterlogged to be helpful.

But the second box looked promising. It had originally housed a Canon printer. The label, with its serial number and individual barcode, was still intact. A team of detectives went to work. They were able to trace the barcode on the box to a Singapore electronic goods store: an important discovery in that it meant the investigators could discard the hypothesis that the body parts had been thrown off a passing boat. There was also a chance that it had actually belonged to the killer.

What the body could reveal

The police's first area of focus had to be the victim's body. Accordingly, Health Sciences Authority (HSA) forensic pathologist Dr Cuthbert Teo was one of the first forensic officers at the scene.

This woman had been dead for less than 24 hours, he told the police.

Teo also observed the precision of the cuts severing the body parts. Could the cuts have been made by a person with some kind of medical or medical-related training?

The body parts were rushed to the mortuary where refrigeration would halt further decomposition. There, swabs were taken from the body, with blood and tissue samples extracted for DNA profiling. A DNA profile would be crucial to proving the victim's identity, once police had a candidate. It would also confirm that both body sections came from the same person, although the cuts lined up perfectly. Swabs of the victim's genital area were taken. If she had been sexually assaulted, they might yield the DNA of her attacker.

At that stage, the forensic pathologist was unable to report on the cause of the woman's death. Her head, shins and feet were still missing. The determination of her cause of death would depend on how quickly those parts were found. Ideally that needed to be soon. A warm and humid climate like Singapore's accelerates the process of decomposition, liquefying the body tissues that a forensic pathologist needs to examine.

As the victim had been dead for less than 24 hours, her body was yet to be affected by decomposition processes that cause the flesh to discolour and the skin to loosen. With her skin still tight, her fingerprints could be taken. CID officers then spent hours searching government databases for a match.

A breakthrough

In an extraordinary investigative exercise, police had a major breakthrough by late that afternoon. Only six hours after the discovery of the body parts in the Kallang River, they knew the identity of the deceased.

The fingerprints taken off the dead body's hands were a match to those of 22-year-old Chinese national Liu Hong Mei. A machine operator for a local manufacturer of circuit boards, Agere Systems in Serangoon North, she had been living in Singapore for three years. Because she was a foreigner who had needed a work permit to get a job in Singapore, her fingerprints were on file.

DSP Lim and his colleagues went straight to Agere Systems. There they discovered that Liu's workmates had reported her missing after she had failed to turn up for her 7 pm shift the previous night.

Liu Hong Mei was well liked, her colleagues told Lim. But she had been promoted very quickly. Some thought this might have been related to the unusually close relationship she had with her supervisor, Leong Siew Chor. At 50, he was more than twice her age, and the pair had been seen kissing at work.

The police also gained access to her locker and personnel file, which confirmed the theory that some of Liu's colleagues had felt resentment towards her. One fellow worker had actually made a complaint about "intimate behaviour" between the dead woman and Leong Siew Chor.

Management had given both of them an official warning as a result.

It was already 8 pm by the time Lim and his colleagues were ready to interview Leong, who had arrived for his night shift at 7 pm. Sitting down with him, Lim framed this first interview as a casual chat. Of course it was the very opposite. It was a careful information-gathering session with a man who, by virtue of his relationship with the deceased, was already a suspect.

The detective didn't inform Leong that his colleague's body had been found in the river. He certainly didn't accuse the man of killing her. At that point there was not a scintilla of evidence to suggest that Leong might be the killer.

A "defensive" interviewee

Yet Leong was "defensive" Lim said later. In particular, he refused to admit to having had any kind of close relationship with Liu Hong Mei, repeatedly insisting he was "a family man". Indeed, he was exactly that. He had a wife and three children, two of them young adults. Slim, bespectacled and balding, he looked harmless and "normal" – nothing like the sort of man who could charm a woman half his age.

But the detective was suspicious. Leong had held his hands clasped tightly throughout the interview. Tiny cuts were visible on his knuckles. Lim asked if he could have a closer look at them.

When Leong extended his hands, they were trembling. Certain that there was more to learn about this man's relationship with the dead woman, Lim asked if he could accompany him home and inspect his living quarters.

Leong's ninth storey apartment was in Geylang, Lorong 3, less than 300 m from the river. There Lim and his colleagues found a stack of Chinese newspapers, similar to the newspaper scraps wrapped around the body parts. They also found stained clothing, green translucent plastic bags like the kind used to wrap Liu's body, a damaged meat cleaver and a heavy, black rubber mallet.

DSP Lim took Leong back to CID headquarters for further questioning. For ten long hours, the man continued to deny having had any special bond with the dead woman.

Then he cracked, admitting that he and Liu had been having an affair for the past year. He confessed to having strangled her in his apartment, while his wife and three children were away.

A supposed "murder-suicide" pact

Leong insisted he had not murdered his colleague. Instead, he told the police, her death had been part of a lovers' murder-suicide pact. The way he told the story, this had been Liu's idea. She had proposed it as the only solution to their hopeless situation. He could not follow her back to China, as she wanted, because he did not want to leave his wife and children. The only way out of that tragic impasse was for them both to die.

He had agreed to her suggestion that he strangle her, and then kill himself. But when he had actually strangled her and seen her face turn blue, his courage had deserted him. In an attempt to hide the crime, he had dismembered her body and parcelled it up into different bags and boxes that he then threw into various Singapore waterways. He had carried out this grisly task in great haste and, it has to be said, with impressive efficiency.

His younger daughter was due back at 6 that evening. He was also due to clock on at work at 7 pm. And he only had a bicycle as a means of transport.

By the time Leong had finished talking, it was well into Friday morning. He was then arrested in connection with the murder.

An arrest after a mere 24 hours

A mere 24 hours after the discovery of the body parts, Singapore police were holding a press conference to announce the fact that they had made an arrest in the matter.

Leong was formally charged the following day in a court hearing attended by his wife and his elder daughter, a teacher. The pair had been on holiday in Bangkok and had rushed home in a show of support. His undergraduate student son was also present in court.

Leong's confession was only one strand in the prosecution case against him. Confessions can be retracted later. DSP Lim and his team needed to collect forensic evidence that would tie the factory supervisor to every aspect of this crime.

During their first visit to Leong's four-room apartment, late on the night of Thursday June 16, they had noticed an array of buckets in the bathroom, presumably where Leong had dismembered his lover's body. It promised to be a treasure trove of forensic evidence.

The following night the investigators brought Leong back to the apartment to assist them with their search. With curious neighbours looking on, police escorted their prisoner, handcuffed and shackled at the ankles, into the building and up the stairs.

The forensic officers began their work in the bathroom. But, although they photographed and swabbed every surface, the area seemed surprisingly free of blood. Leong had done an extraordinarily effective cleaning job in a very short time. He could not have managed it without flushing many buckets of bloodied water down the bathroom drains and the toilet. Yet there were no obvious bloodstains.

A single drop of blood

DSP Lim knew that some killers were able to commit the bloodiest of murders and then do a clean-up worthy of the best professional cleaners. In fact the pristine scene reminded him of a crime scene report he'd read almost a decade earlier. Serial killer John Martin Scripps, executed in 1996, had murdered and dismembered a tourist in the bathroom of Singapore's River View Hotel in 1995. He had then scrubbed down the crime scene so effectively that it looked spotless. Yet one sharp-eyed forensic police officer had found a single drop of blood under the bathroom sink.

Lim looked under Leong's bathroom sink. Nothing. Then he crouched down and examined the underside of the toilet bowl. A 2 mm droplet of what looked like blood was clearly visible. Traces of blood were later discovered on three plastic buckets, on the toilet wall, on a pair of clogs and on the sides of Lift A in Leong's apartment block.

Turning their attention to the rest of the apartment, the officers found pieces of masking tape with strands of hair attached. They also seized a bicycle with small bloodstains on it, Leong's computer, and a towel – the one supposedly used to strangle the victim.

A media frenzy

The media was in a frenzy about the case of the "Cut up China girl", as they called it. The fact that it concerned an illicit love affair was compelling enough. She was also a foreigner. And there were body parts still missing.

The Straits Times took a psychological angle in a piece entitled "What the hack?"

"What goes on in a killer's mind when he chops his victim into pieces?" the paper asked.

Then, a week after the crime was discovered, *The New Paper's* reporter staked out Leong's apartment to speak to the various locals who were visiting.

Some of them came to burn joss sticks for the dead woman's spirit – although one also hoped the experience might help him pick the right four numbers in Singapore's weekly "4D" lottery.

A *Straits Times* article later noted that other locals had visited the apartment block to express their anger at the murder, underlining their feelings by throwing eggs and broken flowerpots at its door. Fortunately, as the author of that piece commented, Leong's wife and three children had not returned to their apartment since his arrest. So they did not have to endure this cruelty and insensitivity.

A DNA match to the victim

Meanwhile back at the HSA, forensic scientists had begun working on the samples taken from Leong's apartment. One crucial piece of evidence was the apparent blood droplet on the underside of the toilet bowl. The Kastle-Meyer test (in which a drop of phenolphthalein reagent is added to the sample, followed by a drop of hydrogen peroxide) suggested that it was. But whose blood was this? DNA was extracted from it, profiled and compared to the DNA profile extracted from the dead woman's body. It was a match.

Although this result confirmed that the victim's body had been dismembered in Leong's bathroom, investigators only had Leong's account of the actual murder. He said he had strangled Liu Hong Mei in the bedroom, using a towel. But had he?

With only the upper and lower torso to work with, and most of the neck missing, Dr Cuthbert Teo was unable to confirm a cause of death that would verify the "strangling" aspect of Leong's story.

Leong had told the investigators that he had dismembered his lover's body in the bathroom using his kitchen cleaver, and had then thrown both her upper and lower body parts into the river at Kallang Riverside Park. The locations where the packages had been found suggested he was telling the truth.

So when he confessed to having thrown his lover's head, feet and shins into the Singapore River, just near Boat Quay, the investigators took him at his word. They consulted the Maritime Port Authority for information on the tides and advice on which way the missing body parts may have drifted.

But by Saturday morning, none of these last packages had been found. Indeed, given their size, it seemed highly likely that they would have been swept up with the general refuse that is sieved from the slow-flowing river every two days. If so, they would have ended up at the giant Tuas incineration plant in western Singapore.

A needle in a haystack of rubbish

It was imperative that those packages be found before they were processed and incinerated. Early on Saturday morning a team of eight officers arrived at the incineration plant to shovel their way through the three tonnes of rubbish that had been collected the day before. The officers had to move quickly. Those tonnes of rubbish were scheduled to be reduced to ash on Saturday night.

Donning masks, which did little to protect them from the unbearable stench, the men picked up their shovels and began working through the mounds of refuse. Every plastic bag had to be opened and its contents checked.

On Saturday afternoon, after eight hours of searching, the unmistakably putrid smell of decomposing flesh assaulted the searchers' nostrils. They recognised it at once.

DSP Roy Lim had encountered his first decomposing body during his time with the Police Coast Guard in 1991, and had seen – and smelled – many since. This was the first occasion that he had welcomed the smell.

It meant that, finally, his officers were working on the right pile of rubbish. Shortly afterwards, the men unearthed a yellow plastic bag containing a newspaper-wrapped parcel. A severed head was inside. Then they found a white plastic bag. It contained two legs, without feet.

Examining a "fresh" dead body, forensic pathologists are accustomed to documenting various indications of strangulation: bruising and abrasion of the neck, engorgement of tissues, fracture of the hyoid bone. Or fracture of the ring of cartilage around the trachea, or windpipe, known as the "cricoid cartilage". In this case, however, decomposition was so advanced that Dr Cuthbert Teo was unable to observe any of these.

It was disappointing, given that police prefer to have every aspect of a confession corroborated by forensic evidence. In fact, Teo could only find a bruise on Liu's head.

Teeth help confirm identity

During his examination, the forensic pathologist had noticed that one of the victim's upper teeth was malformed. Requesting a picture of the deceased smiling, he compared the two. The photo showed an unusually formed tooth in exactly the same position as it was in the head found in the rubbish. It was a comforting confirmation to have, before the DNA test results came back.

The forensic pathologist's examination also uncovered more important physical evidence tying Leong to the crime.

The investigators had already noted that the victim's blood had been found at Leong's apartment. The bags and the newspaper collected there were also of the same type as those found with the body.

Teo found something better than that. Examining the limbs of the deceased recovered from the incineration plant, he found two tiny shards of metal embedded in the muscle of the left leg. They were only a few millimetres in diameter. Might they have come from the damaged cleaver that police had seized at Leong's apartment?

A link to Leong's cleaver

Using a high-powered comparison microscope, scientist Lim Thiam Bon was able to line up the damaged edge of the cleaver with the tiny piece of metal. The jagged edges slotted together. Studying the surface of both the cleaver and the shards, he examined their striations: microscopic marks created in metal when force is exerted on it. Once again, the patterns matched, providing further confirmation that the shards had broken away from the cleaver.

Other HSA scientists were working on the clothes found at Leong's apartment. Tiny traces of fibres clung to some of them. These fibres may have come, the scientists believed, from the cardboard boxes in which the victim's body parts had been packed. Using fluorescence microscopy, the fibres were examined and compared. Unlike conventional microscopy, fluorescence microscopy does not enlarge the fibres. Instead, it directs lights of different wavelengths at them. The light patterns reflected back are different for each fibre. In this case the fibres on the clothing matched the fibres from the boxes. This indicated that Leong had been in close contact with the boxes used to pack Liu's body parts.

Meanwhile other police enquiries were continuing.

Checking the victim's movements over the last few days of her life, the investigators discovered that on Tuesday 14, a day before her death, Liu Hong Mei had reported the theft of her ATM card. That same day someone had used the card to make several unauthorised withdrawals and purchases. More than S$2000 had been drained from her account.

CCTV footage was available of the ATM sites. A man resembling Leong was seen making the withdrawals.

An identical twin

Meanwhile, the police had discovered that Leong had an identical twin brother, who also lived in Singapore. Had it been Leong at the ATM? Was there any possibility that it was his brother?

If there was even the slightest suggestion that Leong's twin also knew the dead woman, the investigation could be in serious trouble. Identical twins have exactly the same DNA profile. Any DNA result linking Leong Siew Chor to the dead woman's body would then lose its power to positively identify him as the killer.

Fortunately, Leong's twin could prove he was far away from the ATM sites when the money was being withdrawn from Liu's account. Nor could police find any evidence to suggest that Liu had even met her lover's twin.

Police then searched Leong's home for the clothes that he was seen wearing in the CCTV footage. They found them.

So they could be certain that it was Leong who stole the money from his lover's account: a detail that did not fit his story of the star-crossed lovers and their suicide pact.

Even when confronted with the CCTV footage, Leong stuck to his "suicide pact" narrative.

He had taken Liu's ATM card on June 13, he told police. It was her day off and they had spent it at Hotel 81 in Geylang, Lorong 20, just down the road from the apartment where he lived with his wife and family. Over the next two days he had almost emptied her savings account. But the thefts were "a prank", Leong claimed, and he had returned the money immediately to Liu. It was a ridiculous-sounding story but the police were unable to disprove it because they were never able to find the cash.

Finally, a confession that made sense

Ten days after his arrest, Leong withdrew his original statement. In another statement made that day (and referred to during his murder trial as "the June 26 statement"), he admitted to killing his lover to stop her from reporting him to the police for stealing her ATM card and then her money.

This confession made sense, psychologically. Liu's threat would have struck terror into Leong. Being arrested for theft would expose their hitherto secret relationship. It would cost him his family as well as his job and reputation. How could he let that happen?

In this June 26 statement, he admitted to police that he had lured his lover to his flat by pretending that he needed to talk to her before she went to the bank to discuss her stolen card.

Unsuspecting, Liu had arrived at the Geylang apartment. Unaware that her lover was the thief who had used her ATM card,

Liu told him that she had already made a police report and was heading for the bank to view the CCTV footage from the ATMs.

However, according to this statement, he had not been able to bring himself to tell Liu that he had taken her ATM card.

"If I had told Liu Hong Mei the truth, everything would be gone," he said.

In this new June 26 statement, it was Leong who suggested that the lovers die together. Yet he never intended to kill himself, he told the police. He didn't dare to.

"I just wanted to know whether Hong Mei was willing to die for me," he said.

Given that she did not argue, he assumed she was.

"Liu Hong Mei did not know that my intention was actually for her to die and not (for us to) die together," he told police. "I knew that she would not struggle or fight me when I decided to kill her."

He then strangled her with a tightly rolled towel as she sat opposite him.

Although their analysis of the forensic evidence had already given the investigators a good idea of what had then ensued, it was useful for them to have the killer's own account. While Leong's suggestion that Liu was willing to die seemed unbelievable, other material that the killer provided was useful.

The investigators had already been able to prove that Leong had used his cleaver to dismember Liu's body. But his various statements contained details they would never have discovered. For example they would not otherwise have known that he had used his bicycle when he disposed of bags containing Liu's feet, shoes and clothes. He had simply loaded the bags into the bike's front basket and ridden along Sims Avenue, only a block away from his home, distributing them into dustbins.

Cycling home, he had dropped his bike and then caught a taxi to the heart of the CBD, alighting at Boat Quay, on the Singapore River. He had dumped the bags containing his lover's head and legs into the water there.

Returning home he had again used his bicycle, making the short ride to the Kallang Riverside Park twice. First he went to dump the box containing his lover's upper torso. Then he returned to dispose of the box containing her lower torso. Later, on his way to work, he had thrown Liu's handbag into a bin outside Ang Mo Kio MRT station.

Strangers also mourned for Liu

Liu's colleagues grieved for her at a midnight prayer ceremony held outside their workplace. And, as had happened less than a year earlier with the murder of 8-year-old Huang Na (see *Little Girl Lost*) Liu's death was also mourned by strangers who gathered across the island to pray for her. A month after her death, her body was released for burial.

Undertakers stitched together her body parts, replacing her missing feet with wax replicas. Their size had been estimated from shoes her sister provided. This procedure was done in accordance with the traditional Chinese belief that a dead person should travel into the next world with his or her body intact.

Liu Hong Mei's funeral, held on July 11, 2005, was attended by 150 people, most of them strangers.

Leong Siew Chor's trial began on May 3, 2006, with the prosecution lining up 33 witnesses to testify. The central plank of their case was the June 26 confession, in which Leong had explained that he killed his lover to stop her reporting his theft of her ATM card and money.

Defence lawyer Subhas Anandan, assisted in court by his junior colleague (and nephew) Sunil Sudheesan, objected to this statement being admitted. They argued that their client had been pressured into making it.

Cross-examined by Subhas, DSP Lim told the court that it was his duty to record whatever the accused man wanted to say.

The barrister reacted with incredulity.

"You are saying," he said, "that without any prompting from you, the accused...out of the blue, decided to give you a statement which will ensure that he will hang?"

Given the chance to testify in his own defence, Leong claimed that, indeed, DSP Lim had induced him into making that statement. In fact he claimed that Lim effectively wrote it for him, winning his trust by buying him a bottle of herbal tea. However, Lim was able to produce his field book and prove that the tea was bought a week later.

Back to the "suicide pact" claim

Leong then proceeded to revert to his initial "suicide pact" confession, in which he claimed the pact had been initiated by Liu and he had strangled her at her request.

It was a novel defence. Under Singapore's Penal Code, it is not considered murder if a person above the age of 18 consents to being killed. But if Justice Tay Yong Kwang were to accept it, he would be the first Singapore judge ever to do so. Leong gave it his best shot, testifying that Liu had been depressed by their affair, and had pleaded with him to commit suicide.

Prosecution investigations, meanwhile, suggested that Liu had been anything but depressed. On the contrary she had been making plans for her future, which included a diploma course in tourism.

There were no independent living witnesses to the strangling. And Leong's account was not to be trusted. But could the "silent witness", the dead body of the victim, tell the court anything?

The dead woman's injuries interpreted

It was time for forensic pathologist Dr Cuthbert Teo to step into the witness box and explain the injuries he had documented in his examination of Liu's head and neck. This was an opportunity for both the prosecutor and the defence lawyers to see if his report could be interpreted to support their respective cases.

There was no argument about the one bruise that the expert had been able to identify on the victim's head.

Leong had told the police that his lover's head had hit the floor while he was dragging her body out of the bedroom and into the kitchen.

This explanation was an exact match for Dr Teo's description of the bruise. The pathologist had described it as consistent with a fall, or with the victim being pushed against a hard object, such as a wall. He had also said that it could have been sustained up to 30 minutes after death.

But what light could the forensic evidence cast on the strangling itself?

According to the Teo report, no overt or defensive injuries were found on the skin of Miss Liu's neck or upper torso.

Both the prosecution and the defence tried to use this evidence as support for their case.

To defence lawyer Subhas Anandan, the absence of "defence injuries" – injuries sustained as a victim tries to protect herself – meant that she had consented to being strangled by Leong Siew Chor. This was just as Leong had explained in all his statements, except the June 26 one, that the pair had made a suicide pact.

The prosecutor, Lau Wing Yum, used the same evidence to argue exactly the opposite point. The victim had no injuries, he suggested, because Leong had attacked her by surprise.

Would a towel ligature leave marks?

Then there was the question of the use of a towel as ligature. What did it mean that no marks had been found on the victim's neck?

Prosecutor Lau Wing Yum asked the forensic pathologist if he would expect to find marks on the neck in a case like this.

A towel wouldn't necessarily leave a mark, the expert replied.

"If the towel is soft and broad, the force being applied to the neck is spread over a large area," he said. "The compression of the neck by a broad, soft towel usually either leaves very few marks, or no marks at all from the towel itself."

However, the defence lawyer wasn't to be put off. He was determined to make something of the lack of defensive injuries.

"In the case of strangulation by towel, could there have been defensive injuries?" he asked.

A victim in this situation might scratch herself while trying to pull the towel off, Teo said. But he had not found any scratches.

If the victim had consented to being strangled, there might not be any defensive injuries. Yet just before a human being loses consciousness, regardless of consent, the natural reflex is to struggle. That could leave marks, he said.

Given that the autopsy evidence could not solve the issue, the focus then moved on to the mechanics of the act.

When recounting the details of the murder to the police, Leong had said that he had been sitting opposite his lover and had strangled her from the front.

The prosecution saw it differently. They were sure that the act had been committed without Liu's consent. In that case, they believed, it was more likely that she had been strangled from behind. And was it even possible to strangle a person with a towel when she was sitting opposite you?

Because the autopsy evidence could not answer any of these questions, the court had no option but to at least explore Leong's account and give him the opportunity to demonstrate that it was possible.

A re-enactment in court

Leong's defence lawyer Subhas Anandan asked his client to demonstrate exactly how he had strangled Liu.

There were gasps and giggles as Sunil Sudheesan walked over to the witness box, holding a towel.

"Don't overdo it," warned Justice Tay Yong Kwang as Leong wrapped the towel around the younger lawyer's neck, crossed the ends behind him, and then pulled.

That was supposedly the way he had strangled Liu as they sat together on his bed in his apartment on June 15, 2005.

The dramatic demonstration may have shown that this kind of murder was possible. But it didn't impress Justice Tay Yong Kwang.

On May 19, 2006, he sentenced Leong to death by hanging.

He dismissed Leong's story of a suicide pact and rejected his account of having strangled Liu face to face.

Describing Liu as "a lively, young woman in the vernal stage of her life", the judge said she was doing well at work, wanted to go on to further study and was looking forward to celebrating her sister's wedding. In short, she had no reason to commit suicide.

"In the classic tragic tale of ill-fated love, the luckless lover committed suicide. Here, Romeo killed Juliet. It was a most disgusting and despicable murder. Liu Hong Mei died a very cruel, heartbreaking death."

Leong immediately appealed but his appeal was rejected by a three-judge panel. An attempt to get that appeal reheard failed, as did a further appeal for clemency. Leong was hanged on November 30, 2007.

The mysteries behind this crime

This case remains puzzling to anyone who expects human beings to commit crimes for reasons that are comprehensible to the average person.

Certainly Leong's lawyer Subhas Anandan continued to puzzle over it until his own death in 2015.

The fact that Leong stole the money was the first mystery. As Subhas wrote in his memoir *The Best I Could*, the theft itself dumbfounded him. Leong was on a good salary. He didn't need his lover's money.

So the lawyer had actually asked his client why he had taken the ATM card and the S$2000. But the answer hadn't satisfied him.

"I suppose it's greed" was all that Leong had told him.

And then there was the matter of the murder itself. Even if it were true that Leong had killed her to stop her telling the police, was such a drastic measure really necessary? After all, the pair were lovers.

"He could easily have confessed to her and asked her forgiveness," the lawyer wrote. "Did he need to kill her because of that? I don't think so."

To Subhas, the motive just didn't make sense. Indeed, during the lead-up to the trial, two different people had phoned him to suggest that Leong had killed his lover because of jealousy. Liu had, both callers suggested, been seen out and about with other men and Leong had been so enraged by this that he had killed her.

The lawyer was unable to use this information because neither of the callers ever came forward. Certainly at the time that Liu was seeing Leong, she was also on the books of a dating agency. Nobody could blame her for that. Her lover couldn't marry her and presumably she was hoping for an introduction to a man who could. Perhaps she was thinking of leaving Leong. Possibly she had threatened to do so on the morning of June 15.

Clearly the police were not the only ones frustrated by the fact that Leong continued to stick to his silly "suicide pact" story. His stubbornness left so many questions unanswered.

Leong Siew Chor would still have gone to the gallows. His crime remains appalling. But knowledge of his true motive would have made it more comprehensible.

Case Six
THE ACCIDENTAL MURDERER

Was Singapore toxicologist Quek Loo Ming a criminal or a klutz? Or both? He stole a drug sample from his workplace – the toxicology laboratory at Singapore's Institute of Science and Forensic Medicine (now known as the Health Sciences Authority). He then used his knowledge of poisons to plan a murder. But he killed the wrong person.

Which kind of forensic expert is best equipped to commit murder? Undoubtedly a toxicologist. After all, toxicologists are the ones who carry out the tests which ascertain the presence of poisons in the human body. So they know which toxins are the most difficult to detect, and which ones create symptoms that most closely mimic "normal" ailments.

Yet cases of rogue forensic toxicologists are rare – an impressive fact. Except you only hear about the ones who made a mistake and got caught. A newspaper search pulls up only two 21st century killer toxicologists: California's Kristin Rossum, now serving life without parole for murdering her husband; and Singapore's Quek Loo Ming, a retired forensic toxicologist sentenced to 15 years' jail in 2002 for poisoning a 62-year-old woman.

In November 2000, Kristin Rossum was working at the San Diego County medical examiner's office when she stole a vial of the powerful narcotic fentanyl, along with 15 fentanyl skin patches, from the drugs locker. She used it to kill her husband.

She then staged his suicide, setting the scene by having her husband found lying in bed, with their wedding photos under the pillow. She left a shredded love letter from her lover, the Australian toxicologist who was her boss, in the dining room. Her own diary, containing an entry saying her marriage was a mistake, was found on the coffee table.

Another melodramatic touch propelled the case into the headlines as the "American Beauty" murder. Her husband had supposedly covered his own chest with rose petals. According to Rossum, the petals were an allusion to the dozen roses her husband had given her for her birthday. But news reports immediately referenced the 1999 hit movie *American Beauty*. It had featured fantasy sequences in which the middle-aged male protagonist, played by Kevin Spacey, imagined the teenage girl he adored lying naked, covered in rose petals.

Rossum knew that her husband had just taken the painkiller OxyContin and the muscle relaxant Clonazepam. As an employee of the medical examiner, she was aware that a test for fentanyl was not one of the routine tests run during autopsies.

Unfortunately for her, the friends and family of her dead husband knew that she had been having an affair, and pressured police to investigate.

A search for other miscreant forensic scientists only brings up a drug thief and a results fraudster. In 2016, Annie Dookhan, a former forensic chemist at a Massachusetts Department of Public Health state laboratory, was released from jail on parole after serving three years for falsifying the results of several thousand toxicology tests and regularly tainting samples so they would produce positive results. Her motive, apparently, was her wish to be seen as more industrious and productive than her colleagues. Also in Massachusetts, the State Crime Laboratory's Sonja Farak was arrested and charged with stealing cocaine as well as tampering with drug samples, adulterating them with innocuous substances to cover her theft of the actual drugs.

More klutz than criminal?

In Quek Loo Ming's case, once you know his circumstances, it's tempting to view him as more klutz than criminal. Yet, like Sonja Farak, he stole a drug sample from his workplace – the toxicology laboratory at Singapore's Institute of Science and Forensic Medicine. And, like Kristin Rossum, he used his knowledge of poisons to commit a crime which resulted in the death of another human being.

It is just that his motive was far less dramatic. And he was so incompetent that he killed the wrong person.

Quek retired from the lab in June 2000 and began spending most of his time at home in the apartment he shared with his wife in the Singapore suburb of Clementi, a traffic-snarled 25-minute drive from the CBD. After his retirement, he served as a volunteer helper to the Bukit Timah Residents Committee (RC): a position with less power and prestige than actual membership of that committee.

Accordingly, the 56-year-old was one of the people called on to help organise the committee's annual New Year's Eve Party, always held at its centre on Clementi Avenue.

On the eve of December 31, five hundred residents had gathered to farewell 2001. But the party mood suddenly evaporated around 10 pm when three of the revellers collapsed with agonising stomach pains. Assumed to be victims of food poisoning, they were rushed by ambulance to Singapore's National University Hospital. The 49-year-old chairwoman of the RC, Doreen Lum, was also taken to hospital. A manager at a manpower consultancy firm, she had suffered an anxiety attack and passed out.

The three stricken partygoers – tea lady Madam Fong Oi Lin, 61; electrician Wong Ah Kim, 38; and retired accountant Richard Ho, 66 – were treated in the intensive care unit. There they underwent the usual stool and blood count tests administered in cases of suspected food poisoning.

Doreen Lum recovered quickly and was discharged. But the condition of the other three victims continued to worsen and worried doctors ordered batteries of further tests.

Blood tests detect an insecticide

On January 3, Madam Fong died. In the meantime, all three patients' blood test results had revealed the presence of an insecticide known as methomyl.

Police were immediately called. The officer in charge of the investigation, Assistant Superintendent of Police Goh Tat Boon, would later win an Operational Excellence Award for solving the crime in just over a week. This was an impressive result given that the 35-year-old detective had been handed a case with no eye-witnesses and no fingerprints. It also featured a crime scene that had been cleaned up three days earlier.

What the officer did know, however, was that the three victims had all eaten chicken satay bought from the Taman Selera satay stall on nearby West Coast Drive. The stall was immediately closed while police questioned its employees. Goh and his team began working their way through all the partygoers' accounts of the evening. As they trawled the background of every single person present, another possible explanation of the night's events emerged.

All three victims had drunk water

First, the investigators became aware that all three victims had drunk water at the party. Wong's wife told police that her husband had drunk some water after putting the lights up for the party. She thought that this water had been poured from a bottle that had been in a refrigerator at the RC headquarters. Her husband had become ill an hour later.

It was also established that Richard Ho had drunk the water.

Madam Fong had swallowed some too. But she had been heard saying that it tasted awful. She had then poured its contents down the sink and dumped the empty bottle in a rubbish bag.

So the satay was off the hook. The relieved stall owners were told they were free to open up for business again and the investigators got back to the business of questioning partygoers. None of their interviewees could name anyone with a grudge against any of the victims. But they were told of one party guest who was believed to be nurturing an intense resentment against the woman who had been hospitalised after fainting at the party, the RC chairwoman Doreen Lum.

Mrs Lum knew that Quek Loo Ming was unhappy with her. When Quek was working as a volunteer assisting the Residents Committee, he had wanted to be appointed to it. But she, along with the two vice-chairmen of the committee, had told him that they felt he wasn't ready. On the night of the fateful party she had phoned Quek at home and asked him to buy 20 packets of chicken rice to feed the volunteers who were helping to set up for the party. He had agreed but with great reluctance. It was clear that he was not happy with her – and that he felt affronted by being asked to run an errand, and at such short notice.

The breakthrough

The breakthrough in the investigation came when police discovered that Quek had been working as a toxicologist with Singapore's Institute of Science and Forensic Medicine and had only retired in

June of the previous year. They knew he would have had access to the methomyl there. The department had a sample of it in storage, having dealt with a case in which a Filipina maid had committed suicide by swallowing the powdered insecticide, dissolved in a cup of coffee.

Quek was initially charged with murder, then a mandatory death penalty offence. Two additional charges of causing hurt were added later.

The toxicologist then hired Singapore's legendarily effective criminal lawyer Subhas Anandan. In exchange for a plea of guilty from his client, he managed to bargain the murder charge down to manslaughter. Meanwhile the two charges of "causing hurt" were amended to the more serious charge of "voluntarily causing grievous hurt by dangerous weapons or means".

When Quek put in his guilty plea the whole sad story came out. As police had surmised, Quek had indeed stolen the methomyl powder from his workplace. Presumably he had been thinking that the illegal but highly effective insecticide might help keep insects off his plants at home. And he had spiked the water that his victims drank in an attempt to punish Doreen Lum for both treating him as an errand boy and giving him insufficient credit for his work.

Revenge was not planned

But his actions were not the result of careful planning.

On New Year's Eve he had done what Doreen Lum asked. He had bought the packets of chicken rice and delivered them. In fact the idea for revenge only came to him on his way home, when he spotted an empty 1.5-litre bottle of Ice Mountain water.

Picking it up, he continued home to his apartment, only a block away. There he filled the bottle with water and stirred in a quarter of a teaspoon of the pesticide powder. He then made his way back to the RC centre and placed the bottle on top of a cabinet that stood in the corridor directly opposite Mrs Lum's office.

His aim, he would explain in the account of events his lawyer presented to his sentencing hearing, was to punish Doreen Lum for treating him as an errand boy. He wanted the poisoned water to give her diarrhea and stomach cramps – an effect that might have followed a tiny dose of the poison. Unfortunately, he had had no way of knowing how much of the poison was "too much". As the deputy public prosecutor would later tell the court during the same hearing, there is no available scientific evidence as to how much methomyl is required to kill a person.

How methomyl works

As a qualified chemist who held a University of Singapore science degree, Quek should have known that methomyl is an anticholinesterase insecticide. This means that it inhibits the functioning of cholinesterase. This enzyme is vital to the appropriate functioning of the nervous system of both humans and insects. In both organisms, the glands, muscles and nerve fibres are stimulated or inhibited by the transmission of chemical messages across switching centres known as synapses.

One particular type of cholinesterase is required to discontinue these signals. When cholinesterase-inhibiting insecticides are present in the synapses, muscle control breaks down. Some muscles will undergo uncontrolled rapid twitching. Breathing may be paralysed. Convulsions – and even death – may ensue.

Symptoms of methomyl poisoning may include nausea, vomiting, abdominal cramps and diarrhea. This is why the illness that struck Quek's victims was initially thought to be food poisoning.

But one has to wonder, as did the public prosecutor, why Quek simply didn't use laxatives. There's probably a simple answer to that:

laxatives rarely come in a form that can be dissolved invisibly into water.

The judicial commissioner who presided over the case made a point of saying that the court "stands between the accused and the lynch mob, not in place of it". He accepted that the retired scientist was remorseful. However he did not agree that the offence was in any way mitigated by the fact that the actual victims were not the intended one.

Quek was initially sentenced to only nine years' jail.

But the prosecution appealed and the Court of Appeal increased his sentence to 15 years.

Case Seven
THE TRIALS OF RAM TIWARY

In 2003 Ram Tiwary was sharing a flat in Sydney with two fellow Singaporeans, Tay Chow Lyang and Tony Tan. All three were in their mid-20s and studying engineering at the nearby University of New South Wales. One horribly unforgettable September afternoon, Tiwary woke to find that his two flatmates had been bludgeoned to death. He was interviewed by police as a witness – as one would expect. But nine months later, he was arrested and charged with the two murders.

At 2.20 on a mid-September afternoon in 2003, a Sydney Emergency Services operator received a panicked 000 call from a man cowering behind a locked bedroom door in an apartment near the campus of the University of New South Wales.

"There's been a murder, two," a male voice gasped down the line.

"I … I need the ambulance and the police… My … my two friends are lying dead outside … There's blood all over the place."

The caller was Ram Tiwary, a 25-year-old Singaporean studying mechanical engineering at the Australian university on a Singapore Armed Forces scholarship. The two dead men were fellow Singaporeans Tay Chow Lyang, 26, and Tony Tan, 27, also a Singapore Armed Forces scholar. Both victims were electrical engineering students at the same university. The apartment, on the upper floor of a red brick duplex on Barker Street, a quiet tree-lined street in the Sydney suburb of Randwick, had been home to Tiwary and Tay since 2002. Tan had joined them at the beginning of 2003.

When the 000 operator asked Tiwary what had happened, he replied, "I have no idea. I was asleep and I heard this screaming."

His friends had been bashed and stabbed, the student said.

"There's a baseball bat and a knife there… there's a knife lying on the ground as well."

The operator then asked if "the person who did this" was still in the flat.

"No, there's nobody outside," Tiwary replied. "The back door was open. I closed the back door and I grabbed the bat, and I came back into my room and called you."

When the operator asked Tiwary if he could leave his bedroom to check if his friends were still breathing, he appeared to panic.

"I'm not going back outside till somebody gets here," he protested. "I'm not f…ing going back outside."

Tiwary sounded in fear of his own life. As he told the operator during the call, which lasted 10 minutes and 27 seconds, he had not seen his flatmates' attacker. But, terrified that the killer might still be around, he had armed himself with the bloodied baseball bat, retreated to his bedroom and barricaded himself in, pushing a cabinet against the door. Only then had he rung 000.

A couple of minutes later, when the operator assured him that the ambulances had arrived, the student agreed to leave the room and check on his flatmates' bodies.

"I'm outside now," he told the operator, after a five-second pause.

"They're definitely not breathing."

"Do you think they are beyond any help or do you want to try and do some first aid?" the operator asked. "I know it's really hard, but I can give you some advice on what to do."

"I know CPR as well," Tiwary replied. "But there's blood… all over his nose, so I don't even know if I can give him CPR…"

The operator then explained that the paramedics would not enter until the police had "cleared" the unit, but told him he could leave the apartment.

Hearing from Tiwary that he was still holding the bat, she gently suggested he should put the weapon down before he walked out into the street.

He initially resisted relinquishing the weapon. Then the operator began to explain:

"Because if you walk out with that in your hand…" Her voice trailed off. The penny presumably dropped for him then. Leaving the bat in his room, he walked out into the street, breaking into a run when he saw the two ambulances parked down the street, about 20 m away.

The two female paramedics in the first ambulance locked their doors at his approach. Tiwary hastily reassured them that he was the person who had called 000.

The ambulance officers' notes on that initial conversation confirmed that Tiwary "appeared to be upset, distressed and bewildered, agitated and breathing heavily". He told an ambulance officer that one of his flatmates was lying on the ground covered in blood, frothing at the mouth. He told another, in answer to a question as to what he had seen:

"I don't know. I was asleep. I heard a noise. I woke up. I saw lots of blood … I think I saw a knife."

In the meantime both uniformed police and plainclothes detectives had arrived and Tiwary identified himself to them. The paramedics duly entered the house and, within two minutes, pronounced both Tony Tan and Tay Chow Lyang dead.

Tiwary's first accounts

Judging by the notes taken by Sergeant Winston Woodward, the first police officer to interview Tiwary, the student gave a clear account of what had happened, one that was consistent with what he had told the paramedics.

Tiwary told the police officer that he had been asleep in his room all day. His girlfriend had called him early that morning, but he had then gone back to sleep until he had been woken by "the sound of things falling". Thinking someone in the flat had dropped something, he'd gone back to sleep until woken again.

According to the notes the detective made, Tiwary had then heard somebody run past. That person, Tiwary had realised, must have been Tony Tan, running from his assailant. The person called out "help", but Tiwary stayed inside his bedroom.

"I didn't go out," he told the detective. "I should have, but didn't. After I heard somebody being hit I should have opened the door." The terrible sounds continued for five minutes.

Some time after that, Tiwary told Woodward, he opened his door. Looking to his right he could see Tony's body lying next to the front door. His dead flatmate's back was against the wall; a baseball bat and a knife were lying near him.

Tiwary picked up the bat and walked towards the back entrance of the flat. It was then that he saw Tay's body. Closing the back door, he locked it, retreated to his bedroom, locked that door and used his mobile phone to call 000.

Detective Woodward then asked Tiwary to accompany him and his colleague Detective Mark Frearson to the local Maroubra Police Station to make a full statement.

At 3.35 pm, when he was on the way there, the first members of an extensive police crime scene investigation team were arriving at the unit.

The police station interview

That police station interview was amicable, with Detectives Woodward and Frearson treating Tiwary with the courtesy that a witness to a murder would expect.

The conversation, recorded both on audio and videotape, began at 4.14 pm and went for three hours. As polite as it was, the encounter was a less than shining example of the art of the police interview, one of the aims of which is to record all the facts while memories are still fresh.

The problem was that the detectives failed to ask Tiwary to explain why he had blood on his feet.

The two officers had begun by asking the student how he had checked for Tony Tan's pulse. So he had shown them how he had placed his fingers on his flatmate's neck.

Tiwary had then started pointing out the spots of blood he had noticed on himself. He had done the same when talking to the first police officers on the scene.

"There's blood here," he was heard saying, as he held up his hand. "… I have some on my leg just here." He then went on to indicate the specks of blood on his arm, most of which the police appeared not to have noticed.

"How do you think you got all that blood on you there?" one of the detectives then asked.

"Because I tried to put Tony's head back, because he was…." Tiwary began.

A fatal interruption

At that point one of the detectives interrupted to tell Tiwary he could put his jumper back on (he had taken it off so that they could check if he had any blood on his torso).

Tiwary then began talking again. He was about to tell the officers how, as he was leaning over Tony Tan, the man suddenly spasmed, sending a spurt of blood out of his mouth and nose. He never got the words out. The audio machine started to beep, indicating that the audiotape was about to run out. It was 5.43 pm.

The interview was at a critical point. But it had to be paused so that the tape could be replaced. When it resumed, fourteen minutes later, both the investigators appeared to have forgotten that they had not finished with this most crucial topic. Instead they moved on to talk about Tiwary's discovery of the body of his other flatmate, Tay Chow Lyang.

This lapse was only one of several in the investigation. What was worse was that, while the audio recording was kept, the first video disappeared. It was somehow "lost". This meant there was no lasting record of the appearance of Tiwary's clothes and hands in the immediate aftermath of the murders and before his clothes were taken for forensic examination.

Even that crucial forensic examination was late, beginning only at 8 pm, more than five hours after his 000 call. Then his clothes were taken away, he was given blue disposable paper overalls to wear, and was finally examined by a forensic doctor.

That night the student wasn't allowed to go back to the murder scene, although all his belongings, including his wallet, were there. He ended up sleeping at a friend's, wearing borrowed clothes.

After their first interview, the detectives would have realised that they had failed to question Tiwary about the blood on his feet. It wasn't a critical mistake. Police can always call a witness back for a second interview. And anyway, Tiwary had agreed to take part in a "walkthrough" of the crime scene three days later.

It was during this re-enactment of his discovery of the bodies of his flatmates that the student told the detectives that he had been leaning over the body of Tony Tan, checking whether he was still breathing when blood from the dying man had landed on his feet.

"When I was right beside him … a spurt of blood came out of his nose and mouth and he spasmed," he told the detectives. "It was just, like, it was like froth … and that made me take a step back … I didn't expect that it would spurt …"

Tiwary seemed nervous

The detectives noted that Tiwary seemed hesitant and nervous and, at that time, unable to give coherent or clear accounts of his actions. He also had difficulty in recalling the exact sequence of events. For example, his account of discovering the bodies varied from the one he had given immediately after the deaths: a variation that would later be regarded as significant.

Yet the police gave no indications that they were regarding Tiwary as anything other than a witness.

After that "walkthrough", three days after the crime, the student had no further contact with the police.

He did his best to resume something resembling a "normal" life – if that was possible, given that everyone he met seemed to be hungry for information about the murders.

The Singaporean's response was to keep the details of the ordeal to himself.

He told only his few closest friends what had really happened, even holding much of it back from his girlfriend. And when people such as the flatmates at his new house found out, he defused their interest by minimising his experience. Sometimes he simply lied about it, suggesting that he had merely returned home to discover the crime scene. Telling it that way meant he didn't have to broach the shameful reality that he had been too frightened to leave his room.

Different theories on the murders

The first police theory on the killings suggested a connection to a recent wave of extortion and kidnapping attacks by local criminals on international students from Asia.

It was first aired in a newspaper article published the day after the murders, with its writer noting that 19 of the previous 30 kidnappings in NSW had involved Asian victims or perpetrators. In late August 2003, the body of a 19-year-old Vietnamese student from the University of Technology, Sydney, had been found strangled in the back of a car after a botched kidnapping attempt. Two weeks earlier a student from mainland China had been kidnapped and assaulted and a ransom of A$120,000 demanded from her Beijing-based parents.

But this theory was quickly dismissed, given that it had been based on nothing but the men's nationality.

The detectives then began looking long and hard at the two victims' personal circumstances, backgrounds and movements on the day. Standard investigative procedure, it was aimed at flushing out any conflicts or secrets that might have led to an attack.

First the officers investigated a possible affair between Tay Chow Lyang and a young woman in Singapore, a former university friend called Jasmine, who was engaged to be married. The theory was that Tay's murder was somehow connected to it, and Tan had been murdered to keep the killer's identity a secret.

Records of the duo's online discussions revealed that they spoke every few days from mid June to early July 2003. Sometimes they chatted for minutes, sometimes for hours, sharing details of their daily lives, their travel plans. The tone of the conversations was sometimes flirtatious and sexual. Yet it was clear that there had been no intimate sexual contact between them. Also a check of immigration records showed that neither Jasmine nor her fiancé were in Australia at the time of the murders. Moreover, both Jasmine and Tay's wife, who was aware of her husband's friendship with Jasmine, denied there had been an affair.

Secondly the detectives began looking into a report that Tony Tan had told friends that he was planning to buy a baseball bat "for protection". One witness, a friend of Tiwary's, David Lee Kay Meng, told police he had seen a baseball bat in the living room of the flat in July 2003. The only bat found in the flat after the murders, however, was the one that Tiwary had bought to actually play baseball with, only two days earlier. The man also said he had never witnessed any arguments among the three flatmates. Other witnesses had told police there had been minor domestic disagreements about washing-up and cooking, easily resolved by the three flatmates doing their cooking separately.

The dead men's final few hours

The most worrying details began to emerge when the detectives started looking closely at the two men's movements in the hours preceding their deaths.

Both Tony Tan and Tay Chow Lyang were conscientious about punctuality and attendance at lectures. On Mondays, when they had the same Mobile and Satellite Communication Systems lecture at midday, they would walk to university together.

On the day of his death, Tay Chow Lyang did not turn up for that midday lecture. Yet his body was found wearing trousers and a jumper, with his wallet in his back trouser pocket. That was the way he dressed to go out. At home he always wore shorts and a T-shirt, only changing into warmer clothes before leaving the apartment.

When the midday lecture began, Tony Tan was also missing. But he arrived late, some time between 12.15 pm and 12.30 pm, according to classmates. One fellow student, C Sun, described him as looking dishevelled, and "like he hadn't slept". Another classmate, a student named Teo, was struck by Tan's demeanour during the lecture because the usually relaxed and focused student appeared "restless and looking around, as if for someone".

Teo had also been expecting to spend time with both Tony Tan and Tay Chow Lyang after the lecture. The previous Thursday the three had made an arrangement to meet and organise a seminar on the topic, Ethics in Engineering. But as soon as the lecture was over, Tony Tan approached Teo and said he had to cancel the meeting. According to another student who made a statement to police, Tan had told him that the afternoon meeting was to be cancelled because Chow Lyang "has got something to do".

Other students interviewed by police described Tony as looking "uneasy" and "shaking from side to side." When another fellow student asked him what was up, he just said that he needed "to go to the toilet urgently". Meanwhile he told another student he was going home to sleep.

Two other students, Jonathan Choy and Sean Murray, ran into Tony Tan on the stairs leading to the university's exit gate. Choy said that Tan looked pre-occupied with something. Usually he would respond to their greeting with a comment and a smile. This time he just kept walking.

A mystery car

All the students were exiting on to a one-way street, Willis Street, an area not covered by the university's CCTV security cameras. As Choy walked out, he saw a four-door white car with three people in it. Parked facing the wrong way, its occupants were clearly there for one purpose alone: they were waiting for someone. They were Asian, he thought, but he didn't recognise them.

He would later describe the atmosphere, as he watched Tony Tan get into the car, as "tense". Murray, also watching, described the car as dark – not an unusual variation in real-life eyewitness accounts of the same event – and its occupants as Asian.

The car left Willis Street at about 1.50 pm or 1.55 pm to make a trip of a few hundred metres: a distance so short that none of the flatmates had ever driven it. It was little more than a minute's drive.

Tony Tan certainly arrived home. In fact, in the minutes before his death, he had begun preparing a meal. One of the first police officers to enter the flat after the 000 call found the stove on, and a saucepan containing several chicken wings cooking away. While the heat was on high, the chicken was only burnt rather than on fire. So it seemed that it had been cooking for just a short time.

But who was he cooking for since the amount of food could have fed two? After the resolution of their minor dispute about washing up, the flatmates were not in the habit of cooking for each other.

Exactly what happened in the next 15 minutes will never be known for certain, although the car that had dropped Tan home was spotted elsewhere in the following 30 minutes or so.

Other sightings of the car

A University of New South Wales student who arrived in Barker Street around 2.25 pm on the day of the murder (while Tiwary would have been on the phone to 000) told police that she saw an olive-skinned man, neither Indian nor Caucasian, "looking around" as he walked towards a white sedan parked in front of the house next door to the murder scene. Just before 2.30 pm, he pulled out from his parking spot, and she took it.

A local resident, a Mr Timothy Cousins, told police that he saw a pale car parked in the laneway near the premises after 1 pm. Another witness had also described a car that sounded like the same one, being driven erratically away from the Barker Street area at around 100 kph.

The mystery car would remain a focus of police enquiries in the months after the murder.

In December, police began a publicity campaign aimed at flushing out its driver, a man "last seen driving a light blue or white car resembling a Toyota Echo". They said the man had picked up Tony Tan less than half an hour before his body was found in the hall of the Barker Street duplex. They described him as potentially "the vital link" in solving the murder of both Tan and his flatmate. Anyone with any information or who had seen a car like that in or around Barker Street, Kingsford, on September 15 was urged to contact Maroubra police. But nobody did, prompting police to intensify their efforts and send out an international press release seeking information.

What the autopsies revealed

Sometimes autopsy results can provide a clue to the identity of a perpetrator; for example, the manner in which a cutting implement has been used may suggest a perpetrator with medical knowledge.

The autopsy results on the two Singaporeans told only of the ferocity and ruthlessness of their killer. And they clarified the timeline of the two deaths.

Forensic pathologist Professor Johan Duflou's autopsy report on Tony Tan confirmed that his ordeal was one that would have woken even the heaviest sleeper: a man such as Tiwary.

The extent of his head injuries suggested Tan had received between five and ten blows to the head and a number of blows to the front of his face. His nose was smashed and he had broken teeth.

Dr Duflou believed that after the injuries were inflicted, Tan would very likely have been deeply unconscious.

Tan was also stabbed five times on the right-hand side of the neck, which left him with inhaled blood in his lungs, and frothy blood in his nose and mouth. In addition, he had defensive stab wounds on the backs of both hands. He had tried to fight his attacker off, but had failed.

Tay's attack, on the other hand, would have been a quieter affair.

Given that he was found lying on the living room floor, it appeared that he had been assaulted while sitting on the floor using his computer, which sat on a low table behind the couch. His assailant had hit him from behind, bashing him twice on the back of the head with a blunt object, possibly a baseball bat.

During the autopsy on Tay, Duflou documented two wounds on the man's head, describing them as the cause of death. The expert also noted one blunt force injury to the left hand, probably a defensive injury, sustained when the man's left hand flew up to his head after the first blow. This meant that his left index finger took some of the force of this second blow, which was so powerful that it almost amputated the top of the left index finger, fracturing the bone.

Meanwhile an examination of his brain revealed that Tay had survived for at least two hours after the initial attack. The bashing of his head created catastrophic and extensive brain injuries. But microscopic examination of the brain tissue showed an accumulation of amyloid precursor protein, or APP. This protein, Duflou explains, is "a substance in nerve fibres in the brain which is only seen under the microscope if the person has survived for a minimum of two hours after a serious brain injury has been sustained".

Tay had also suffered a potentially lethal stab wound to the neck. But the fact that there was no bleeding from it into the lungs suggested that this wound was sustained either at the time of death or after it.

The first sudden attack on Tay would have immediately rendered him deeply unconscious and immobile. This made it credible that Tiwary could have slept through the attack. In fact he recalled later that he had woken for a few seconds. Hearing only the loud TV, he had assumed that sound had woken him.

The fact that Tay survived two hours or more after this attack indicated that it took place some time after midday, after Tony Tan had left for his lecture. The fact that he was stabbed when he was dead or almost dead also suggested a scenario in which his assailant returned two hours later when he drove Tony Tan home. Seeing what he believed was some sign of life in his first victim, he had then stabbed him to ensure he was dead.

But who was that attacker?

By late December 2003, the Maroubra detectives were no closer to an answer.

Their publicity campaign for information about the mysterious white car had produced no useful results.

The Maroubra detectives were not showing any obvious interest in Ram Tiwary. But they had not yet ruled him out.

After all, the murder weapon had been his baseball bat: he had bought the aluminium bat two days before the murders from Rebel Sports in Sydney's CBD.

Police focus turns to Tiwary

Meanwhile it appeared that Tiwary did have a possible motive. It wasn't an obvious one but it was clear that the police believed that it was credible that Tiwary had murdered Tay because he owed him A$5000 in back rent – and had then committed the second murder so that Tan could not report him for the first. Tiwary had denied this, and said the money had been paid. The detectives did not believe him.

Yet they made no signs of moving in on Tiwary. Presumably they were waiting until they had more evidence.

It is impossible to know when – or even if – they would have arrested Tiwary if he had stayed put in Sydney.

In May 2004, when Tiwary expressed his intention to leave Australia and return to Singapore, they appeared to have panicked. Perhaps they were worried by the fact that extradition can sometimes be a complex and expensive affair. Singapore and Australia are signatories to the London Scheme, by which Commonwealth countries agree to extradite fugitive criminals to each other upon the presentation of *"prima facie* case evidence" and in the absence of an extradition treaty.

At this point the detectives didn't have enough evidence to even think about a committal hearing.

To be fair to Tiwary, he had every possible innocent reason for returning home. The academic side of his life had been a struggle since he first arrived in Sydney in 2000. The Singapore Armed Forces bursary gave him a stipend that he supplemented with his part time job as a security guard. But it brought its own pressures.

It seemed that all the Singaporean student's energy had gone into his social life which, unlike his academic life, was a great success. He had many friends, a close relationship with his girlfriend, and was generous with his money, spending some of it at the casino. His partying meant that he would often sleep until late in the morning and into the afternoon. Or he would get up for a morning lecture and then go back to bed.

Being on a scholarship, he was supposed to produce good results. Yet, he had failed a number of subjects: a fact that he sought to hide both from the army and his parents. In 2001 he had told the army that he had passed all five of his semester two subjects. In fact he had failed four of five subjects in semester one and three of five subjects in semester two of that year. On another occasion he sent his girlfriend's transcript to his parents, and passed it off as his own: an episode of dishonesty which the police interpreted in the most sinister way possible.

He was already doing poorly before the murders. In 2002 he had failed four of seven subjects in semester one, and four of his six subjects in semester two. He did not re-enrol in semester one of 2003. He kept studying after September 2003 and even managed to get through two of five subjects. At the same time, he received special consideration in relation to the other three, due to the death of his flatmates.

But he wasn't keeping up with his student fees.

University fees outstanding

In March 2004 Tiwary had been blocked from re-enrolment because he had outstanding student fees. He owed the university A$5650, due by July 16, 2003. In fact he had sought permission to withdraw from the course. If that were granted he would have to repay the army for his university fees. Otherwise his brother and his cousin, who were the guarantors for his scholarship, would be liable for the debt.

By May, he realised that he was going to have to go back to Singapore and face the music. His mistake was to share that thought with Detective Mark Frearson.

The fateful call to Detective Frearson

On May 27, 2004, Tiwary telephoned the detective to check that it was OK for him to return to Singapore. When Frearson asked him why he was leaving, the student told him the truth. University hadn't been going well and he had commitments in Singapore that he needed to fulfil. Asked when he was flying, Tiwary replied that he hadn't decided on a date and hadn't even bought the ticket. He then asked whether the police needed any more assistance from him.

Frearson said he would check. Ten minutes later he called back and asked if Tiwary could come to the Maroubra Police Station the next morning at 7.30 am. The student agreed. While he was unhappy at the early hour, he accepted the detective's assurance that his colleague had to be in court the next morning and could make no other time.

Clearly it never occurred to Tiwary that the police had begun to regard him as a suspect.

The next morning's interview began with Tiwary being read his rights. Detective Frearson and Detective Paul Thierjung also offered him a lawyer, but he refused.

Charged with the murders

Tiwary only realised what dire trouble he was in when the interview ended and the detectives told him he was being charged with the murder of his flatmates.

"What about the people in the car?" he asked, as he was led downstairs from the interview room to the custody area, where he was strip-searched and his belongings confiscated.

Neither detective answered.

The wheels of the justice system had begun to turn.

Tiwary was told that his flat was going to be searched and that he had the option to accompany the detectives. When he learned that this meant he would be taken in handcuffs, he declined. Instead he spent the day in a custody "cell" at the police station, a concrete and perspex structure that was more like a cage. That night he was transferred to the Surry Hills police centre, on the edge of the Sydney CBD.

The next morning he was taken to the Parramatta Local Court. There he spent hours sharing a filthy holding cell with four other prisoners before he was finally taken up into the courtroom and charged.

He was refused bail. Not only was he on two murder charges but he had told the police that he was intending to return to Singapore. He was therefore, by definition, a "flight risk".

Nothing happened for the next two months. Except that the NSW police dredged up 11 new charges to add to the murder charges. They included using a fake security licence and false academic results to gain "financial advantage" – arguably a very heavy-handed reaction to the fact that he had been hiding his poor academic performance.

The police continued to be unimpressively slow in compiling their brief of evidence against Tiwary. It appeared that they believed he had killed his flatmates. But they still had to prove it.

The blood

This was not an easy task. The murder scene had been an absolute bloodbath: the "absolute worst" crime scene – in terms of brutally bloodied victims – that NSW police crime scene examiner Sergeant Phil Elliot had seen in his 22-year career. Yet Tiwary had so little blood on him.

There was also no evidence (no blood-filled drains or wet towels) that Tiwary had washed himself or left the flat between the murders of the two men.

Detective Elliott had been able to come up with some forensic evidence which could point to Tiwary as the perpetrator. He had detected bloodstains on the front, rear, inside front, and inside right cuff of Tiwary's long-sleeved top. These stains were consistent with transfer stains, which could have come from the man's bare skin.

There were, however, no stains on the top that the detective could connect to the assault.

Elliott also examined the shorts which Tiwary had been wearing. He found a number of stains, three of which were later confirmed to be human blood, and which, he said, were consistent with medium velocity blood spatter.

The police also had to be able to dispute Tiwary's claim that the blood on his feet had landed there after one of his victims "spasmed" and coughed it up. If a forensic expert were to say this was not possible, the only other explanation would be that the blood had spattered on to Tiwary during one of the attacks.

Yet the detectives did not appear to have hurried to find a forensic scientist who could help their case in this way.

Additional questions

Four months after Tiwary had been charged, the detectives running the investigation wrote to Dr Johan Duflou asking him for an additional report on the last few minutes of Tony Tan's life.

Could the dying Tony Tan have "spasmed/coughed or spurted blood some minutes after he was inflicted with his injuries and rendered unconscious", they asked the forensic pathologist.

"If this is possible, what is the likelihood of this happening?"

Duflou's answer was that, if the dead man survived for a number of minutes after sustaining his injuries, then it was "probable that the entry of blood into his airway would have caused a degree of airway irritation and coughing".

The detectives also wanted to know about the force with which this blood could be expelled and the distance it might travel. Could this sort of cough mean, they asked, that "blood would be scattered in fine droplets far enough to cover the hands and feet of someone standing or crouching beside them"?

Duflou said it could.

"A person standing or crouching beside a person coughing in the approximate way described could have a fine blood spray deposited on his hands or feet if the coughing was in the appropriate direction and was of a forceful enough nature. Even when a person is near death, there can be significant coughing."

This would not have been an opinion that the detectives wanted to hear. They needed an expert who believed that the blood that landed on the student could not have been coughed on to him in the way he had described.

They found one: trauma unit doctor Dr Gordian Fulde, the director of the emergency department at Sydney's St Vincent's Hospital. He could honestly say he had never seen it. He believed that Tony Tan would have been too deeply unconscious to have coughed and was prepared to testify to this in court.

By May 2005 Tiwary had been in custody for a year and the police brief against him still wasn't complete. His solicitor Peter Doyle complained bitterly about the delay during a "directions" hearing (in which the prosecution checks in with the court to report on the progress of their brief). The critical comments were reported in the newspapers, but the process was not speeded up.

His "committal", a hearing in which a magistrate reviews the evidence to decide whether a case should proceed to trial, finally took place on September 13, 2005. It was just two days short of the two-year anniversary of the murders.

The trial began in June 2006, with the prosecution in the hands of the highly experienced and articulate barrister, Tim Hoyle, SC.

The Crown case against Ram Tiwary

The case Hoyle was making against Ram Tiwary sounded, initially, quite believable. After all, the Singaporean student claimed to have been sleeping in his room while the first murder occurred and to have only been woken by the sounds of the second. Some jury members would certainly be sceptical of that, though others may have accepted Tiwary's girlfriend's evidence that he was a famously heavy sleeper.

Then there was the fact that Tiwary had stayed in his bedroom during the attack. He had had training as a commando. Was it not odd that he had heard his friend call for help, heard sounds of hitting and failed to investigate? He could have had no idea of the ferocity of the attack that was about to happen. So why not check?

And what about the baseball bat, the murder weapon in at least one of the deaths? He had bought it only two days earlier. And there were blood spots on his feet and blood smears on his hands.

Painting the portrait of a liar

Hoyle did an excellent job of portraying the Singaporean student as thoroughly dishonest, describing him as a "cunning and crafty liar" who devised an elaborate "big lie" about sleeping through the attack on his housemates.

The prosecutor was right about the small lies. Tiwary had lied about his poor academic results to both the army and his family. And he had given friends different versions of his movements on the day of the murder. He had told some he was at university at the time. He had even told one friend he had been at work, while he had told the detectives that he had been cowering behind the door of his bedroom.

Hoyle underlined the point by calling several of Tiwary's friends to testify in detail about the various and different accounts the student had given of his whereabouts on the day of the murder.

The barrister also went to town on the discrepancies between what Tiwary had said on the 000 tape and what he had said in his interview at Maroubra Police Station. On the 000 tape, Tiwary is heard telling the operator that he had seen the bodies of both his flatmates. But in his taped interview, he told the police he had only seen one body when he made the call. The prosecutor told the jury that Tiwary hadn't known the 000 call was being recorded so he had given a different story to the police to make himself look innocent. There were also problems with his reconstruction of events on the day of the murders. For example he had said that he had picked up both the bat and the knife and had checked to see whether Tay was still alive while holding both weapons. How likely was that? Especially given that he had apparently done so without having any of the man's blood transferred on to him in the process.

Debt as a motive

Hoyle also made much of the "rent debt" motive, tendering Tiwary's bank account details as supporting evidence. These documents indicated that, as of September 5, 2003, Tiwary had A$7.26 in his account, suggesting he didn't even have the money to cover the rent. Tiwary disputed this detail later. But during the trial, the jury was free to see him as broke and desperate.

Then there was the blood. That was a challenge. For someone who had supposedly bashed two men to death with a baseball bat, Tiwary had a preposterously small amount of blood on him.

It was such a minimal amount that the first detectives on the scene had effectively ignored it.

In the context of the trial, the prosecutor needed to turn those few blood spots into proof that Tiwary had bashed both his flatmates to death.

Hoyle did well even at that task. His first witness, crime scene officer Sergeant Phil Elliott, had an answer for the lack of blood spatter on Tiwary. He said that a weapon such as a baseball bat had a "wide end" meaning that the blood of a victim bashed with it would be projected to areas away from the bat. This would mean that an attacker would be protected from it.

The crime scene specialist also had a reason why Tiwary had none of Tay's blood on him. He described the bloodstain near Tay's body as "very directional", meaning that there had been no "back spatter" landing on Tiwary when he attacked him.

Elliott remained adamant that the small amount of blood on Tiwary was consistent with him being the attacker. This statement did not sit well alongside his comment that this had been the "absolute worst" crime scene – in terms of brutally bloodied victims – that he had seen in his 22-year career. This was a case full of contradictions, it seemed.

The officer even had an answer for the absence of Tay's blood on the weapons. Perhaps it had been present, he suggested. Just not in the places on the weapons that he had chosen to swab. He also accepted that it was possible that the bat and knife were not the weapons used on Tay (although it was not incumbent on him to explain what had happened to those weapons).

Hoyle then wheeled out the doctors. Dr Gordian Fulde told the court that Tan would have been too deeply unconscious to have coughed up blood. Meanwhile forensic pathologist Professor Johan Duflou had revised his original view on the coughing. During cross-examination, he told the court that his view had changed after discussions with emergency physicians. He now believed, he said, that after sustaining the blunt force head injuries it was highly unlikely Tan would have coughed.

The defence case

The defence had called two highly reputable experts to explain the blood spots on Tiwary. They were both adamant that a dying man's cough was a highly possible cause.

Dr Mark Hersch, director of the neurology department at Sydney's St George Hospital, had done research on the cough reflex after brain damage. His conclusion was that Tan "would have coughed". The experienced Sydney consultant neurosurgeon Dr John Matheson could go one better. He had seen a severely injured patient cough in exactly that way.

Blood from a cough? The judge seemed convinced

The prosecutor didn't even attempt to cross-examine Matheson. And it was clear that the trial judge, Justice Michael Adams, was impressed by this evidence. In his summing up, he told the jury that the blood on Tiwary's feet could have come from Tan coughing and any other finding was not open to them.

Justice Adams may also have been aware of a famous NSW case in which two forensic scientists had proven that a badly injured person can cough blood and create bloodstains that are different from "impact spatter" – but capable of being mistaken for it by the non-expert. They had done so in an experiment that effectively re-created the crime scene. One of them had filled his mouth with blood and then coughed it on to the other's white lab-coat. They had photographed the blood spatter patterns that resulted.

In 1965 Alexander McLeod-Lindsay had been jailed for the attempted murder of his wife, with the prosecution pointing to the blood spatter on his jacket as proof that he had bashed her with a steel bar, breaking her facial bones and teeth. McLeod-Lindsay continued to maintain that he was innocent, that he had come home to find his wife injured and had crouched over her, trying to help. A 1989-1991 judicial enquiry looked at the experiment conducted by the scientists, agreed that the blood spatter could have been "expirated blood" and pardoned him.

But Justice Adams wasn't deciding Ram Tiwary's guilt or innocence. The jury was. This group of twelve lay people was being asked to assess evidence from a whole line-up of scientists, several of whom were casting extensive doubt on the prosecution scenario.

One of them was the prosecution's own: crime scene witness Sergeant Christopher Clarke. He said that the blood on Tiwary's feet could have been caused by spatter from repeated blows to Tan's head by a blunt instrument. Or by Tan coughing blood.

Clarke testified that there would have been a reasonable likelihood of back spatter landing on the killer of both Tan and Tay. And under cross-examination he said he also would have expected to see Tay's blood on the weapons.

Meanwhile, as would be expected, the defence's bloodstain expert, Warren Day, a former police crime scene officer, bolstered the idea that blood on Tiwary's feet had been coughed.

Impact spatter spots tend to be "tadpole-shaped", he told the jury. But the photos of the blood spots on Tiwary showed a number of stains that were round and that seemed to have a hollow inside. To Warren Day, that suggested exhaled and respirated blood.

The common sense view?

Warren Day also stated what begs to be described as the "common-sense" view of the way that a killer from this scene might be expected to look. The man who killed Tay, he said, would be expected to have been covered in blood spatter. It would be on his hands, legs and front. Cast-off blood would even have landed on his back, dripping from the baseball bat, when he pulled it back for a second swing at his victim.

The only explanation for the lack of blood on the man in the dock, he said, could be that he had washed himself or he wasn't the killer.

The final forensic argument in favour of Tiwary's innocence involved water. Or the lack of it.

The prosecution had floated the idea that the student must have washed himself (and the weapons) after the first murder. But they didn't linger on it, because their own evidence contradicted it.

In fact, there was not a single skerrick of evidence anywhere in the flat to suggest that Tiwary had washed any blood off himself, or off the baseball bat.

At 3.35 pm on the afternoon of the murder, Sergeant Phil Elliott had inspected the kitchen sink and the bathroom. He found no signs that they had been used in an attempt to wash or remove blood from Tiwary or his clothing. He even conducted a presumptive test for blood in the bathroom. He did manage to obtain a weak positive on the hot water tap and a strong positive on the hand basin. But all that meant was that the test, which reacts to iron, was reacting to something. Most probably it was rust.

His most significant finding was that the shower recess, the laundry tub and the basin were all dry. Nor were there any wet towels to be found.

The bat handle was also dry

In his summing up, Justice Michael Adams also brought up the fact that the handle of the bat was covered in fabric, which would have been wet if the bat had been washed as thoroughly as the prosecution was suggesting. And if it hadn't been washed, then why didn't it have any of Tay's blood on it?

According to the Crown case, and despite the lack of forensic evidence tying it to Tay, the bat that Tiwary had purchased – brand-new and shrink-wrapped – was still the weapon used in both murders. Never mind that it had none of Tay's blood on it. Never mind that pieces of the plastic shrink wrap were found on Tony

Tan's body but not on Tay Chow Lyang's. This made no sense, given that Tay was killed first.

The prosecution made a point of glossing over the lack of any evidence tying Tiwary or his bat to the death of Tay Chow Lyang. This was an issue they needed to avoid because it opened the door to a more logical explanation of the crimes. This explanation – one that was begging to be raised – was that Tay's killer was the driver of the white car that had collected Tony Tan from university.

This man had left the flat after killing Tay, taking the murder weapon with him. He had then returned with Tan, killed him, and departed again.

Can the absence of evidence itself be "evidence"?

It is a precept of forensic crime scene examination that "every contact leaves a trace".

Yet this investigation, oddly enough, had been full of absences of forensic traces. Not enough blood on the alleged killer. No evidence that he could have washed blood off himself. None of the first victim's blood on the murder weapon.

These absences were so striking that, like the famous "dog that didn't bark" in Sir Arthur Conan Doyle's Sherlock Holmes story, *The Silver Blaze*, they could almost be regarded as evidence in themselves.

The Silver Blaze is a story about the midnight disappearance of a racehorse from its stable. A stranger had been suspected of the theft. But Sherlock Holmes identified the horse's trainer as the thief because a dog at the horse's stable failed to bark on the night in question. Clearly the midnight intruder had been someone the dog knew well.

To Holmes, this absence was itself an event. He called it "the curious incident of the dog in the night-time". When a Scotland

Yard detective argued that there was no "incident" because nothing happened, Holmes rebutted him. The silence itself was "the curious incident", he explained.

The Ram Tiwary case had three separate "curious incidents" of forensic evidence that, if the Singaporean student were the killer, should have been present. Anyone taking good notice of them might have wondered if there could, at least, be "reasonable doubt" that he was the killer.

No "CSI effect" here

But the jury did not see it that way. It is often claimed that many modern juries suffer from "the CSI effect". This means that, overly influenced by their viewing of TV forensic dramas such as *CSI* or *Silent Witness*, they want forensic evidence to help them come to their decision. It makes them dissatisfied with cases where no DNA or other scientific evidence is presented.

If "the CSI effect" exists, then the jury in *R v Ram Puneet Tiwary* was not one of the juries affected. They deliberated for four days before returning on June 20, 2006, with a verdict. Guilty.

The verdict was a shock to Tiwary's lawyers, who immediately engaged the services of Tim Game, SC, a senior silk with a big reputation for winning appeals.

It is possible that the verdict also came as a surprise to Justice Michael Adams. In his summing up, he had made comments that could have been interpreted as suggesting that he found the defence case credible.

The prosecutor certainly thought so. At a time when the jury was absent, Hoyle had complained that Justice Adams was "rubbishing" his case to the jury and had used body language that was "dismissive" when he, the prosecutor, was speaking. He also requested that the judge spend more time explaining the Crown's case to the jury.

Justice Adams had responded with the explanation that his face might have worn a "puzzled" look when the prosecutor had been speaking. The judge had also criticised some of the prosecutor's arguments as *non sequitur.*

But one Sydney lawyer who studied the trial closely was less surprised by the verdict. Not because he believed that Tiwary was guilty, but because he thought that the trial had, as he put it, "gone off the rails". He felt that too much time had been spent on two particular areas of evidence that were very unhelpful to Tiwary. The result was that the jury might very well have ended up thinking these topics were the two crucial issues in the case.

One area was the evidence given by the prosecution's medical expert, Dr Fulde, the director of the emergency department at St Vincent's Hospital. He had suggested that Tony Tan would have been too deeply unconscious to have coughed. Dr Fulde's arguments were ably and convincingly rejected by the defence's experts. But they were also echoed by his fellow prosecution expert, Johan Duflou.

The other was the length of time spent on debating the implications of the variations in Tiwary's accounts, such as whether he had seen the second body by the time he made the 000 call. The prosecutor, arguing that Tiwary was the killer, had used these supposed discrepancies to suggest that Tiwary had fabricated a version of events to make himself sound innocent.

In truth, it was irrelevant, but, according to the lawyer, it added more depth to the prosecution's portrait of Tiwary as a liar and a generally unpleasant person.

Anyone who has never sat through a criminal jury trial might think that the lawyer is being unfair to the jury in suggesting that they could assume issues were important simply because a lot of time was spent on them.

So it is necessary to remind readers that criminal jury trials bear no resemblance to television courtroom dramas. In these very entertaining programmes, opposing barristers air neat, easily comprehensible, logically arranged alternative sequences of events. The jury then votes for the one they find more convincing.

Nothing could be further from the reality of a real court. A real-life prosecution's narrative will circle and swivel for hours. Occasionally it will swoop down to drill into one area in so much detail that those trapped in the court dream of leaping to their feet to run shrieking from the room.

The questions posed are often long and rambling. The answers, even more so. Double negatives and "questions within questions" abound. The cross-examination of forensic experts can be a particular agony. It may go on and on, circling in upon itself. Even the court reporters, concentrating fiercely to take notes, struggle to follow. Bludgeoned by detail, jurors often seek relief in sleep.

Some modern judges use their iPads to give juries timelines and "decision maps" to help them come to their verdicts. The jury in *R v Ram Puneet Tiwary* was given no such assistance. They would inevitably have been struggling to keep track of the torturously detailed timeline of the case's narrative. And they needed to really understand this timeline to come to a verdict that truly reflected the evidence.

Guilty

So what made them so certain he was guilty?

Tiwary later wrote a memoir about his experiences in Sydney. In it he suggested that racism might have played a part in the verdict. He quoted a prisoner whom he met in his time on remand as saying: "If you are brown-skinned and are charged with a violent crime, you will be convicted; if you are yellow-skinned and charged with a drug crime, you will be convicted; if you are Aboriginal, look it, and are charged with any crime, you will be convicted. If you fall outside those groups, only then does reasonable doubt come into play with the jury."

The lawyer who studied the trial doesn't think racism applied in this case. But he identified a factor that may have been nearly as powerful: the jury as a whole just didn't like Tiwary. Therefore, they didn't believe a word he said.

After all, he had certainly been lying to the army and his parents about his academic results and hadn't been paying his rent. He had "lied" to friends about whether he had been at the flat during the murders. So how could he be believed when he said that he was in his room asleep during the first murder, and had stayed in his room during the second?

In November 2006, Justice Adams sentenced Tiwary to 25 years' jail for the murder of Tay Chow Lyang and life imprisonment for the murder of Tony Tan.

Fortunately for the prisoner, his engagement with the NSW court system did not end with that sentence.

In the five months between the jury verdict and his sentencing, Tim Game, SC, had already begun working on an appeal that was finally heard in October 2008. The judgement, released on December 17, 2008, justified Game's reputation as the "go to" expert for appeals. The verdict in the 2006 trial was quashed and a new trial ordered.

The second trial

This trial, held in 2009, was effectively a re-run of the first one. The police crime scene expert, Detective Elliott, appeared again. He repeated his statement that, in his view, the blood spatter on Tiwary's feet was "impact spatter" that landed when Tiwary was bashing Tony Tan, and not, as the defence suggested, "expirated blood" coughed up by Tan in his last minute of life.

Needless to say, a test exists that could have resolved this question. The blood on Tiwary's feet could have been analysed for the presence of saliva. But this test was not done.

At the previous trial the police scientist had offered a possible explanation for the absence of Tay's blood on the weapons. Perhaps it had been there, he had suggested. Just not in the places on the weapons that he had chosen to swab.

In the time before the second trial, the bat and knife had both been tested, from top to bottom. There was none of Tay's blood on either weapon. Unabashed, Elliott repeated his assertion that the "shape of the bat" had restricted the direction of the blood spray and spatter.

Of course a simple re-enactment by police, using the same bat, could have confirmed or contradicted this. And a re-enactment may even have been attempted. Police documents confirm that a Maroubra detective bought the same bat as Tiwary's in November 2003. A police statement at the time confirmed that it was "later... used by crime scene for scientific tests". If such tests were done, their results never made it into the brief of evidence. There is a temptation to conclude that these test results were not used because they contradicted the police case.

Once again, as in the first trial, the jury was asked to believe that Tiwary had emerged with none of Tay's blood, and hardly any of Tony Tan's blood, on him because he had washed himself. And they were asked to believe this in spite of the absence of wet towels or any trace of the washing away of blood in the flat.

Once again, a jury found Tiwary guilty, with the second trial judge imposing a sentence of 48 years.

A second appeal

Tiwary's barrister, top Sydney silk David Dalton, SC, immediately began working on an appeal.

The advocate was "shocked" by the verdict, he recalls. The evidence against his client just wasn't there, he believed. There was also solid forensic evidence – in the form of fingerprints on the back of his bedroom door and dust marks on the floor – which supported his client's account of having dragged a cabinet in front of his door to barricade himself in when he heard what sounded like an assault going on outside.

"I am not usually shocked by jury verdicts," the lawyer says. But the ones that he finds difficult to predict tend to be found in cases where an accused has been the subject of extended media attention. Local media interest in the Tiwary case in Sydney had been sparse and he had never considered it as a factor. Afterwards, however, his attention was drawn to the blanket coverage the case had received in Singapore. Reading some of the very negative pieces published, he found himself wondering whether some jury members had quietly defied the trial judge's standard warning against using Google to do their own research. One article, "Killer's smiles hid an angry dark side" published in *The Straits Times* after the first guilty verdict, had included a range of negative anecdotes, mostly anonymous, accusing Tiwary of everything – from stealing an army mate's rations to slapping a girlfriend (according to an unnamed ex-girlfriend who emailed the paper after his conviction).

As his memoir later revealed, Tiwary also spent a great deal of time pondering why this jury, like the previous one, had found him guilty.

One lawyer told him, privately, that he had been "too composed". This was an angle also taken by the prosecutor in the second trial, who had told the jury to not only look at "what" Tiwary said, "but how he says it".

Tiwary ended up concluding that it made most sense to attribute his convictions to "human nature".

"When tragedy strikes, we want someone to blame," he wrote later. "And when a receptacle for the anger we feel is presented to us in the form of an accused sitting in the defendant's box, with the authorities asserting his guilt, it is all too easy to be prejudiced in favour of the prosecution."

Unsurprisingly, by the time that second jury found him guilty, Tiwary had already spiralled deep into despair and depression.

The filth of the prison environment had also set off a serious case of Obsessive Compulsive Disorder. This made it impossible for him to sit on or even touch most of the surfaces in the various jails in which he was confined over his eight years and three months of incarceration. He became a compulsive hand washer, using first "a dirty initial soap" and following up with a second "clean" bar of soap. He scrubbed and disinfected his cell daily. He even disinfected the rubber gloves he donned before touching the paper towels that he would soak in disinfectant before wiping all surfaces in his cell.

His one distraction was the appeal. He spent the next two years obsessively studying transcripts and evidence, so he could feel as involved as possible in the process.

The appeal bench judges assess the forensic evidence

That second appeal was heard on July 20 and July 24, 2012. Two days later, the three judges on the appeal bench overturned both murder convictions. They acquitted Tiwary on both counts and ordered him to be freed.

Their written judgment, published in September 2012, drew the conclusions that a cool and logical assessment of the facts and the forensic evidence demanded. The judges did what the police had been unable and unwilling to do. They treated as plausible the theory that the murders might have been the work of the driver of the car that collected Tony Tan from the university that fateful day. They did, however, wonder if Tiwary might have had some idea about who this man was.

They then explained that it was this possible involvement of others, combined with the dearth of forensic evidence connecting Tiwary to the murders, that created the "reasonable doubt" about him being the murderer. This justified an acquittal.

Their judgement provided a comprehensive summary of the forensic evidence presented to the jury. They drew particular attention to the absence of any signs of washing – a state of affairs that contradicted the prosecution case.

"If …. the bathroom had been used by the appellant to wash himself," the judges wrote, "he would have had carefully to dry the bathroom surfaces and himself. This would have required clothing or a towel which would have been wet. No such wet clothes or towel were or was placed into evidence."

The judges also skewered the implausibility of the prosecution's theory of the timing of that supposed clean-up.

"Having just bludgeoned and stabbed Mr Tan in a violent and ferocious attack, this careful and cold-blooded murderer must carefully and thoroughly wash and dry not only himself, but also the bathroom. Sloppy or careless work will see him undone. The killing was in all likelihood done some time after 2.05 pm, possibly after 2.10 pm. By 2.20 or 2.21 pm, he has called 000. Not only is this barely enough time to undertake the task of despatching Mr Tan, washing and drying himself and washing and drying the bathroom, but it raises the question why he would place himself under such time pressure."

They pointed out the inherent absurdity of Tiwary calling 000 at 2.20 pm if he was calling to cover up his murder by pretending to find the bodies.

"There was no need to call 000 at 2.20 or 2.21 pm. The importance of the cleaning task for exculpation would logically have dictated (to such a careful planner, on this hypothesis) some further delay of the call."

And they noted the tone of that 000 call, describing it as having aspects that "tell in favour of innocence".

"Whilst emotion can be faked, of course, the tone, verging on hysteria, of the appellant when he was transferred, resonated with fear. Further, he asked to remain on the line with the ambulance officer until the ambulance or police arrived, in a tone of residual fear and distress. This would not appear to be the action of someone who has methodically planned and effected the execution of both Tay and Tan."

Acquittal but not freedom

Acquittal did not mean Tiwary was free to walk the streets of Sydney. He was allowed to shed the green prison issue clothing that he had been wearing for the last eight years. But he was transferred to immigration detention, where he spent the next six and a half weeks, awaiting the release of the Court of Criminal Appeal judgement.

Nine days after it appeared, he boarded a plane home to Singapore.

A few days later, the NSW Director of Public Prosecutions confirmed that there would be no appeal against the acquittal.

Tiwary did not speak to the media on his return home, a decision he made out of respect for the families of his dead flatmates.

And neither he nor any of his family members would agree to be interviewed when Channel NewsAsia made a short film about the case, called *Get Real!: The Sydney Murders Mystery*, and aired on TV the following year.

Two years later, in September 2014, the then 35-year-old published his memoir, *Ninety-Nine Months*, which became a bestseller in Singapore. Since then he has done no interviews and made no public appearances.

Case Eight
SAVED BY THE DIRT UNDER HIS FINGERNAILS

Hong Kong-based truck driver Chan Sum-yau had been charged with being involved in one of the most daring and dangerous bombing plots in Hong Kong history. Residue of ammonium nitrate (the main component of the planned bomb) was found under the man's fingernails. This was proof, the prosecution said, that he was involved in the plot. But was it?.

You could call Hong Kong-based truck driver Chan Sum-yau an idiot. Or you could call him simply unlucky. But it is fairer to sum him up as typical of the kind of man who would one day find himself in desperate need of a criminal lawyer.

Neither criminal masterminds nor overly law-abiding, men like Chan can live their lives without attracting serious police attention. Then, one day, they do something both mildly illegal and stunningly stupid. Suddenly they're facing a long prison sentence.

A divorced father of four, Chan had obtained his Hong Kong residency after "sneaking in" from mainland China in 1972, at the age of 21. He made a living by dividing his time between the former British colony and China, driving trucks back and forth. At the same time he was maintaining relationships with both a "lady friend" in Hong Kong and a fiancée in Guangzhou.

The one spectacularly foolish thing he did was to accept a delivery job that involved him using a false name to buy a piece of property for somebody else. He failed to ask any probing questions about the use to which this property would be put. And, crucially, he never bothered to find out who was behind the whole operation.

As a result, he landed himself a small but important role in one of the most daring and dangerous bombing plots in Hong Kong history. It was a plan that involved two of the most notorious gangsters to have ever picked up an AK-47.

The extraordinary plot and the two gangster kings

The first gangster, a crime boss known as "Big Spender", had hatched a plan to blow up Hong Kong's Stanley Prison in order to free the second. This man was his colleague and former partner in crime, Yip Kai-foon – alias "the king of thieves"– then serving a 41-year sentence behind its five-metre walls.

Chan knew none of this. At that point he only knew "Big Spender" and Yip Kai-foon as characters on the evening news.

The truck driver's unwitting involvement with Big Spender had begun one night in late 1997, when he went to a mahjong hall in Guangzhou. There he had got talking to a man named Ah Chui, who was involved in gambling on horse races. Ah Chui had several small but lucrative jobs to offer him. One of them was to make a property investment in Hong Kong for him. Chan knew there was something dodgy happening. He assumed it was to do with illegal gambling.

Following the instructions he'd been given, he bought a rusting ivy-covered hut in the remote New Territories village of Yuen Long, near the border with Shenzen, and registered it under a false name.

Then, on Saturday January 17, 1998, he carried out the rest of the job exactly as he had been instructed. Along with a man called Wong Fung-kei, a tailor by trade, he bought and delivered a load of plastic barrels to the Yuen Long hut. From the outside, the place looked just the same as the derelict shack he had purchased some months earlier. But in the meantime its interior had undergone a complete renovation. It now had two new rooms and a secure interior cockloft.

The trap closes on Chan Sum-yau

The two men had just finished carrying the last load of containers inside when Chan became aware of a sudden flurry of movement in the undergrowth around the hut.

Within seconds he was lying flat on his face in the dirt as camouflage-wearing police from the Organised Crime and Triad Bureau emerged from the bushes and wrestled him and his fellow worker to the ground.

He was put under arrest. Suddenly he was in urgent need of a lawyer – a necessity that became even more pressing when he discovered that the crime he was being arrested for had nothing to do with illegal gambling.

Together with Wong and another man, a mobile phone shop proprietor called Lau Cheuk-fan, Chan was charged with the possession of a huge quantity of explosives.

A week later he and his co-defendants were being treated like newly captured terrorists.

As a crowd of reporters looked on, the three men were herded into the dock of Hong Kong's Eastern Court by eight police officers. More police, all armed with submachine guns, stood at the back of the court, their fingers tense on the triggers of their weapons.

All three were being charged with possessing 818 kg of explosives, 497 m of safety fuse, almost 2000 detonators and two gas masks, both of which contained traces of explosives trapped inside the filters. A load of explosives this size, the prosecutor told the court, could bring down a multi-storey building.

The slightly dodgy job that Chan had taken on had involved delivering barrels to a lonely hut in the New Territories. But the charge wasn't for being a gangster's delivery boy. He was being charged because the hut where he dropped off the barrels was a store for boxes of explosives. And the barrels were going to be employed to transport those explosives to their next destination. Some big and dangerously criminal enterprise was underway. By taking the job – and being there when the police arrived – he had made himself part of it.

By then Chan had made the first sensible decision since the night he met Ah Chui. He had chosen lawyer Peter Lavac to represent him.

Lavac was an Australian barrister who had arrived in Hong Kong in 1986 and spent his first eight years as a crown prosecutor for the Hong Kong Director of Public Prosecutions. In that position, he had worked on a daily basis with police from the Organised Crime and Triad Bureau. A world-class athlete, the former Sydneysider had set a world record in 1990 when he led a six-member surf ski team more than 900 km across the South China Sea from Hong Kong to the Philippines. In 2002, he would also win gold and bronze medals at the World Lifesaving Championships at Daytona Beach, Florida.

Despite having crossed over to criminal defence work at the private Bar, the lawyer had maintained good police contacts. He was very familiar with the criminal histories of both Big Spender and Yip Kai-foon – and he had heard all the rumours about Big Spender's plans. So he knew exactly how much trouble his client was in.

Yet it wasn't his job to lecture his client on the stupidity of his actions. His job was to get him off.

Lavac's new client had lots of problems. The most serious was the sheer quantity of the explosives involved. Memories were still fresh of the 1993 Oklahoma City bombing in which native-born

US terrorist Timothy McVeigh had exploded a homemade bomb made of 1816 kg of ammonium nitrate fertiliser. The blast had brought down the Alfred P Murrah Federal Building and destroyed or damaged more than 300 other buildings in surrounding blocks. The death toll had been 168, with 680 others injured.

But there were other difficulties ahead – especially the potential "guilt by association" implied by his client's apparent connection with Big Spender. The police had evidence that the two other men with whom Chan had been charged were well acquainted with the gangster kingpin. Lavac would have to convince a jury that his client was the only "cleanskin" in the group. He needed them to believe that Chan, like the jury members, was just a Hong Kong resident who read the papers and therefore knew all about the exploits of both Big Spender and Yip Kai-foon. But, like them, he didn't even know what either man looked like.

The Big Spender: his life and times

By 1998 Big Spender had such a high media profile in Hong Kong that he was almost a folk hero. At times, it seemed that the authorities couldn't lay a glove on him.

Yet he had actually been one of the first targets of the Hong Kong Government's Organised and Serious Crimes Ordinance, created in 1995 with the aim of fighting organised crime by seizing convicted criminals' assets. Around HK$160million worth of his properties had been seized by authorities. But these were later restored to his family because of lack of evidence.

Born Cheung Tze-keung, Big Spender had earned his nickname from his lavish lifestyle, funded by the armed robberies and kidnappings he carried out. He bought flashy cars, including a yellow Lamborghini, and a large real estate portfolio of luxury apartments. He also dropped huge amounts of money in casinos from Macau to

Cambodia. He was reportedly in the habit of gambling millions of dollars in a single session. Once he lost HK$200million on a single game. Or so the story went. And journalists loved him because he actually talked to them – and could speak English well.

Big Spender had started his working life as a teenage apprentice, helping in his father's illegal lottery business. He first gained notoriety in 1991 when, at the age of 36, he was charged with executing one of the world's biggest-ever cash robberies: the theft of a sum of HK$167million in US and Hong Kong currency from a security van at Hong Kong's Kai Tak Airport.

The money, the property of a New York bank, was about to be loaded on a flight to Taiwan. It was in a security van heading towards the airport's air cargo terminal when three men, one of them allegedly Cheung, hijacked it and drove it to a nearby location. There the guards were tied up and the money loaded into another van that was found, abandoned, 36 hours later.

Cheung was convicted and jailed for 18 years for his role in this heist. But he was freed in 1995 after serving only three years. A judge ordered his release on the basis of the unreliability of the evidence of the one witness who had claimed to be able to identify him. The judge even ordered police to return the HK$262,000 seized from him years earlier, after police found it in a hiding place behind a fish tank at his mother-in-law's business premises.

His reputation newly restored, with newspapers describing him as "a businessman", Big Spender emerged from the court to pose for newspaper photographers. He was also free to move on to an even more profitable business: kidnapping for ransom.

In 1996, Cheung masterminded the kidnapping of Victor Li, son of Hong Kong's richest man Li Ka-shing. A year later, he abducted tycoon Walter Kwok, the chairman of real estate behemoth Sun Hung Kai Properties. Each man was snatched while driving between home and work, taken to a house in Fan Ling, in the New Territories, and imprisoned in a wooden box with a few air holes in it. Neither the victims nor their families ever called the police and the two crimes netted Cheung HK$1billion and HK$600,000 respectively, half of which the crime boss kept himself.

The king of thieves: his path to Stanley Prison

In his days working as a prosecutor, Lavac had learned more than he wanted to know about "the king of thieves": the man whom Big Spender wanted to free from his cell at Stanley Prison.

Yip Kai-foon was a legendarily violent criminal who had been Hong Kong's most wanted man until his arrest the previous year.

He was also said to have worked together with Big Spender on a series of brazen daylight robberies on Hong Kong jewellery stores in the early 1990s.

In one, Yip and his balaclava-wearing colleagues had threatened shop staff with AK-47s and stolen HK$3million worth of jewels. They had then fired more than 50 shots at pursuing police as they fought their way down Tai Po Road in Sham Shui Po district.

The lawyer had seen TV news footage of a balaclava and combat boot-clad Yip. Filmed at a busy Kowloon intersection after the robbery, it showed the gangster in combat stance, feet planted wide apart as he fired long automatic bursts from his AK-47 at approaching police cars. The cars were riddled with bullets as pedestrians scattered – having finally realised they were not watching a cops and robbers film shoot. As was his habit after carrying out a big heist, Yip had then vanished back over the border to the mainland.

But by January 1998, as Lavac's client and his new workmate Wong were dropping off barrels at a remote New Territories hut, Yip was not only behind bars – he was also in a wheelchair.

Everything had gone wrong for the gangster in the early hours of the morning of May 13, 1996, when he had covertly re-entered Hong Kong by boat. At the time it was rumoured that he had come to help Big Spender with the kidnap of Victor Li. His plan came unstuck when police literally stumbled over him and five of his henchmen as they attempted to land their small boat at Kennedy Pier. Mistaking the group for illegal immigrants, the police started firing questions at him. They had no idea who he was – and didn't find out until they got him back to the police station and fingerprinted him.

Yip's underlings fled. But their boss dropped his bag to his feet and pulled a gun. In the exchange of fire that ensued, he was shot in the spine and left paralysed from the waist down. The bag had contained another handgun, a high-powered machine gun, ammunition, 1.8 kg of explosives and two remote-control detonators.

Yip was later wheeled into court to face charges of possessing arms, ammunition and 1.8 kg of explosives, and of using a gun to resist arrest. For that, as well as charges relating to an earlier escape from custody back in 1989, he was jailed for 41 years.

What was the evidence against Chan?

Lavac's first job, as Chan's lawyer, was to find out all the details behind the charges that had been laid against his client.

What evidence did the police actually have on him? And how much did they really know about the supposed plot to bomb Stanley Prison, let alone Chan's connection to it?

In this respect, Lavac's extensive police connections served him well. He learned that a paid informer had told police about Big Spender's alleged preparations to blow up Stanley Prison in order to free Yip Kai-foon.

To Lavac, this crazy plan had sounded quite believable. For a start, Big Spender was a generous friend. He was known to be extremely angry about the treatment being meted out to several of the imprisoned drug criminals with whom he had become close during his own time in Stanley Prison. And he was especially perturbed by the plight of Yip Kai-foon.

The lawyer knew that Hong Kong police had already suspected Big Spender of organising a series of attacks on Correctional Services Department buildings in 1996, during which sentry posts were demolished and an officer's car was torched. Big Spender was also presumed to have ordered the draping of a banner outside the prison, which read: "Treat my colleagues better or eat dog shit." This was a reaction, supposedly, to rumours that prison officers had forcibly injected Yip with sedatives.

A prison bombing almost sounded like the logical next step he would take.

Lavac was soon aware that the police had no proof that Big Spender had actually intended to bomb Stanley Prison. But, as the quantity of explosives indicated, he had been clearly planning some kind of bombing campaign.

His client's bad luck: Big Spender was a police target

The lawyer also realised the extent of his client's bad luck. Chan had taken a job for the gangster kingpin at exactly the time that Hong Kong police had finally decided to crack down on him once and for all.

By late 1997, not long after Chan had made his ill-fated purchase of the shack in Yuen Long, Hong Kong police had officially ended any apparent tolerance of the infamous gangster's exploits.

They had not been happy that Big Spender's high-profile kidnap victims had never called on their help.

And now, it seemed, there was a possibility that more kidnappings would follow.

Informers had begun reporting that the crime boss had further "rich lister" kidnap victims in mind. Macau casino king Stanley Ho was one name that kept coming up. One of Hong Kong's wealthiest men, Ho lived in an exclusive low-rise enclave of streets in Deep Water Bay, on the southern shore of Hong Kong Island – as did the gangster's previous targets. There were also whispers that Big Spender had been plotting to kidnap Hong Kong's Chief Secretary, Anson Chan, to use her as a bargaining chip for the release from jail of Yip Kai-foon.

It was time to move against the gangster. A special task force was set up to track his every move.

Round the clock surveillance of Big Spender began in December 1997. Within a few weeks, police had gathered what looked like promising material for a future prosecution of the gangster.

Big Spender was believed to be the owner of a number of properties in Hong Kong, including a 5,000-sq ft dwelling in Cumberland Road, Kowloon Tong, which later sold for HK$30million. He also owned three villas in South Bay and a 3000-sq ft apartment, where his partner and two sons lived.

Police surveillance soon focused on a high-walled hideaway in Fanling. This luxury residence was also thought to be the place where Big Spender's affluent kidnap victims were held while negotiations continued over their ransoms. Most of the surveillance film that ended up as evidence for the prosecution's case against Chan and his two co-accused had been shot outside this house.

Lavac wasn't thrilled to discover that the place had actually been bought by Wong Fung-kei, the man with whom Chan had been delivering barrels when they were both pounced on by undercover police. It was Wong who had filled out all the appropriate documents in the name of his 78-year-old mother. But the furnishings, which included a life-size iron bust of Big Spender, suggested the actual identity of the hideaway's owner. The lawyer was immensely relieved when he was sure that police had no evidence linking his client to this property.

The undercover operation caught Chan in its net

Undercover police teams set themselves up in bushes some 500 m away from the high-walled compound. On January 8, 1998, they captured extensive footage of Big Spender himself.

Stripped to his underwear, he was seen hefting polystyrene boxes labelled "fresh scallops" from a truck and loading them into a silver Mercedes Benz. Several other men were helping him. Wong was one. Another was Lau Cheuk-fan, the third man who would later be standing in the dock with Chan and Wong. Again, Lavac was relieved to discover that his client had not been there.

The silver Mercedes made several trips to the hut that Chan had purchased, and forty boxes were unloaded. At that point, police were still unsure of their contents. Some officers had assumed they would contain heroin.

Once the delivery team had left, police officers took swabs of the soil near the boxes. They hoped the soil samples would give them a hint to the boxes' contents. And they did. The tests showed traces of ammonium nitrate: the main ingredient of the explosive known as ANFO, or ammonium nitrate fuel oil. Used regularly in mining – and in bombs – it comprises 94 per cent ammonium nitrate and 6 per cent fuel oil.

A group of surveillance officers from the Organised Crime and Triad Bureau then dug themselves into a position with a clear view of the entrance to the hut where the explosives were stored.

Their orders were clear: they were to arrest the next visitors to the hut.

On January 17, Wong and Chan arrived and began unpacking their load of empty plastic barrels. Police were entitled to assume that the contents of the boxes already in the hut would soon be transferred into these barrels before being transported to the places where they would be put to use. Whether the boxes contained heroin or explosives, their owners and transporters were breaking the law.

When the men had finished unloading, the officers pounced. Lau Cheuk-fan was arrested later that night at his home.

Big Spender's escape: was the president of China involved?

Oddly enough, the man who was supposed to be the organiser of this operation was not arrested.

Big Spender had been the target of a 24-hour-a-day surveillance operation. And yet Hong Kong police officers had failed to move against him. Worse, it seemed that they had stood by and let him slip over the border of Hong Kong, into mainland China and out of their jurisdiction. The official handover of the former British colony to China had taken place on July 1, 1997. "One country, two systems" was its mantra. It meant that Hong Kong kept its British-style legal system, and its police maintained their control of its territory.

It was later confirmed that the gangster had left Hong Kong on January 15, 1998. At this point police were keeping surveillance on the Yuen Long hut. It was two days later that Chan and Wong would be arrested there.

At the time, however, there was no official news of Big Spender. It later emerged that he had been arrested by mainland police on

January 26, as he attempted to go through the border control point that divided the Zhuhai Special Economic Zone from the rest of China.

Rumours had begun to circulate that Big Spender was missing, that he was somewhere on the mainland and had been arrested. But they were not published in the newspapers until March 1998. Mainland authorities did not confirm his arrest until July.

One big question remained. Why had Hong Kong police allowed Big Spender to leave their area? There was a logical answer to it. But it came in the form of an intriguing conspiracy theory.

The China connection

Back in 1996, when Cheung had kidnapped Victor Li, the son of Hong Kong's richest man Li Ka-shing, neither the victim nor his family had contacted the police. It appeared that the gangster had escaped with a HK$1billion ransom. He had even, it was rumoured, had the cheek to ask Li Ka-shing for advice on the best way to invest his windfall – a detail that Li would confirm many years later.

But, according to police gossip, the magnate had his revenge. And he had done so with the help of his powerful friends on the mainland, most notably President Jiang Zemin.

Li, the gossip went, was frustrated with the fact that Big Spender's top gun lawyers had always been able to get him out of charges brought in Hong Kong. And he was still smarting from the loss of the HK$1billion ransom. So he had spoken to his friend, the Chinese president. The message had then gone down to Hong Kong's Crime and Triad Bureau. The crime boss was not to be arrested in Hong Kong. In the former colony the death penalty was a distant memory. It had been formally abolished in 1993, 27 years after the last execution had been held.

Accordingly, Big Spender was to be allowed to escape into China – and to think he was getting away. For him there would be no Hong Kong jury trial, held under a British-style system.

Instead he would face the mainland's draconian legal system – with its speedy trials, regular guilty verdicts and subsequent executions.

This theory was first aired in print in August 1998, a month after mainland authorities confirmed that they had Big Spender in custody. An article by journalist Agnes Cheung Wai-sum in *Asiaweek*, entitled "Exit Big Spender", had spelt it out. The order to let Big Spender escape to China had come from Chinese President Jiang Zemin himself, she wrote. It was supposedly the leader's response to the kidnapping of the son of his good friend Li Ka-shing.

The theory was also outlined in Jonathan Fenby's *Dealing With The Dragon: A Year in the New Hong Kong*, with the former *South China Morning Post* editor placing the episode in the "realm of generally believed probability which remains unprovable".

Lavac watched out for every scrap of news or gossip about Big Spender's fate. If the gangster boss were to be tried in China, the trial would be quick and secret. Some extra details might also emerge of the crimes for which Chan had been charged.

Also in August 1998, Hong Kong's *South China Morning Post* had published an article airing mainland authorities' claims that Big Spender had confessed to intending to use the explosives "to threaten the Government, blow up prisons and kidnap more tycoons". During that confession he also reportedly told police that he had feared that his luck had run out when a jade pendant he always wore broke a short time before his arrest. In Chinese culture, jade symbolises nobility, perfection and immortality and it is considered lucky to receive a gift of jade jewellery.

The *South China Morning Post* article was short. Lavac hoped that the potential jurors in his client's trial had missed it.

On October 20, 1998, after months of imprisonment and interrogation, Big Spender, along with 35 alleged accomplices, was finally brought to trial in the Guangzhou Intermediate People's Court. He was found guilty of importing more than 800 kg of explosives from China into Hong Kong and of kidnapping Victor Li and Walter Kwok. Along with four of his former gang members, he was executed by firing squad in early December 1998.

Two months passed, during which articles about Big Spender's trial and execution continued to appear.

Chan's trial begins

The trial of Chan and his two co-defendants, Wong Fung-kei and Lau Cheuk-fan, opened in February 1999 in the court that had once been known as the Supreme Court. Since the British handover it had been renamed the Court of First Instance.

As the prosecutor began his opening address, it was clear that the authorities had realised that the power of Big Spender's reputation would have prejudiced the three accused men's right to a fair trial. They did not want to risk the possibility of their defence lawyers applying for an indefinite stay of proceedings on this ground.

Therefore, Chan and his two co-accused were described only as accomplices of a criminal, whose fingerprints had been found at the hut and who was known, cryptically, as "Person A".

Lavac was relieved, although the evidence against his client still didn't look good for him.

Chan had only been filmed unloading the empty containers, which were presumably meant for further transport of the explosives being stored in the hut. But police had swabbed his client's hands and clothes after his arrest – and found substantial traces of ammonium nitrate. This fact, the prosecution was alleging, meant that Chan had handled the explosives. It also indicated that he had been inside the hut for purposes other than delivering the empty barrels. If he had handled the explosives, then that would imply that he knew he was involved in some kind of criminal bombing attack.

At least the jury didn't know that Chan had been working on a job organised by the notorious "Big Spender".

The involvement of Big Spender is revealed

That all changed on the fourth day of the trial when the jury was shown the video of the infamous gangster loading boxes of explosives into his car. None of them would have recognised the ordinary-looking guy in his underwear as the charismatic Big Spender, who was most usually seen in newspaper photographs posing with his Lamborghini.

But then one of Lavac's fellow defence lawyers, Peter Cosgrove, who was defending Wong, blew the cover of "Person A".

The lawyer was cross-examining Acting Sergeant Lam Chun-kwong, 33, the officer who had shot the covert video of Cheung loading boxes of explosives into the boot of his silver Mercedes-Benz, assisted by Wong.

Suddenly Cosgrove asked Lam if he could identify the man previously referred to as "Person A".

Sergeant Lam paused for a minute.

"Cheung Tze-keung," he replied.

"And that's the same Cheung who was recently executed in China?" the barrister asked. "Who had the nickname Big Spender?"

The officer agreed. Journalists in the court leapt to their feet and rushed out to phone their editors. The case had already been attracting good coverage because of the amount of explosives involved. Now the name "Big Spender" was in the headline of every news report about it.

Lavac remains mystified by his fellow counsel's decision. It certainly didn't help the man's own client, who had been captured on video in conversation with Big Spender and therefore looked to be the closest of the three to the crime kingpin. The fact that it was Wong's lawyer who asked the question made his client look even more directly identified with Cheung.

From that moment on, Chan and his co-accused were referred to in press reports as "henchmen" or "alleged henchmen" of the gangster. But, in contrast to his two co-accused, no evidence was ever produced to prove that Chan had even met the extroverted crime king.

Yet, while the ghost of Big Spender remained a constant presence in the courtroom, no mention was ever made of his plan to bomb a Hong Kong prison. It was puzzling. After all, this allegation had been aired in a documentary shown on mainland television: one that had featured excerpts from Big Spender's filmed confession to authorities.

The allegation was repeated in the "Exit Big Spender" *Asiaweek* article, which appeared while Chan and his two co-accused were in jail awaiting trial.

Why didn't the prosecution mention the prison bomb plot? Perhaps the charges Chan was facing "of possessing explosives with an intent to endanger life and property" were already serious enough. More likely, they believed that their star expert witness would give evidence that would make the planned attack sound even more damning: so damning they didn't have to dress it up with a prison escape plot which the defence could argue was just a rumour.

Enter the forensic expert from Central Casting

With his trademark white panama hat and silver-tipped ebony cane, 39-year-old Dominic Brittain, the prosecution's star expert witness, was every crime show scriptwriter's idea of the eccentric forensic expert. The officer in charge of Hong Kong police's bomb disposal unit, Brittain was a Wagner fan who moonlighted as an opera critic for Hong Kong's *South China Morning Post*. He gave his testimony the full Götterdämmerung treatment.

He focused on the fact that the 818 kg of explosives seized from the boxes in the hut had been divided into 326 separate bags, each containing 2.5 kg of an incendiary mix of ammonium nitrate, TNT, fuel oil and wood chips. This suggested, he told the court, that they were intended for a series of explosions in a deadly "campaign of terror". Any of its bombs, detonated in a medium to large room, would kill or maim all its occupants. His nightmare scenario of injury to innocent victims sounded far bloodier and more cruel than a prison bomb plot where the destructive effect of the explosives would have been aimed at thick stone walls, not innocent passers-by.

The expert described the haul of explosives as "extraordinary", displaying "a level of evil I hoped I would never have to look at again". Asked by the prosecutor to describe the effect of this load of explosives being set off all at once, he asked the court to imagine it loaded into a van and detonated in "Central" – the heart of Hong Kong's business district.

"An intense fireball will light up everything in the area," he said. "The blast will expand like a semi-circular wall of air moving extremely rapidly. Anybody within a 50-m diameter has almost no chance of survival… The blast will literally rip the lighter parts off the body – traumatic amputation of arms and legs, and in several cases, heads will be removed as well… As it moves outwards, people will have a higher chance of survival. Their lungs will explode and, at the outer limits, eardrums will burst. Beyond 100 metres, people will suffer pain from the noise."

And then there would be the effect of the shrapnel. The blast would cause the van itself to disintegrate into "missiles travelling several thousand metres per second that can be lethal at a range of 200 m".

Broken glass would rain down from the windows up to 40 storeys in an area 600 m in any direction from the blast. If the bombs were planted inside, any building in the SAR (or Hong Kong Special Administrative Region, as the former British colony was renamed after the handover) would collapse "like a pack of cards".

The jury was transfixed, Lavac recalls. Open-mouthed, eyes wide.

The government prosecutor Mike Arthur didn't need to play to the jury. His star witness had done that for him.

"It's obvious," Arthur said in his summing up, "that this amount of high explosives was not intended for anything innocent."

It is hard to imagine a defence barrister not feeling ill at the sight of a jury turning to putty in the hands of a prosecution barrister. But Lavac was not allowing himself the luxury of emotion.

"In any trial I am totally unemotional," he says. "I function like a robot. It's the only way to survive as a criminal lawyer. A lot of people can't do this job because they can't switch their emotions off."

The card up the defence lawyer's sleeve: their own forensic expert

Lavac also had a killer card up his sleeve. He had found it when he was looking at the forensic evidence.

The first question for the three men's defence lawyers had been a very basic one. Could they provide any evidence that their clients had no knowledge of the fact that they were involved in the storage and transport of a deadly load of explosives?

In fact Brittain had provided some evidence that, in theory, might have given the three accused men an "out". Under cross-examination, he told the court that the powder in the zip lock bags would not be recognisable to somebody untrained in the use of explosives. An amateur's eye would also have failed to identify the cardboard detonators.

The contents of the boxes were so dangerous that they had the potential to be detonated by the static electricity that can come off the human hand.

"The little spark that jumps from a finger is a source of fire," he told the court. "It sounds unlikely but that static has caused explosions to happen and kill in the past."

The fact that Chan's co-accused Lau had been shown on the surveillance video smoking while loading the boxes of explosives could have been taken as evidence that he didn't know what he was handling.

Lau's barrister asked Brittain to comment on the wisdom of smoking in the same vehicle as the explosives. He replied that it would have been "incredibly stupid".

"Lau's barrister made a big deal out of this to the jury, telling them that, by smoking, he couldn't possibly have known he was handling explosives at the time," recalls Lavac. "It was a good point."

The best evidence to support a convincing argument that the men had no idea of the goods they had been dealing with would have been an absence of any trace evidence of explosives on their hands.

But, as Lavac explains, the prosecution's forensic evidence suggested the exact opposite.

"After they were arrested the cops took them back to the police station and had them forensically examined," the lawyer recalls. "They tested their fingernails, shoes and clothing. And they found ammonium nitrate residue under their fingernails, on their shoes and on their clothes. There was enough of it to have the prosecution say 'this is conclusive evidence that these guys both handled the explosives inside the hut on that day'."

This was classic forensic science evidence. It illustrated the forensic science precept first set out more than a century ago by the French police scientist Edmond Locard and known ever since as "Locard's exchange principle" or, simply "Locard's principle".

According to Locard, who set up the world's first police lab in the French city of Lyons in 1910, there could be no such thing as a "clean contact" between two objects.

"When two bodies or objects come into contact, they mutually contaminate each other with minute fragments of material," Locard wrote.

It was the prosecution's theory that the ammonium nitrate on the hands and clothing of the suspects meant they had been handling the packages of explosives in the hut and that they therefore were involved in the whole enterprise. Chan had only been caught in the act of delivering barrels. It was the prosecution's case that all three had been doing more than that.

But could this trace evidence be interpreted to mean something else? Might the presence of ammonium nitrate on the men's hands and clothing be evidence of a different kind of contact altogether?

Peter Lavac's first step was to look closely at the actual process by which his client had been arrested. In particular he focused on the fact that Chan had been tackled to the ground by the undercover surveillance officers. He had only been handcuffed after a struggle featuring a lot of rolling around in the dirt.

Imagining the scene, he visualised soil flying through the air as the men scuffled. His client had dirt on him from the ground. And he had ammonium nitrate on him.

The prosecution said that it came from the contents of the boxes. But what if the soil outside the hut had also been contaminated with ammonium nitrate? The substance was a fertiliser, after all.

There was one person who could help provide a definitive answer: forensic scientist Sheilah Hamilton, who had spent two decades with the Forensic Science Division of the Hong Kong Government Laboratory before setting up her independent consultancy, Forensic Focus. At the time she was away teaching in her native Scotland. Lavac phoned her and she agreed to look into the case. If her report was needed, she would come back to Hong Kong to testify for the defence.

The jury was well positioned to understand the significance of any evidence about soil because Lavac had insisted – with the agreement of the judge – that the jury be taken on a tour of the hut and the area immediately outside it.

"For me it was very important that the jury should see that for themselves," the barrister recalls. "Particularly where the accused was tackled to the ground by the cops and where the struggle occurred, involving a lot of rolling around in the dirt."

The lawyer could only shake his head as the police then proceeded to turn the jury's day trip into a media circus. It looked designed to make the public view his stumblebum of a client as a dangerous terrorist. What was worse was that the jury would also be coming to a similar reassessment of Chan.

"My client was taken to the scene in a prison van escorted by a dozen police cars. He emerged from the van with a black hood over his head and both his wrists and ankles shackled. Just to make sure, when he shuffled to the site, he was surrounded by a phalanx of police officers, wearing bulletproof vests and armed with sub machine guns. Meanwhile we were deafened by the clatter of at least three police helicopters hovering overhead.

"It was totally surreal. There were at least 100 journalists, photographers and TV crews, all tipped off by police."

When it was finally aired in court, Hamilton's report would prove devastating to the Crown case. The first hint of its contents, interestingly, came out during the testimony of the prosecution's forensic expert, Kwok Lai-chu.

Under cross-examination by Lavac, the government expert had agreed that the swabs taken from the bodies and clothing of the accused men contained only ammonium nitrate. This was only one of the ingredients found in the haul of greyish white powder explosives being stored in the hut. The actual explosive powder contained TNT, fuel oil and wood chips in addition to the ammonium nitrate.

Peter Lavac asked Kwok if he had tested the soil outside the hut. The forensic expert had to agree that he had not.

Lavac then told the court that more than 3.2 million kg of ammonium nitrate had been imported into Hong Kong in 1997, mostly for use as fertiliser.

"Bearing in mind that this is a rural area," he asked Kwok, "if the soil contained ammonium nitrate, it could contaminate the hands and feet of anyone who came into contact with it. Correct?"

The prosecution expert had to agree.

The court then took a break for the Lunar New Year holiday. Lavac was pleased with the timing. The defence had delivered their first big blow to the prosecution's version of events. The seven-member jury now had a break, with no new information to displace this theory in their thinking.

For the defence barrister, the court story in the next day's newspaper was the perfect way to start a holiday. He smiled as he cut the article from the paper and dropped it in his case file. He couldn't have asked for a better headline. "Explosive traces may be fertiliser, expert testifies," it read.

The first sitting day after the holiday was his client's day in the witness box. Letting your client get up and speak for himself is an option that defence lawyers often refuse. But Lavac was confident that the jury would accept his client's version of events: that he had taken a job thinking it only involved some work for an illegal gambling operation.

Moreover, as he later explained, he really had no choice but to let his client speak.

"Chan had to tell the jury under oath that he had no idea he was working for the Big Spender and that he had no knowledge of any of the explosives. He was just a delivery boy, delivering empty containers. Sheilah's forensic evidence on its own would not have been enough. The jury had to believe him as well. But he came across as a fairly harmless dope – and they obviously accepted his story."

Sheilah Hamilton's day in court was devastating for the prosecution. In contrast to her work in some cases, she did not carry out any separate special tests herself. She did however commission an aerial map of the area around Ma Tso Lung, the part of Yuen Long where the hut was located, showing the many farms in the vicinity. She also produced figures indicating that almost all the farms used ammonium nitrate fertiliser. She explained that, when the wind blows, ammonium nitrate dust would fly into the air and be deposited in soil all over the area.

She was then able to destroy the credibility of the prosecution's test results simply by highlighting the basic scientific procedures they had failed to follow. The prosecution's test results, she told the court, were "worthless" because they had missed one basic and vital scientific step. They had failed to take "control samples" from the hands, shoes and clothing of other people who had also been in the vicinity of the hut where the explosives had been stored. Tests should have been conducted on the police who had been hiding outside and who had then scuffled in the dirt with the two accused as they arrested them.

She also lambasted the tests of local soil that were carried out for the prosecution.

The scientist told the court that the government forensic officers had tested soil at an address some 30 minutes' drive from the alleged crime scene – and they had done so almost a year after the seizure of the explosives.

"It was nearly a year later . . . and more to the point, it wasn't the same part of the New Territories," she told the court. "[The result] doesn't help in the slightest."

She then agreed, in reply to a question from Lavac, that ammonium nitrate traces found under the defendant's fingernails could "certainly" have come from fertiliser.

Lavac watched the jury's faces as she answered.

"They were smiling at me and nodding their heads in agreement," he recalls. "I knew I had them."

Had the Scottish-born scientist just saved his client from a long jail sentence? That afternoon in court remains one of the highlights of his almost 40-year career as a barrister.

He laughs.

"You know, if the cops had just tested their own clothes they may not have had ammonium nitrate on them. That might have been enough to contradict Sheilah Hamilton's evidence. But, stupidly, they never did. Typical bungling Hong Kong Keystone Cops."

Lavac's reading of the jury's faces proved correct. On March 9, after 13 months in custody, his client left the court a free man. But without a backward look at his lawyer.

"During the trial Chan Sum-yau promised me several times that if I got him off he would take me and my legal team on an 'all expenses paid' Mediterranean cruise," Lavac laughs. "But after he was acquitted he never even shouted me a drink."

Chan's co-accused Lau Cheuk-fan was also found not guilty. But the jury clearly thought that Wong Fung-kei knew more than his mates in the dock. They found him not guilty of possession of explosives with intent to endanger life and property, but guilty on an additional charge of possession of explosives.

The following month, according to Jonathan Fenby's *Dealing With The Dragon*, Big Spender's famous yellow Lamborghini V12 Diablo, on the market since the previous December for HK$900,000, less than one-third of the cost of a new model, finally found a buyer.

POSTSCRIPT:

In 2013 Li Ka-shing broke his 17-year silence and spoke about the night that he handed over a HK$1billion ransom to Big Spender in exchange for his son. In an interview with a mainland newspaper, the tycoon said he had advised the gangster to run away and start a new life with the money. But Cheung failed to take this advice and gambled the money away, ringing Li Ka-shing some months later for investment advice.

In 2014 Thomas Kwok, the brother of Walter Kwok, kidnapped by Big Spender in 1997, spoke about the three bargaining sessions he had with the gangster before they reached agreement on a figure of HK$600,000 for the ransom. A colleague from the family's Sun Hung Kai real estate company had to make two trips to deliver the money because he could only fit HK$300,000 worth of banknotes into his car.

Case Nine
THE BODY IN THE COUCH

Retired Salvation Army major Janet Gilson was on one of her regular visits to her Hong Kong-based niece, Julia Fareed, when she disappeared. When her body was found in a couch at Julia's flat, suspicion fell on Julia's estranged husband Ahmed. He denied any involvement. But the forensic evidence had its own story to tell.

Julia Fareed met her husband Ahmed in 2003 when they were both working in the same hotel on the idyllic tropical paradise of the Maldives: a chain of 1192 coral islands in the Indian Ocean. They married in Hong Kong in 2007 and their daughter Jasmine was born in March 2008.

In Hong Kong, the couple found another idyllic place to live, settling down on Lamma Island. Just 3 km off the southwest coast of Hong Kong, Lamma was – and still is – famous for its unspoiled rural beauty, its beaches, its excellent seafood restaurants and its population of endangered species: Romer's tree frogs, green turtles and porpoises. An attractive destination for expatriates and bohemians, the island also boasted rents that were (then) far below the usual astronomic mainland China or Hong Kong Island rates. And it was only a 40-minute ferry ride away from Julia's job on Hong Kong Island: a journey that a *New York Times* travel piece described as "one of the most delightful commuter runs in the world".

Julia Fareed's married life on Lamma was less idyllic. Her husband's ongoing drug use became a continuing source of conflict. In 2009 he was convicted of possessing dangerous drugs. The following year he was jailed for two months after being found guilty of "criminal intimidation".

By 2011 the couple had separated. Julia and Jasmine moved to a small two-bedroom ground floor flat in Yung Shue Wan, and Julia began divorce proceedings. Although they had agreed on a schedule for Ahmed to have access to their three-year-old daughter, Jasmine, Ahmed's aggressive behaviour prompted his ex-wife to go to court to get a "non-molestation" order, preventing him from entering her home.

In March 2011 Julia was happily awaiting the pleasant diversion of a visit from her UK-based Aunt Janet.

More of a mother figure to Julia than an aunt, Janet Gilson was a retired Salvation Army major who lived in the UK town of Leigh-on-Sea in Essex and had made regular trips to Hong Kong in previous years. In fact this trip was her fifth in as many years. As usual, she would be staying at Julia's flat. The place had no guestroom but Julia was happy to sleep on the living room couch, so she could give her aunt her bedroom.

Janet Gilson arrived on March 5. But Julia had the chance to enjoy only the first week of her stay before the ongoing difficulties with her ex began, once again, to blight her happiness.

A row with her ex

Hostilities flared on Sunday March 13 when Ahmed failed to return Jasmine home by 5.30 pm, and Julia had to go looking for him. After she finally tracked him down at a local restaurant and retrieved their daughter, he came round to her flat – a breach of the "non-molestation" order. Claiming that he had Jasmine's water bottle and hat, he insisted that she let him in.

When she refused, he started banging on the door, swearing at her and threatening to cause her "big trouble". She called the police, who promptly arrested him. The next morning, Monday March 14, the couple were back in the Family Court where the judge told Ahmed off and ordered him to return to court in a week's time.

The only positive aspect of this dispiriting situation was that they had at least been able to reach one agreement. Ahmed was unemployed and unhappily dependent on his wife for money. With their final divorce only weeks away, he had agreed that he had no future prospects in Hong Kong and would be best off returning to the Maldives. Julia would be paying his fare.

That night Julia arranged for Jasmine to stay at her maid/babysitter Karen's place. The day's events had been exhausting. She wanted to sleep in her child's bed and enjoy a better night's rest than she had been getting on the sofa.

The next day, Tuesday March 15, 2011, she left home at 7 am as usual, catching the 7.20 am ferry to Hong Kong Island where she worked for a local hedge fund.

Her morning was plagued with interruptions, all of them related to Ahmed.

Phone calls and texts from Ahmed

His first call had come when she was still on the ferry. He wanted Karen to collect a suitcase of Julia's from him. Supposedly this was part of his preparations to pack up his stuff, leave Hong Kong and return to the Maldives.

Julia was at her desk by nine. But there was more to-ing and fro-ing by text. Ahmed hadn't turned up for the meeting with Karen. Then he asked her to re-schedule it. Shortly after 11.30 am, she received a text message from her Aunt Janet. The message was entirely innocuous.

"Went to Sok Kwu Wan," it read. "Going to have some food here and then will take the ferry to Aberdeen. I will tell you when I come back later. Love, Jane." Sok Kwu Wan was a village, a couple of kilometres away from Julia's home.

The text arrived at exactly 11.37 am on Tuesday March 15, 2011. Later Julia would recognise that moment as the point at which her life changed forever.

At the time, however, she had simply read the text and got back to work. As a personal assistant, she always had plenty to do. Certainly she had enough time to note that it was a bit strange to be receiving a text from her beloved aunt, who was not a texter. Like many retired 64-year-olds from sleepy British seaside villages, Janet Gilson had a mobile phone but used it like an old-fashioned landline: just for phone calls. The text was also signed "Jane" rather than Janet.

But Julia wasn't a worrier by nature and she was too busy at work to let her mind start wandering. After all, this was her aunt's fifth trip to Hong Kong and she knew her way around. If she'd had time to think about it, Julia might have wondered if her aunt had got talking to someone – a friendly woman at an adjacent restaurant table perhaps. Maybe that person had taught her how to text, in between chatting about the delights of the seafood restaurants of Aberdeen.

She didn't think any more about the mysterious text until she got home and found that her aunt was still out.

Had something happened to her aunt?

It was then that she started to worry that something could be seriously wrong. For a start, her aunt wasn't answering her phone.

More perplexing was the fact that she seemed to have left the house in a terrible hurry. Her room was in a mess and she had left the bathroom water heater on.

Janet Gilson's handbag and its contents, including keys to the premises, a wallet and her passport were missing, as expected if she had headed off for a day of sightseeing. But she hadn't taken her glasses, or the shoes she usually wore when out and about. She had also put clothing out on the bed, presumably to wear after taking a shower. The garments were still lying there.

Something had caused her to leave the house in a mad rush. But what?

Julia continued to try her aunt over the next few hours. She waited until 10.30 pm, in order to check that she was not on the last ferry from Aberdeen, which docked at that time. Then she went to the local police post and reported Janet Gilson missing.

The police responded quickly.

On Wednesday morning an extensive search was launched. Police took a quick look around the house. Then 20 police officers with tracker dogs scoured the area between the village of Yung Shue Wan and nearby Sok Kwu Wan, where the text supposedly sent by Janet said she'd gone.

There was no sign of Janet Gilson. The following day, another 20 police and 20 Civil Aid officers joined the search. Meanwhile Julia posted photos of her aunt around the island and went from shop to shop trying to find someone who might have seen her.

Julia felt more distraught with each passing day. But she had to pretend to behave normally for her daughter's benefit.

Red stains on the floor

On Saturday morning, when she was lifting her daughter on to the sofa she noticed some red stains on the floor tiles. They hadn't been there on the Monday night when she'd been sleeping on the sofa. She also noticed an unpleasant smell in the house – a sickly odour that refused to budge even when she opened all the windows.

Once again she called the police.

Requesting Julia to remain outside, senior inspector Chung Shing Keung immediately ordered his men to lift the sofa. A long cut had been made into the black material undercover of its yellow foam base, creating a cavity. In it they found Janet Gilson's body. It was obvious that she had met a violent and undoubtedly painful death.

There were no signs of a forced entry into the apartment. Mrs Gilson had either let her killer in because she knew him – or the killer had used a key. Julia's spare keys had gone missing. Who would have both the opportunity and motive to steal them? There was also only one person to whom Janet would have opened the door.

That individual was, of course, Ahmed Fareed. According to his daughter's maid/babysitter, he had been rifling through drawers at his ex-wife's house some ten days earlier.

Ahmed arrested

Late on that Saturday afternoon, Ahmed was on a ferry travelling from Lamma to Central when a police motor launch came alongside, ordering it to stop. Police then boarded the ferry and arrested him. He was later charged with the murder of Janet Gilson.

Ahmed Fareed's jury trial began in Hong Kong's Court of First Instance in June 2013.

Forensic evidence was crucial to the prosecution case against Ahmed. And plenty of it appeared to link him to both the scene and the victim's body.

Yet he pleaded not guilty. Perhaps he was emboldened to do so because there was no evidence of him having any motive or reason for killing Janet Gilson.

Why would Ahmed kill Janet Gilson?

While he might have been understood to have a motive for killing his wife, he had no reason to kill her aunt. The woman didn't even live in Hong Kong and had expressed no intentions to stay on longer than her arranged visit.

So why did he kill her? Reflecting on this case, its prosecutor Ms Audrey Campbell-Moffat, SC, now a Judge of the Court of First Instance of the High Court, still believes that he did not enter the apartment with the intention of murdering his ex-wife's aunt.

It was – and still is – her view that he most probably arrived planning to steal something he could then sell to buy drugs. And somehow Janet Gilson got in his way.

"He was an inept murderer. He was a drug addict. He came around that morning, thinking that Janet was not there, thinking he was going to nick something."

The prosecution, of course, was under no obligation to prove that Ahmed had a motive.

It just had to prove that he was Janet Gilson's killer. And Ahmed may well have thought he had a fighting chance of escaping that charge. After all, there were no witnesses to his arrival at or departure from the crime scene. And there were certainly no witnesses to the crime itself.

Ahmed appeared to have worked very hard to establish an alibi for the morning that the murder took place. He had been very busy during those few hours: dropping off his ex-wife's suitcase to the babysitter and making phone calls from the public phone at the Green Cottage, a restaurant in Yung Shue Wan village's Main Street. It seemed that he was trying hard to be seen in public by lots of people.

Unfortunately for him, the only witnesses who were willing to testify to the court spoke of seeing him before 7 am.

The 9 am meeting with the maid

Meanwhile, his fixing of a 9 am meeting with the maid – and his failure to show up – may actually have worked against him. Instead of being an alibi for his defence, it begged to be interpreted as his way of ensuring that Karen would not arrive at his ex-wife's house at a time when he intended to be there. It is very possible that he may only have been trying to arrange a time to be alone at the flat so he could burgle it. It made him look as if he were planning something.

Ahmed Fareed told the court that he had actually spoken to Karen in the street outside the Green Cottage at around 9.15 am on the morning of March 15. Karen contradicted this, testifying that she had been in the street at that time – and that she had not seen him.

Despite all Ahmed's efforts, police were easily able to narrow down the time of the deadly assault. It had to have taken place after 7 am, when Julia would have left home to make her way to the ferry. Most probably it had taken place after 7.43 (when he had called Julia from the Green Cottage restaurant to arrange for Karen to meet him at Tai Peng village at 8.45) and before 10 am, when Karen arrived at Julia's flat. By then Janet Gilson's body had probably been in its hiding place in the couch for at least an hour.

It was clear that it was Ahmed Fareed who had sent the text from Julia's phone at 11.37 am: an act that the presiding judge, Michael Stuart-Moore, highlighted as evidence of his cold and calculating nature.

"The defendant locked both doors when he left the house after killing Janet," the judge told the court as he sentenced Ahmed. "And later, using Janet's mobile phone, (it must have been) the defendant who sent a text to Julia to set a false trail, making out that Janet had gone to Aberdeen. In fact, of course, she was dead. These were the acts of a calm and very calculating killer and I have no doubt whatsoever when the mood takes this defendant that he is highly dangerous."

Information from the victim's body

The body of the unfortunate victim, of course, provided the police with plenty of information.

Police forensic pathologist Dr Lai Sai Chak inspected Janet Gilson's body at the murder scene, noting that the dead woman, clad in pyjamas and a dressing gown, had a rope ligature around her neck. Part of that rope had also been used to tie her hands in front of her. Meanwhile a towel had been stuffed deep into her mouth, well behind the teeth, gagging her.

Later, when the forensic expert performed an autopsy, he noted the bloodstained fluid covering her face, and the fractures to her nose and three of her ribs. Blood had flowed out of the dead woman's nose as a result of the suffocation caused by a rag being stuffed into her mouth.

One of her ribs was fractured in two places: the result, he suggested, of a blow with the force of a karate kick. The cause of death, he concluded, was the lack of oxygen supply caused by the obstructions to her nose, mouth and neck, with the blockage to the blood supply through her neck possibly hastening her death. The condition of Janet Gilson's body, the scientist told the jury, suggested that she had been dead for between three and five days.

The prosecution's key evidence against Ahmed Fareed was a textbook example of Locard's "exchange theory": the basic principle of forensic science, first set out by French police scientist Edmond Locard in his 1931 book *Traité de criminalistique: Les empreintes et les traces dans l'enquete criminelle* that "every contact leaves a trace".

The forensic evidence against Ahmed

Audrey Campbell-Moffat, SC, outlined the forensic evidence against Ahmed in her opening address. The prosecutor's argument was a compelling story told in fibres and bloodstains. Fibres and bloodstains on Ahmed's clothing had come from his alleged victim, while fibres found on her had come from him, her alleged assailant.

Slowly and methodically, the barrister detailed the forensic findings. Twenty-seven fibres found on Janet Gilson's body and clothing matched fibres from Ahmed's clothing (26 matched his jacket and one matched his shirt).

Meanwhile five fibres found on Ahmed matched the fibres of the dead woman's purple dressing gown. The prosecution also relied on the fact that nine fragments of material found on various items of Ahmed's clothing matched the yellow spongy foam padding found inside the sofa.

The defence's answer

The defence had theoretical arguments to explain how the various fibres could have found their way on to both Ahmed and the victim in an innocent way. In the first place, Ahmed had helped move the couch into the apartment when his ex-wife moved in. So the fibres could have migrated to his clothing on that occasion. He had been cuddling his little daughter, who had been held by Janet Gilson when she had been wearing that purple dressing gown. So the purple fibres could have landed on his clothing via a process that forensic crime scene officers call "secondary transfer". The same process, in theory, could have transferred fibres from his clothing on to the victim.

But the defence lawyer had no adequate answer to the bloodstains on a jacket belonging to Ahmed. This jacket was the crucial piece of evidence against him and the only story Ahmed could come up with to explain its stains was preposterously unbelievable.

Supposedly he had walked in the rain on the afternoon of the day that Janet Gilson died. After arriving at the home of a friend, where he was going to stay that night, he had changed out of his wet clothing. He had then left his jacket, shirt, jeans, a sweater and a belt on an outside table to dry. Of course he didn't know how Janet Gilson's blood got on to his jacket. But, as his lawyer told the court, he had left property out on a public table in an area where anyone could have gone to it and put the blood on it "in some mischievous way".

The blood spatter expert's testimony

The jury listened to this explanation. They also heard from forensic chemist and blood spatter expert Dr Ho Siu Hong. He told them that the three bloodstains on the chest of the jacket were an "impact pattern", reflecting the projection of blood caused by the impact of a direct blow on a live human body. After DNA profiling the blood of both victim and accused, he had examined the bloodstains on the clothing of the accused and concluded that there was only a one in 324 quintillion probability that they came from a donor other than the deceased.

The jury was convinced, returning a unanimous guilty verdict. Justice Michael Stuart Moore then handed down a life sentence.

"There was no doubt whatsoever that you killed Janet Gilson," he told the court. "Her blood on your shirt and jumper and trousers and jacket speaks louder than any words ever will that it was you who killed her. There were many other forensic clues as well in the form of fibres that were transferred from your clothes on to her body and from her clothes, her nightclothes, on to your clothing. She was still wearing her nightwear when she was killed.

"The evidence of your guilt is overwhelming. You have committed the ultimate crime and you did so in a fashion so terrible, that words failed to describe the true horror of what she had to go through and of what you did."

Apparently undeterred, Ahmed applied for leave to appeal against his conviction, representing himself although he had been granted legal aid and assigned a lawyer.

His application cited a raft of failings by both the judge and his own lawyers, whom he slammed as incompetent. He was particularly annoyed that they had failed to call their own forensic witnesses. (In fact his lawyers had commissioned independent forensic reports from the well-respected UK-based former Hong Kong scientist Dr Sheilah Hamilton and from the DNA expert Dr Terence Lau. They had not been called to give evidence because they could not fault the prosecution experts' reports.) Ahmed Fareed complained that one juror did not understand English. He also claimed that the judge erred in refusing to allow the jury to watch a video in which he was shown eating at the Man Kee Restaurant at 6:30 am on the day of the murder.

But three judges of the Court of Appeal declined to grant him leave to appeal.

A case that stayed with its prosecutor

Five years after this trial, Justice Campbell-Moffat recalls it in extraordinary detail. In particular she remembers the frustration of not being able to get the forensic pathologist to commit to a precise explanation of how the victim died: so she could give the jury an exact and compelling narrative of her death.

There was nylon rope around the woman's neck, there was a rag stuffed in her mouth, and there was damage to her face (possibly caused by the frame of the sofa). And the victim suffocated. But how, exactly?

"Something caused the death," the former prosecutor recalls. "Not the rope on its own. Not the damage to her nose on its own. It was to do with the rag in her mouth. But the rope also told a story about what was happening. It didn't look like an attempt to kill. It looked like the product of an attempt to subdue her.

"Maybe there was panic. Maybe she passed out or even suffocated. Maybe she was still alive when she went under the sofa. It could have been a mix of all three.

"But what was happening in her lungs caused blood to spatter on to her pyjamas – and on to him."

Fortunately the blood spatter expert, Dr Ho Siu Hong, was very good at explaining to her – and then to the jury – what had then happened.

Justice Campbell-Moffat also still finds herself wondering whether Ahmed might have had help. At the time she remembers noting his skinny frame and wondering whether he would have had the strength to put his victim into the sofa without assistance.

She certainly remains mystified by the fact that Mrs Gilson's body remained undiscovered for so long.

"There were blood spatters on the tiles and on the Ikea cushions on the couch. A maid that was doing her job would have seen them. That was odd."

And then there was the fact of a decomposing body in an apartment where the air-conditioning would not have been on all the time.

This was not an aspect of the case that she wanted to dwell on in court, with the victim's niece present every day of the trial.

"Sometimes it is overly cruel to go into those details."

Case Ten
MURDER OR ACCIDENT?

The marriage of Hong Kong mechanic Chan Sai-kit and his wife Gloria Mak Wai-ngor, both aged 40, had been rocky. But they were still together. One night Chan was working on his car and asked his wife to help him by trying to start it. There was a sudden explosion and a fire, in which she died. Chan was later arrested and tried for murder. But was this catastrophic event an accident? The answer, the jury was told, was in the forensic evidence.

Just for a moment, put yourself in the shoes of a man who has just found out that his wife had secretly recorded all their worst marital arguments.

Imagine that these bitter exchanges took place several years ago, when things were pretty bad between the two of you. Some ugly things were said – mostly by you. Your wife certainly goaded you, it's true. But you always took the bait. You even admitted to an affair which you hadn't actually had – just to annoy her. That's how toxic your relationship was at the time.

Then, imagine that the transcript of those recordings is going to be read out in front of other people. Embarrassing enough?

It gets worse. Those other people are sitting in a courtroom. They are members of a jury. And they are eventually going to have to come to a verdict. On you.

Why? You're on trial for murder.

The above scenario may sound like a nightmare. But it was exactly the situation in which Hong Kong mechanic Chan Sai-kit found himself.

In October 1989 Chan and his wife Gloria Mak Wai-ngor, both aged 40, were living with Chan's uncle in the rural New Territories area of Lam Tei. The couple had been married for ten years and had been living in Canada where they were both citizens. They had returned to Hong Kong in March that year.

Chan, who had qualified as a mechanic in Ontario, had been working on his car in the shed adjacent to his uncle's house.

On the night of October 23, 1989, he had decided to sort out the problem that had been making his car so hard to start.

He thought the issue might be the oil pump. So he needed to see what would happen when the ignition switch was turned.

As he would later explain to police in a statement taken the next day, his wife was inside the house, already in her pyjamas. Chan asked for her help to try and start the car. She actually agreed: not a foregone conclusion. But the pair were not fighting at this time. In fact three years had passed since she'd made those tapes of their ugly arguments, back in Canada.

It was cold out there in the shed, and Chan gave his wife a pullover to put on. She got into the car, sat in the driver's seat, flicked on the radio and then switched on the ignition. While she did that, Chan was crouching over the bonnet, using a special tester lamp he'd made himself, to check whether the spark plugs were working. They were.

Next, he thought about testing the oil pump pressure. Once again he was going to need his wife to start the car. But first he wanted to change the carburettor pipe, so he moved to the bench several metres away.

A few clicks, and then a small explosion

He had his back to the car when he heard his wife make several more attempts to start the engine. There were a few clicks, and then a small explosion. A red glow suffused the garage. In shock, he turned around. The car was a ball of fire.

Chan called his wife's name but there was no response. He assumed she must have escaped. The flames, meanwhile, were getting bigger and the heat more intense. So he rushed outside to connect a water hose to douse the flames.

Gloria Mak's charred remains were found behind the car.

The police, when they arrived, were immediately suspicious – as they always are. When a wife dies in an accident, investigators always look closely at the husband. Anyone who's ever watched a TV crime drama knows that.

Chan was arrested but released on bail while police investigated. There were no eye-witnesses, except the alleged perpetrator.

Forensic evidence would be crucial

This was a case where the forensic evidence would be crucial to determining what had happened. There would be two potential sources of this evidence: the crime scene itself, and the "silent witness" – the body of Gloria Mak.

The crime scene is always especially important in the case of a fire. Many fires that are initially considered accidental are reclassified as arson, or arson/murder following the discovery of some kind of trace evidence.

Sometimes traces of an accelerant are found. Or crime scene evidence reveals that a fire victim had been tied up, or drugged so they would be trapped in the flames.

In one case, in Melbourne, Australia, a house fire that killed a baby and badly burned its mother was initially reported as an accident, in which an aromatherapy burner had toppled over into a box of tissues. This deadly conflagration was later deemed to have been fuelled by ether. A highly volatile and flammable liquid, ether was also used as an anaesthetic in hospital surgery until the late 1950s.

In this Australian case there was no physical evidence of the accelerant because ether leaves no trace. The baby's mother, who lost an arm in the fire, had woken in hospital with a strong recollection of being "held down" and smelling an odd odour.

Her husband, hearing this, quickly produced a story to match. He explained that his wife had had a cold at the time, which was the reason for the presence of the aromatherapy burner by her bed. Hearing his wife's laboured breathing, he had soaked a tissue with a decongestant called "Vick's Vaporub" and held it to her nose, to help her breathe better.

The speed and ferocity of the fire led Victoria Police's forensic fire examiner to believe that some kind of accelerant had been used. The husband also had ready access to ether at his place of work.

The scientist attempted two reconstructions of the fire. The only way he could replicate a fire like the one he was investigating was to pour a small amount of ether on to both the bedside table and the corner of the mattress nearest it. His experimental ether-fuelled fire caused exactly the same burn patterns as found in the house fire, with the flames burning down the side of the mattress and underneath it.

The HK government scientist had no suspicions

Back in Hong Kong, government forensic scientist Tang Man Hin had no similar suspicions when he visited the New Territories hut where Chan had garaged his car.

Examining the scene, he could find no evidence of foul play or any indication that the fire was anything but accidental. In his view, he told police, Chan's account of the fire was entirely consistent with what he found at the scene.

As a result Chan was released and was permitted to return to Canada.

Three years later, in July 1992, Chan returned to Hong Kong voluntarily to attend the inquest into the death of his wife. But he was arrested at the airport, and remained in custody until his trial for murder began in September 1993 in Hong Kong's High Court.

Chan's defence counsel Gary Plowman, SC, would have loved to have fought his client's case purely on its forensic evidence. It was, after all, up to the prosecution to prove that his client planned the explosion that caused the fire that killed Gloria Mak. And nothing had been found at the scene to indicate that Chan had deliberately set up the fire. But the barrister knew that the jury would want more than that. They also needed to be convinced that Chan was not the sort of man to have committed this crime.

Tang was the first forensic expert to testify in the five-week trial. He repeated his initial 1989 statement that his findings were consistent with Chan's account of the fire.

The prosecution then called in University of Columbia forensic pathologist Professor James Ferris, an expert on fire deaths, to examine Gloria Mak's remains. The fire was intense enough to melt metal and strip paintwork. The damage it would have done to a human body doesn't bear thinking about.

Gloria Mak's body was still a highly articulate "silent witness". In this fire, smoke and fumes would have created a high concentration of carbon monoxide in the air inside the car and in the entire garage. The expert's careful reading of the levels of carbon monoxide in Mak's blood could tell him what happened in the last minutes before her death.

The carboxyhaemoglobin levels: the key test

The key test for Ferris to carry out was an examination of the levels of carboxyhaemoglobin in the dead woman's blood. Haemoglobin is a protein in red blood cells that carries oxygen to the body's tissues. In this process oxygen binds to the protein, creating an oxygen-loaded form of haemoglobin known as oxyhaemoglobin. But when carbon monoxide is present in the air a person is breathing, this process changes. The carbon monoxide binds itself to the haemoglobin instead. Carboxyhaemoglobin is created instead of oxyhaemoglobin.

Normal healthy people tend to have carboxyhaemoglobin levels of about one per cent, while a smoker may have a level of 6 per cent. People who die of "smoke inhalation" in house fires will often have levels as high as 60 or 70 per cent. They have inhaled so much carbon monoxide that it has effectively replaced oxygen in their blood.

The carboxyhaemoglobin levels of 23 per cent found in Mak's body were very significant, Ferris told the court. They meant that the unfortunate woman had not died of carbon monoxide poisoning. Instead, she had died from her burns, or, from the shock associated with them. Her vital organs had failed before she had inhaled enough carbon monoxide to render her unconscious.

This scientific information was crucial to the prosecution because it appeared to cast doubt on Chan's account of the night, in which he had last seen his wife in the front seat of the car. And if he was lying about that, what else was he lying about?

Was Chan's wife in the front seat when fire broke out?

As the prosecution's expert told the jury, Mak had died with only a level of 23 per cent carboxyhaemoglobin in her blood. This meant that she had only breathed the carbon monoxide-filled air of the car for between three and five seconds before she died of her burns.

Both this low carbon monoxide level and the presence of soot in her throat meant that she was alive when the fire started. But she was burnt to death very quickly – most probably within a minute or two.

It was Ferris's view that she had died in the spot where her body was found: behind the car. This, he told the court, would also have been the place where she was standing when the fire took hold.

If this interpretation was correct, Gloria Mak had not been in the driver's seat of the car turning the ignition when the fire broke out, as Chan had told police.

Chan had insisted that he had not seen his wife when he turned around to see what had happened. He assumed she had left the car in the intervening seconds. There was one problem with this account. Chan was supposed to have been standing at a bench three metres away. He would have had a clear view of the driver's side of the car from there.

Gary Plowman wondered if there could be a credible alternative explanation.

Cross-examining Ferris, he suggested that it would only have taken three to five seconds for Mak to get out of the front seat and reach the spot behind the car where, presumably, she had succumbed to the flames. There was still a discrepancy about what Chan should have been able to see. But the man had to have been in shock at the time. And so-called "eye-witness" accounts of traumatic events can be notoriously unreliable. There is more than a century of research, beginning with the work of German-American psychologist Hugo Münsterberg, author of *On The Witness Stand*, suggesting exactly that.

It was crucial for the defence that the jury accept this part of Chan's version of events: that his wife was in the driver's seat when the car exploded.

Plowman managed to get Ferris to agree that, in theory, it was possible that Mak might have survived long enough to escape from the car. Yet the expert continued to maintain that the woman's low carboxyhaemoglobin levels were a strong argument that she had not moved.

If Gloria Mak had survived long enough to get out of the car, perhaps with her clothing on fire, the forensic pathologist explained, she would have breathed long enough to get a higher level of carbon monoxide in her lungs than the one she died with.

Did Chan's wife escape from the car and then collapse?

Plowman wasn't thrilled with this theory. But, while he could not shake the prosecution's forensic pathologist on it, his battle on this point was not yet over. He would continue it when the prosecution had finished presenting its case and he had his turn to present the case for the defence.

The defence lawyer would be offering evidence from another forensic scientist witness, New Zealand-government forensic pathologist Dr Martin Sage. Dr Sage had a different view of the way events could have unfolded that night. He would tell the court that, in his view, it was certainly possible that Gloria Mak had escaped from the front seat of the car, only to collapse behind the vehicle.

This version of events was, at least, consistent with Chan's account of the fire. Plowman was also able to get the prosecution's forensic pathologist to confirm that he had found no evidence to suggest that Gloria Mak had been tied up, or that she had sustained any other injuries except burns. In particular, her body showed no sign of any internal injury which might indicate that she had been disabled by an assault, or by drugs, alcohol or poison.

In principle, the defence lawyer believed, the jury had been equipped with enough information to make them query the prosecution argument that Chan was lying about what happened on the night.

Certainly the prosecution could suggest that Chan had carried out some nefarious plan in which he planned an explosion serious enough to kill his wife but not injure himself. And all without leaving any clues as to the way he might have set it up! But they had failed to explain exactly how he might have tinkered with the engine to guarantee an explosion. Nor had they found a shred of evidence pointing in this direction.

Would the jury be seeing it this way? That was a different question. Plowman had spent six years as a prosecutor with the Hong Kong Attorney-General's Chambers and had then gone into private practice as a criminal barrister in 1984. In his time he had watched hundreds of juries come to their verdicts.

An accused who refused to testify

He had one serious problem. His client did not want to testify. And the lawyer knew that he might have a better chance of winning over the jury if he did.

The jury had been reminded that the Hong Kong legal system – like the British one on which it was based – enshrined an accused person's right to remain silent. It was up to the prosecution to prove a person's guilt; an accused person had nothing to prove. But jurors are human beings. Many of them just want to hear the accused speak for himself.

Certainly, every jury is different. This one, Plowman could sense, comprised people who would make an adverse judgement on his client for refusing to testify. A couple of hard-nosed banker types, in particular. He could practically read their opinions on their faces.

On the other hand, it could also be a bad mistake to let an overly nervous defendant like Chan testify. Hesitance and a reluctance to look the jury in the eye could easily be interpreted as shiftiness and dishonesty.

Anyway it was out of Plowman's hands. His client was, as he recalls him, "nervous and ineffectual". He could not be persuaded to stand in the witness box and give an explanation of exactly what happened that night. It had been explained to Chan that there were problematic discrepancies between his police statement and the findings of Professor Ferris. In principle, the man recognised that a more personal account of the night – from him and in his own words – might help reconcile them.

Unfortunately it wasn't to be. Chan was just too frightened of submitting to cross-examination by prosecutor Gary Alderdice, QC. A close friend of Plowman's since their days as law students together in New Zealand, he had spent years as a Crown prosecutor before leaving to join the private criminal bar in 1984.

Nicknamed "Never Plead Guilty Gary", Alderdice was highly-rated as a defence lawyer. He was an equally aggressive prosecutor and a formidable cross-examiner.

Plowman wasn't to know it at the time, but the Chan trial would be the last time he would get to cross swords with his good mate. Less than a year later Alderdice would be murdered in the Russian city of Vladivostock.

The defence lawyer remained optimistic

Still, Plowman remained cautiously optimistic. The prosecution's forensic evidence against Chan sounded impressive. But looking at it closely, it did not "prove" anything at all "beyond reasonable doubt". There was no evidence at all that the mechanic had set up the fire.

After all, the first person to examine the fire scene, government scientist (and prosecution witness) Tang Man Hin, had said that his findings were consistent with the mechanic's story. Certainly,

Professor Ferris's evidence had been damaging. But Plowman felt that he had got the point across to the jury that an alternative explanation was still possible.

Furthermore, even Ferris had conceded, under cross-examination, that it was *possible*, if less likely, that Mak might have escaped from the front seat, only to die behind the car.

An industrial training consultant, Charles Close, had also testified that Chan's qualifications as a mechanic, which he had gained in Ontario, were such that he would have understood the potential dangers of a repair such as this one. He could point to no specific failing on Chan's part that might have indicated homicidal intent.

The "hostile" Chan marriage

The real damage to Chan's chance of acquittal, Plowman feared, would be done elsewhere: through the prosecution's detailed depiction of the Chan-Mak marriage as one plagued by hostility and ill will.

Chan, as presented by the prosecution, was a man who had committed violent acts against his wife on previous occasions. He was also, the prosecution alleged, a man with a motive to kill his wife. He had, as Alderdice told the jury, taken out travel insurance on his wife a mere seven months before the fire. You might think a would-be killer might have insured his wife for more. The amount Chan insured his wife for was only C$100,000 – half the amount she would get if he lost his life.

The terms of the travel policy, the prosecutor conceded, did not cover the circumstances of Gloria Mak's death. But the Crown would be arguing that Chan must have thought the policy would cover this kind of accidental death because he had actually attempted to claim on it back in July 1991, two years after the death, but a year before he was arrested for murder at Hong Kong Airport.

There was also the question of the couple's will. A friend who liked to play the role of amateur lawyer gave evidence that he had drafted a joint will for the pair. At one point Gloria Mak had wanted to include a clause which said that, in the event of her death under suspicious circumstances, there should be an investigation and their joint assets should be given to a scientific research centre in China.

A couple of days later, this witness said, Chan phoned him to say that his wife had changed her mind. In the event of their deaths, Chan's brother was to be the beneficiary. And the clause about investigating her death was to be dropped.

The tapes of the arguments not ruled out

The prosecutor also spent a lot of time detailing the content of the taped arguments between husband and wife. This was material that Plowman had fought hard to have excluded. He had argued that the tapes, made in 1986, were too old to be used as proof of enmity between the couple in 1989 and therefore were not appropriate to be used as evidence to establish a motive for murder.

Plowman was shocked that the judge did not rule this material out, despite the fact that it was clear from listening to the tapes that Chan's ex-wife was deliberately provoking her husband. Presumably she had done this with the aim of obtaining evidence which she could use against him in divorce proceedings.

Either way, the tapes painted a picture of Chan tha the defence counsel would have preferred the jury not to hear. In the first place Gloria Mak made reference to an episode of violence in Canada, for which Chan had been charged, and during which he had stabbed her in the hand with a knife. In one of these taped conversations, the couple were heard negotiating about this. Chan asked his wife to tell the prosecutor that she did not want to proceed with the case. His wife then asked for some financial concessions in return, along with a promise that he would seek marriage counselling.

Even more damaging (unless you believe that people who talk about killing never actually do it) were the segments on the tape where Gloria Mak accused her husband of adultery and of wanting to kill her and have her body shredded and her bones burned. To this, Chan was heard to reply that if a dead body were not found, then there would be no evidence of murder.

On the tape Chan had also told his wife that he had not meant what he'd said about disposing of the body. "I said that only in a moment of anger," he was heard to say.

Later, when police questioned him about the threats he had been heard to make, he told them that his remarks were "just words".

Putting all these elements together, the prosecutor invited the jury to conclude that Chan had a good motive to kill his wife. Not only was their relationship toxic, but he stood to gain, financially, from her death as well.

Yet some witnesses contradicted the overwhelmingly negative view of the Chan-Mak marriage presented in the tapes. Chan's uncle, with whom the couple had been living in the seven months before Gloria Mak's death, told the court that the Chans were a "close and loving" couple.

Plowman could also show the jury something in Gloria Mak's own words: letters she had written to two cousins in China in September 1988 (two years after she had made the tapes and a year before her death) in which she had said that her husband was "behaving better".

Unfortunately for the defence, the prosecution also had the dead woman's younger siblings on their witness list. And they told a different story. Gloria Mak's younger sister told the court that the couple had stayed with her on a visit to Hong Kong in 1987 and had argued a lot. She saw them on their return in 1989, and agreed they were getting on better. But she also described an incident in September 1989, only a month before the accident, in which Chan had apparently given Gloria some tonic soup after which she had felt ill. That night Gloria had said she did not want to go home with her husband because he would "set another trap and do her in".

Meanwhile Mak's younger brother said that, as recently as December 1988, less than a year before her death, his sister was complaining, in her husband's presence, about his ill-treatment of her. At this point, he told the court, he saw Chan hit his wife, hard, on the stomach with the back of his fist.

Verdict and appeal

It seems obvious, at least in retrospect, that this was the kind of evidence that swayed the jury. Their verdict was announced on October 12, 1993. Guilty. Chan received a life sentence.

Shocked and disappointed, Plowman immediately announced he would appeal. The jury, he felt – and still feels – had been swayed by prejudicial evidence that the trial judge should not have allowed the prosecution to air. In his view, the judge had erred in allowing the tape recordings to be used as evidence. The judge had also been wrong, he believed, in allowing the jury to hear the evidence about the insurance policies and the will.

The appeal was heard in 1995; Plowman didn't represent Chan in this one but he followed it closely and was shocked and disappointed to see it fail.

Back in 1993 Gary Plowman had believed his client was innocent. Now, more than 20 years later, he has not wavered in his view.

"I think his decision not to give evidence counted against him with the jury. The tape recordings were at least three years old and, as the Court of Appeal acknowledged, there was a clear indication from the contents that the wife was deliberately provoking the accused in order to obtain evidence which she could use against him in divorce proceedings.

"There was also evidence that the accused had made false admissions of adultery in response to her taunting. Once that motivation is established it was dangerous to allow this evidence to go to the jury. Furthermore there was compelling evidence that the relationship between the two had improved by the time of the offence."

Chan is now back in Canada, having been transferred there on a prisoner exchange scheme after the 1997 handover of Hong Kong to China.

THE PHILIPPINES

BACKGROUND NOTE:

In some areas of forensic science, the Philippines is a relative newcomer. Dr Raquel del Rosario-Fortun, the country's first forensic pathologist and a professor at the University of the Philippines College of Medicine has even described some aspects of forensic science practice in the Philippines as being "like the United States in the 1960s". Speaking in 2016 at the country's third Forensic Science Symposium, in Diliman, Quezon City, Fortun singled out ballistics and forensic pathology as areas in need of both qualified personnel and the people to train them.

But the area of DNA is a splendid exception to this rule. There are four operational DNA laboratories in the Philippines. According to Dr Maria Corazon de Ungria, who heads one of them – the DNA Analysis Laboratory at the University of the Philippines' Natural Sciences Research Institute – Philippine research into DNA is equal to that being done elsewhere in the world. Together with a team of lawyers and student volunteers, Dr de Ungria launched the Innocence Project Philippines Network (IPPN) at the National Bilibid Prison in 2011. A network of law school clinics, scientific and academic laboratories and non-governmental organisations, the Innocence Project uses DNA evidence to seek justice for wrongfully convicted persons.

Case Eleven
A SURPRISE PATERNITY TEST RESULT

One of the DNA Analysis Laboratory's "routine" tests was done for a man who was contesting his partner's claim that he was the father of her child. The test confirmed his belief that he was not the father. But the second result that it delivered was a complete surprise.

The Philippines is yet to pass the legislation required to set up a national DNA database of the country's convicted criminals. Instead, the caseload in DNA work in the Philippines is dominated by paternity testing cases. A significant number of these paternity testing cases are carried out in the context of criminal investigations, particularly those that involve human trafficking. In the Philippines, an estimated 60,000 to 100,000 children have been victims of human trafficking.

The DNA Analysis Laboratory headed by Dr Maria Corazon de Ungria also does a great deal of "routine" DNA testing, the kind that is requested by mothers requiring proof of their child's paternity to back a claim for child support. These tests are also requested by fathers needing evidence to dispute such a claim.

One of these "routine" cases produced such an extraordinary result that de Ungria and her team published a paper about it in the 2016 edition of the Asian Forensic Sciences network newsletter, *Forensic Asia*.

The case was brought to the lab by a man who was contesting a woman's claim that he was the father of her child. The lab took blood samples from the man, the woman and the child. It then ran the standard "Powerplex" test, made by Promega and used by many police labs around the world. This test, which examines 15 different markers or "loci" on the DNA strand, showed that the man was not the father of the child.

This result was not a surprise to the man. But the testing procedure delivered a second result: one that came as a surprise to the testers. This woman was not the biological mother of the child either.

To be sure of this, the scientists had to run another test, the AmpFiSTR Identifiler. The Powerplex test had shown two markers where the mother and child's DNA did not match: a result that could have been explained by a rare gene mutation.

The Identifiler examined two markers not tested in the Powerplex test. These further excluded the woman from being the child's mother. There were now four places on the DNA strand where the supposed mother's DNA did not match her child. This meant conclusively that the woman was not the child's biological mother.

Could this be a case of child trafficking? The supposed father asked that the Department of Social Welfare and Development investigate.

The department was already accustomed to dealing with identity enquiries through its involvement with the DNA-Prokids programme, a joint initiative by the University of Granada's Genetic Identification Laboratory and the University of North Texas Center for Human Identification, aimed at fighting human trafficking, especially in women and children.

So now there was one more test to take, in order to check whether the supposed "mother and child" were related in some other way.

This was a mitochondrial DNA test. While conventional DNA testing looks at the DNA found in the cell's nucleus, mitochondrial DNA testing analyses DNA from a cell's cytoplasm, the gel-like substance surrounding the nucleus.

Mitochondrial DNA (known by the abbreviation MtDNA) is passed through the female line, from a mother to both male and female children. But in subsequent generations of a family, it is only passed on through females. So it can show whether different people are related through a common female ancestor.

The extra advantage of mitochondrial DNA is that it can be extracted from old samples of bone, teeth and hair. While each cell contains only one nucleus, it may contain hundreds of mitochondria. This increases the chances of obtaining a usable sample from old material.

MtDNA profiling cannot offer the same level of discrimination as nucleic DNA profiling, because all the children of the same mother have an identical MtDNA profile. But they have a different nuclear DNA profile.

The mitochondrial DNA sequences of the two samples taken from the supposed mother and her child were identical. This meant that they were related through the maternal line.

Without further investigation, it would have been impossible to know exactly what that meant. So a social worker from the Department of Social Welfare and Development investigated the family, and discovered that the woman was actually the child's maternal grandmother.

The woman had taken her own daughter's child in an attempt to get support from her boyfriend, because the daughter was, in her view, financially unstable.

After counselling and advice from the social worker, the woman gave the child back to his biological parents.

Case Twelve
SOLVING A GIANT GENEALOGICAL PUZZLE

The identification of 23 children who died in an orphanage fire in Manila in 1999 was an extraordinary forensic team effort. The victims had been buried, each with a number instead of a name, in a special above-ground concrete burial vault. The bodies were later exhumed and a team of experts had to use forensic anthropology and DNA to identify them.

On December 3, 1998, a fire swept through the 73-year-old timber headquarters of an orphanage run by the Asociacion de Damas de Filipinas, a charitable organisation that was started in 1913 by the wives of members of Manila's nationalist Columbian Club.

Settlement House, a shelter for orphans since 1925, was a collection of wooden buildings two- and three-storeys high. It was a home to "foundlings" who had been left on its doorstep. But at the time of the fire it was also occupied by the children of loving but indigent parents. These parents had left their children to be cared for by "Damas", as the institution was known locally, and they would visit them regularly. They planned to take their children back home when they could afford to look after them.

The murderous blaze broke out at 1.30 in the morning. Burning out of control within half an hour, it razed two buildings to the ground. Although there were fire escapes, the doors leading to them had grilles that were padlocked. The children and babies sleeping on the upper floors had little chance to escape the flames and smoke.

Forty-three workers and children survived the conflagration. But after the site had been thoroughly searched, 23 children aged between six months and eight years were still missing. Twenty-two charred bodies were eventually found, huddled together in rubble or buried under the debris of collapsed wooden floors and ceilings and burned iron bedsteads and cotton mattresses.

No immediate move to identify the dead

Local forensic pathologist Dr Raquel del Rosario-Fortun, then based at the Philippine General Hospital, a tertiary state-owned hospital operated by the University of the Philippines, had had no involvement with the recovery of the bodies from the ruins of the orphanage building.

But when she and her colleagues heard news reports that the dead children were about to be buried, they contacted relatives of the dead and offered help. One doctor, a graduate from the University of the Philippines with a masters in forensic medicine from Scotland's University of Dundee, formally wrote to the Manila Mayor, offering help from the University of Philippines in identifying the dead.

The doctors were surprised to be told that no help was needed. It appeared the children's families had been promised that the country's National Bureau of Investigation (NBI) would conduct DNA tests, with the Mayor's office issuing death certificates.

Nothing happened, however. Later, stories emerged of grieving parents waiting for hours at the NBI, only to be ignored.

Burials and exhumations

Instead the children's burials went ahead, despite the fact that no identifications had been possible because the small bodies had been too charred to be positively identified by sight. Each set of remains was assigned a number and buried separately in a special above-ground concrete burial vault. The sole exception was one eight-year-old boy who had been positively identified by his grandfather.

As weeks dragged by, the children's relatives grew increasingly distressed that so many victims remained unidentified. Some of them decided to take the initiative, contacting the activist group, Volunteers Against Crime and Corruption (VACC). This non-government organisation championed victims' rights as well as a range of justice causes.

VACC referred the relatives to Dr Fortun and her colleagues. Their professional advice was that an exhumation of the bodies was the only possible solution, with DNA profiling used to identify the victims.

On February 2, 1999, nine parents signed a VACC-organised petition to the Mayor for the exhumation of the children's bodies. On March 19, after six weeks of paperwork-induced delays, the exhumations began. Only 21 victims were exhumed however. The child who had already been named was not included in the exhumation order. (And, while 23 children were missing after the fire, only 22 bodies had been found.)

At the morgue

After the 21 small coffins had been removed from their burial vaults, they were taken to the morgue at the University's College of Medicine.

Each set of remains was assigned a number, X-rayed and examined for any remnants of identifiable clothing. This was an unreliable indicator, given that clothes may be borrowed or swapped. But it was still worth doing.

Categorising the victims by their gender was an important first step in the identification process. This was especially relevant here, where 17 of the missing children were male.

Dr Fortun had also enlisted the help of the University of the Philippines' Natural Sciences Research Institute. Its DNA lab, staffed by specialists such as its head scientist Dr Maria Corazon de Ungria, would be key to the success of the identification project.

The team's first step was to try and reconstruct what had happened in the immediate aftermath of the fire. It was then that the forensic pathologist discovered the extent of disorganisation that had characterised the recovery operation.

Chaotic recovery of the bodies

"The people who recovered the bodies had no sense of coming up with a system and simply picked them up," Dr Fortun later explained. "In fact, when we were trying to reconstruct what happened, we found out that one of the firemen was apparently a volunteer who was at the same time employed in a funeral parlour."

The bodies had been taken to this man's place of work.

Even more frustrating, in retrospect, was the discovery that the children's bodies had been located in the three rooms where they slept. This meant that a simple map of where each body had been found (a standard forensic crime scene procedure) might have helped the identification effort. Most victims were found in Cottage One. But only three children slept in Cottage Two. Meanwhile the orphanage's six babies were located in the nursery where they were sleeping when the fire broke out. It was even known which baby had slept in which crib.

If only these bodies had been properly tagged, and their location mapped, "presumptive" identifications could have been made at the beginning.

But this chaotic response was typical of the times, as Dr Fortun would later write in *Responding to Health Emergencies and Disasters,* a 2005 report for the Philippines government's Department of Health.

"When multiple fatalities are encountered in mass casualty incidents, the common response locally is for the emergency personnel to turn over the remains to the funeral parlours without regard for (these) forensic needs," she wrote.

Instead, she suggested, the country desperately needed "an efficient death investigation system". This new system should be able to establish the identity of deceased people and determine the cause and manner of their deaths. To do this it would have to involve the immediate recognition, collection, documentation, and preservation of forensic evidence.

A team effort: autopsies, and dental examinations

Dr Fortun began by carrying out autopsies, during which she was able to identify the sex of some of the babies and older children. Despite the severe charring and decomposition, she was successful in 14 of the cases. Meanwhile the remaining seven bodies were so badly burnt that DNA had to be used to determine gender.

A team of volunteers, mostly students from the Anthropology and Molecular Biology Department of the University of the Philippines, then helped remove soft tissue from the bones, so they could be better examined.

The next step was to prepare the children's teeth for dental examination, a process that was run by Dr Danilo Magtanong, of the UP College of Dentistry.

With adult fire and disaster victims, the comparison of ante-mortem dental records and X-rays with post-mortem jaw X-rays is a very useful method of identification.

But these children, not surprisingly, had no ante-mortem dental records.

"So we went back to the relatives to ask them if they recalled any identifying marks on the teeth of the children," says Dr Fortun.

"Some of them reported that ... there were cavities or the teeth were eroded ... or the teeth were just fine. Although these were very non-specific, the information was useful to our colleagues at the College of Dentistry. The dentists really helped a lot."

The dentists were able to use their own observations, along with information provided by anthropologist Dr Francisco Datar who had examined the children's bones in order to approximate the age of the children.

The bodies, ranging in age from six months to eight years, were classified into three age groups: under two years, two to five years and over five years.

The team was then able to establish that they had three male bodies, aged between six and eight. These bodies certainly belonged to the three eldest missing boys. But which was which?

Enter the scientists from the DNA Analysis Lab at the Natural Sciences Research Institute (NSRI) of the University of the Philippines at Diliman in Quezon City.

Preparing the DNA samples

Dr Fortun had isolated the atlas bone, the first cervical vertebra of the spine, from each child's remains. It would serve as a source from which a bone marrow sample could be taken.

The work of processing these samples and obtaining a DNA profile from each was done by scientists Dr Maria Corazon de Ungria and Ms Gayvelline Calacal. Ms Calacal had just returned from a year's internship at the prestigious Institut der Rechtsmedizin at Berlin's Humboldt University. She became the primary scientist involved with the processing of the samples.

The two scientists also collected as many "reference" blood samples as possible to compare with the children's DNA profiles. Reference samples are samples from a known source such as the child's parent or parents, grandparents and siblings. DNA profiles are then extracted from them and used for comparison.

In two cases, the scientists had actual ante-mortem DNA samples to compare with the post-mortem samples. Two of the families with a missing child had kept the child's umbilical cord, a common practice in many cultures, including Hispanic ones. They could therefore give the scientists their child's dried umbilical tissue, a rich source of DNA.

In one case the scientists were given reference samples from both parents. In eleven cases, they had a sample from one parent and there was also one grandparent sample.

The fact that there were four sets of brothers amongst the children promised to simplify the process. Given that all children inherit half their DNA from each parent, the DNA profiles of siblings are similar. But in these cases, no simple assumptions could be made about the degree of similarity to expect. The fact that a sibling pair had been brought to the orphanage together might indicate that they shared the same mother. There was no guarantee that they were the progeny of the same father.

What then ensued can be best compared to a giant genealogical crossword puzzle, with the investigators using their collection of DNA profiles to eliminate non-parents, and sort out pairs of likely matches. The aim, ideally, was to identify all 21 sets of remains.

What is DNA?

DNA (or deoxyribonucleic acid), a double-stranded molecule in the nucleus of most human cells, is "the blueprint for life". It is composed of four different substances, often described by scientists as letters in a four-letter chemical alphabet. These letters, representing the building block molecules adenine, thymine, guanine and cytosine, are used in the same way conventional letters are. They can be ordered in specific sequences that create particular meanings within the DNA molecule (as a gene which codes for a particular function). Or they can be in random order without any as-yet known meaning associated with them.

More than 99 per cent of the DNA of all human beings is identical. The remaining amount, less than one per cent, carries individual differences.

Every human being inherits half of his or her DNA from each parent. Different areas on the DNA strand feature patterns that carry the code or gene for general human characteristics, such as heart function, or for variations such as hair, eye colour, height, or predisposition to disease.

Between these sections of DNA that code for specific functions, there are many sequences, first identified by US geneticists in 1980, which do not appear to hold any genetic information.

Known as STRs or "short tandem repeats", these sections contain short DNA sequences of adenine, thymine, guanine and cytosine (ATGG or GATA, for example) repeated a large number of times. The number of repetitions in each STR can vary between people. Some versions of the STR may have 15 ATGGs repeated one after the other. Another version may only have 9 ATGGs.

Each person carries two copies (or "alleles") of each STR – one from their mother, and one from their father. Thus, an individual's genotype can be referred to as 9,15 for that marker.

The system that Dr de Ungria's lab was using at that time tested nine of those areas, known as "loci". This system also used a gender marker, the amelogenin sex gene, which shows if the DNA donor is male or female. (Today's systems use 22 markers, plus the sex marker.)

The genotype at each of the nine STRs was then put together to produce a DNA "profile". It featured nine sets of numbers, plus the gender marker. This set of numbers could then be compared to others on a computer database.

It was information in a form that was very well-suited to the complex cross-matching assignment that the lab's scientists had been given.

The first two identifications

There were two cases where the team could make a positive identification quite quickly. These were two young boys (cases 1756 and 1758) where the investigators actually had ante-mortem DNA samples to compare with the post-mortem samples. They were the children whose families had kept their dried umbilical cords.

The other cases were all going to present much more of a challenge. In most standard "missing person" cases, the identities of both parents are available, so the "inferred profile" of their child can be worked out.

Here, the scientists usually had only one parent's DNA to work with. Meanwhile, to make the puzzle more difficult, the state of the children's remains meant that the scientists could not always get results for all of the nine loci on the DNA strand that they were testing.

But the team had another DNA testing trick up their sleeves: a technique that would prove especially useful for this particular group, where 17 of the victims were male, with four pairs of brothers among them.

A technique to use for male DNA

The technique was Y-DNA typing. This is the analysis of specific loci, or testing regions on the Y chromosome, the chromosome that indicates male gender. Males have one Y chromosome and one X chromosome, while females have two X chromosomes.

Because the Y chromosome is passed directly from a man to all his sons, Y-STR testing can be used to trace a direct paternal line.

This test tends to be of limited use in criminal cases because all the male members of a family will have the same profile. Nevertheless, it was this test that, in 2013, enabled police in the US city of Boston to definitively nail the identity of the notorious 1960s killer, The Boston Strangler – almost fifty years after his last victim died (see story at the end of this chapter).

Dr de Ungria's team did not need to be able to tell the male family members apart. They just needed the Y-STR test to help them find the four sets of brothers in the group. The technique achieved everything they asked of it. It allowed the scientists to identify three of the four sets of brothers amongst the dead children. They could then use teeth and bone examination to establish the elder and the younger of each pair.

The test also clarified the situation of the fourth set of brothers. It helped them establish that the younger brother in this set was the only one of the 23 children whose body was never recovered from the rubble.

The key to this mystery was the "reference" profile provided by a paternal grandfather who had two grandsons at the orphanage: an 8-year-old and a 23-month-old toddler.

When the investigators had done all the DNA profiles, they only found one set of remains (case no 1773, a body that looked about eight years old) which was an exact match for the grandfather's Y-STR profile. They should have found two. This meant that the 8-year-old's little brother was the child whose body was never found.

Another mystery solved and a mis-identification discovered

This testing also solved another mystery. This particular grandfather was not expecting the scientists to be examining his

8-year-old grandson. He was the grandfather who had visually identified the body of his 8-year-old grandson at the time of the fire. He had had the child's body buried. Believing he was certain of the identity of this particular set of remains, he had refused to have the body exhumed.

Sadly, he had made a mistake. The DNA testing could account for all the boys, except the 23-month-old toddler. And a 7-year-old boy.

It became suddenly clear. This grandfather had mistakenly claimed the body of the 7-year-old as his grandson, who was eight.

It was a salutary reminder of the danger of allowing relatives to make visual identifications of loved ones, based on information such as clothing.

In the end, 18 of the 21 sets of remains were identified. The multidisciplinary team of scientists was then able to share their experience with the international forensic science community, publishing a paper about it in the *American Journal of Forensic Medicine and Pathology* in 2005. It was an extraordinarily good result, given the chaos of the recovery operation.

The three identification mysteries in the group of 21 were all female.

These three girls, cases 1772, 1768 and 1761, were aged between three and five. Two of them (cases 1772 and 1761) had DNA profiles that were a partial match to one of the mothers (mother No 5) who said she had lost a child in the fire and had given a DNA sample.

But in the absence of the profile of a father, there just wasn't enough information to say for certain.

Although 23 children died in the orphanage fire, the scientists only received 21 sets of remains. The success of their operation, and the fact that the last two missing children were male, meant that relatives were able to deduce the identities of the two bodies that the scientists never saw. And know what happened to them.

One was the 23-month-old toddler whose body was never found. The other was the 7-year-old who remained in the grave where he had been buried after the fire because he had been mis-identified by the grandfather mentiond earlier.

Working on this case affected Dr Fortun deeply. She got to know the bereaved parents well and, twenty years on, her memories of their grief are still fresh.

"The fire happened after their Christmas party and I've got a group picture of most of the kids who died," she says. "They were so cute. I think only one or two were really orphans. Most were kids of single parents (widowed, separated and other circumstances). I was told they were paying Damas for taking in their children because they couldn't bring them to their workplaces. So the kids were boarders."

The forensic pathologist will never forget the day that the children were ready to be returned to the cemetery after the identification work was completed.

"I got spooked," she recalls. "It was late in the afternoon and getting dark. I was alone in the morgue with all the little coffins around me. I was placing the wrapped remains in the caskets, (being) careful that the labels were not mixed up.

"I suddenly had this overwhelming sense of anxiety that the little kids were around me. I am a sceptic, being a scientist, but sometimes there are things I can't explain."

Dr Fortun kept a close watch on the labelling of the children's remains until they were reburied.

The consequences of mistakes in identification

A correct identification process is the least of the courtesies that the living owe the dead. This is a maxim that all forensic scientists who have dealt with the identification of victims in disasters swear by.

An incorrect identification isn't just a problem for the family who makes it. It also creates a difficulty for another set of relatives.

Dr Fortun came to the orphanage fire with direct experience of the huge grief and trauma generated when there is no proper system for establishing the identities of people who die in a mass accident or disaster.

Her chapter "Who's who" in the 2005 Philippines government health report describes the chaotic aftermath of the infamous 1996 Ozone Disco fire in Quezon City. In that disaster, 162 people, mostly students celebrating the end of the academic year, were incinerated.

The Ozone Disco fire

The Ozone Disco had no fire exit. Equally disastrous was the fact that its lone exit had an inward swinging door, which swung shut against the stampede of frantic patrons trying to get out. When the fire was over, there were 144 dead bodies piled up in front of this closed door. Other bodies were found elsewhere in the building.

Dr Fortun was part of a group who volunteered to unravel the chaos created by a situation in which relatives were permitted to visually identify badly burned bodies and take them away for burial.

The team soon discovered that there were more claimants than bodies. This ghastly situation had been created by a few individuals who had stolen the identities of the dead and used them to claim compensation.

Investigating further, the volunteers discovered that one man had been able to carry away two bodies after claiming to be the father of two of the students who died in the fire. He had photographs and documents, including fake birth certificates, to support his claim and managed to net at least 70,000 pesos in compensation. He had even joined the Justice for Ozone Victims Movement and attended their meetings.

The volunteer doctors were able to identify some of the bodies. But at the end of their efforts they were left with eight bodies. These individuals remained unidentified and unclaimed because they could not be matched to any of the eight families looking for their missing children. Clearly the bodies of these eight families' children had been taken by other families and buried or, in many cases, cremated – making it impossible to trace errors.

"In other words," Dr Fortun wrote, "eight families ended up with no bodies to claim and grieve over, while those who managed to recover their dead most likely obtained the wrong remains."

The process, as she pointed out, could not have been less scientific. Families were simply going to the various funeral parlours where the dead had been laid out and looking for some physical attribute that they felt they could recognise.

According to Dr Fortun, some relatives became very defensive when questioned about these identifications.

"One ... declared defiantly: *Hindi nagkakamali ang kutob ng ina!* (A mother's intuition cannot be wrong!) Many families just picked out dead bodies, claimed them and the funeral parlours were only too glad to dispose of the bodies quickly."

The Boston Strangler mystery

In 2013 a group of Texas-based DNA scientists made world headlines by using Y-chromosome testing to solve a 50-year-old mystery. Their testing proved that Albert DeSalvo was responsible for murdering at least one of eleven women raped and strangled between 1962 and 1964 in the US city of Boston, Massachusetts. DeSalvo had been thought to be the infamous "Boston Strangler". Now it was known for certain.

The murders had taken place more than 20 years before the development of DNA profiling in 1986. But in the 1990s, police began searching through all the evidence they could find from the original 1960s crime scenes for body fluid samples that could be used in the then "new" testing.

All they could find was a semen sample taken from the body of the Strangler's last victim, and a semen-stained blanket found at the scene of the woman's murder. Finally, after repeated attempts to extract a DNA profile from the blanket failed, a 2012 effort worked.

DeSalvo, of course, had long been dead and buried. Permission for an exhumation and a DNA test would only be granted if scientists could present credible evidence to support one. So the scientists looked to male family members of DeSalvo's. Their Y-chromosome test results would all be identical.

In 2013, police covertly followed Timothy DeSalvo, a nephew of Albert's. When he discarded a water bottle, they picked it up and tested it. His Y-chromosome DNA matched the crime scene profile.

It wasn't a conclusive identification of Albert DeSalvo as the Boston Strangler. It only indicated a family member as the perpetrator. But it was enough to order an exhumation of his body. Samples from his teeth and femur were analysed.

They yielded a DNA profile that matched the semen samples. The odds that it belonged to a white male other than Albert DeSalvo were one in 220 billion.

Case Thirteen
THE MARIVIC GENOSA CASE

A heavily pregnant Marivic Genosa killed her violent and abusive husband Ben on the night of November 15, 1995. She was sentenced to death for it in 1998. At the time, her case was judged simply as a wife's brutal murder of her husband, with the prosecution taking no interest in how Ben Genosa actually died. Five years later, when feminist lawyer Katrina Legarda took up Marivic's appeal, she looked at the case's forensic science evidence and used it to mount an appeal.

The Marivic Genosa case made legal history in the Philippines. The case began with the murder of Ben Genosa in 1995. He was "a drunk, a gambler, a womaniser and wife-beater". At least that is the way that the Philippines Supreme Court's Justice Artemio Panganiban would later describe him. His wife, office administrator Marivic Genosa, was sentenced to death for his murder in 1998.

Her crime was described by Judge Fortunato L Madrona of the Regional Trial Court of Ormoc City as a brutal one. She had, the court found, bashed her husband to death.

Otherwise this case seemed more sad than special. After all, Ben and Marivic Genosa had been childhood sweethearts. And they had two children.

What made this case unique was that it prompted an appeal that featured a historic legal "first". This appeal, filed in 2000, was the first time that a Philippines court considered "Battered Woman

Syndrome" as a defence to murder.

The appeal succeeded – at least in part. The 2004 appeal judgement set aside the death sentence, substituting a jail sentence. What made it historic was the fact that this judgement led to the enactment of a new law: one that recognised "Battered Woman Syndrome" as a defence to murder in the Philippines.

But with all that has been written about this case, one fact never got the attention it deserved. This appeal was enabled by forensic evidence.

How did Ben Genosa die?

It was forensic pathologist Dr Raquel Fortun's report on the actual cause of death of Marivic Genosa's husband that gave crusading feminist lawyer Katrina Legarda ammunition to help her overturn that first Regional Trial Court judgement against Marivic Genosa.

That court had found Marivic guilty of bashing her husband to death with a lead pipe as he lay sleeping in bed. No notice was taken of Marivic's own insistence that she had shot her husband with the gun with which he had previously threatened her and that she had done so in the dining room.

The suggestion that the dead man had been bashed also affected his wife's sentence. It led Judge Madrona to find there was the aggravating circumstance of "treachery" because Ben Genosa was supposedly defenceless when he was killed. This seems to have contributed to the judge's decision to impose a death sentence.

When Katrina Legarda began working on Marivic Genosa's appeal against her death sentence, she turned to Dr Fortun for help.

At the time the medical expert was the only qualified forensic pathologist in the country. It was clear to her that the forensic examination of Marivic's dead husband had been slipshod.

The most glaring problem with it was that the doctor who had done the autopsy had no forensic pathology qualifications. Physician Refelina Y Cerillo was the health officer of Isabel municipality in Leyte, at the time. She had a medical degree, but no training to qualify her to examine a decomposing body and establish its cause of death. She also had no special equipment to perform autopsies, and no morgue.

When Legarda filed the urgent "omnibus" motion for an appeal, she had "Battered Woman Syndrome" in mind. She asked for a re-examination of her client's psychological state at the time of the murder. She was also keen to query the narrative that "this woman bashed a sleeping man".

Marivic's own account of shooting her husband to defend herself from another beating was a typical way for a desperate wife to finally fight back. Certainly the literature on "Battered Woman Syndrome" is peppered with US cases of women who suffer years of abuse before finally picking up one of their husband's weapons and shooting him.

The lawyer believed Marivic. But she needed a proper forensic opinion to back her up. She wanted the body of Ben Genosa exhumed so that Dr Fortun could do a second autopsy and establish his actual cause of death.

Dr Fortun's re-examination of the case

Dr Fortun started looking into the case and found more than enough to justify this request.

The authorities didn't make her task easy for her. She was given all the exhibits, including the autopsy report, and Marivic Genosa's testimony. Yet she had no access to the original crime scene photos. Instead she had to work with black and white photocopies of photos of the dead man's head injuries, which she looked at in the context of the examining doctor's report.

Despite those difficulties, her conclusion was that the description and photos of the death wound at the time of the post-mortem did not match the damage caused by a beating with a lead pipe. Instead it was a better fit for a wound caused by a gun shot.

The lawyer attached a letter from the forensic pathologist to her appeal motion. It explained Dr Fortun's opinion and requested a complete re-examination of the cause of death of Ben Genosa, including an autopsy.

Dr Fortun's disappointment

Although the request for an appeal was granted and the appeal had such an important result, Dr Fortun looks back on this case with frustration, describing it as "a disappointment from a forensic point of view".

She felt let down on two counts. First the request for an exhumation was not granted.

A full bench of the Supreme Court rejected it for legal reasons. Justice Artemio Panganiban ruled that it was not the superior court's job to establish the facts of the case. Instead, he said, "the matter of proving the cause of death should have been made before the trial court".

Dr Fortun was also disappointed by the fact that the Supreme Court went on to review the case as a battered woman case without taking any interest in reviewing its key facts.

"To me the court practically said they didn't really care how the crime was committed," Fortun recalls.

"So how was the guilt of the accused proven beyond reasonable doubt? (The actual ruling was that, in this appeal, the specific or direct cause of Ben's death had 'no legal consequence'.) I don't get that part because I'm in the forensic sciences. For us, it's the truth and nothing but."

The lawyer's view

Katrina Legarda sees it differently. For her, the forensic pathologist's work was valuable because it gave her another ground for her appeal.

"I said I wanted an exhumation to prove that (Marivic) wasn't lying," says Attorney Legarda. "If she wasn't lying about cause of death then she wasn't lying about battery."

Certainly, despite Dr Fortun's frustrations with the court system, her work helped Attorney Legarda make the name "Marivic Genosa" part of legal history in the Philippines.

Without their work, that first 1998 judgement against Marivic Genosa would have cemented her place in Philippines criminal history as a cold-hearted killer rather than as a victim, deserving of pity.

How did the first trial get the case so wrong?

The answer, again, is forensic evidence. Neither the prosecutor nor Marivic's defence lawyer took enough interest in the actual forensic evidence against Marivic.

They focused only on the fact that Marivic had killed her husband. The prosecutor accused her of beating her husband to death with a metal pipe. Found leaning against a wall in the bedroom where the dead man's body had been discovered, it was more than a metre long and 38 mm wide. It had a red stain at one end.

No time seems to have been spent on analysing how this murder was carried out and how, exactly, Ben Genosa died. Neither was there any interest in establishing where he had been killed. There was no evidence confirming that Genosa had been in bed when he was killed. Certainly he had been found lying on the bed, wrapped in a bedsheet. But had he been killed there? To Dr Fortun's great frustration, no efforts were made to find out.

Her personal theory is that Marivic shot him when he was in bed, as opposed to in the dining room.

"I doubt if she could have done it elsewhere and then set up his body like that." And, of course, shooting him would have been far easier for her to do in this situation.

Actual "cause of death" is – and clearly needs to be – a crucially important issue in a murder trial. But in this case, the prosecution was happy to assert that Marivic Genosa had killed her husband by bashing him over the head with a lead pipe. It did not matter that there was no expert forensic evidence supporting this. All that seemed to concern the prosecution was that Marivic had confessed to the killing. The prosecution didn't believe her and simply ignored this testimony. And the judge appeared to have accepted the prosecution's scenario without question.

An unlikely criminal

Marivic Genosa was the last person one would ever expect to end up in the dock, facing murder charges.

A university graduate with a degree in business administration, she had a good job as a secretary to the manager of the Port of Ormoc City, in the province of Leyte, some 1000 km south of Manila. She had started work there as a port traffic officer but had been promoted two months later because of her efficiency.

She had done only one thing wrong. At least that was what her parents thought. She had married the wrong man.

She had known Ben Genosa since elementary school. They had been neighbours when they were growing up, and they were also third cousins.

Interestingly both sets of parents had objected to the match and had done their best to stop it. But Ben had been a persistent suitor. He was also Marivic's regular dance partner at fiestas. This gave him the opportunity to court her while keeping other potential suitors away from her.

The first year of their marriage had been happy. Subsequently, however, Ben Genosa's serial infidelities, drinking and gambling – especially on cockfighting – had had a toxic effect on the marriage and, no doubt, on the couple's children.

There were violent arguments, especially when Ben Genosa had been drinking, during which Marivic sustained injuries. Although Marivic made at least five attempts to leave, her husband would always go after her and the pair would reconcile.

At the time of the murder, they had been married for 12 years.

Extensive evidence of abuse

A key witness to the damage caused by this marital discord was Dr Dino Caing, a physician at the clinic in Leyte, where Marivic had also worked at one time. He told the Ormoc City Regional Trial Court that she had been treated there on six occasions between 1989 and 1995 for physical injuries.

The court heard extensive details of these injuries. All of them, Marivic had told the various doctors who saw her, had been caused by her husband.

They included: hematoma (swelling and bruising caused by ruptured blood vessels) on the lower right eyelid (1990); and contusion and hematoma of the left eye socket (1992). In April 1995, seven months before the murder, she had been treated for trauma and tenderness on the right shoulder. Then in June of that year, five months before the murder, she had suffered multiple abrasions, trauma and swelling on the left leg. At the time she was already five months pregnant.

Marivic herself gave detailed evidence to the court about the arguments with her husband. She said they took place about three times a week, and often featured slaps and beatings as well as raised voices. There were also witnesses to the violence she endured. A former neighbour gave evidence about hearing quarrels between Marivic Genosa and her husband, and seeing her bruises.

Meanwhile, her cousin Ecel Arano testified that Marivic had often asked her to sleep over at the Genosa house because of her fear that her husband would come home drunk and hurt her.

On one night when the cousin did sleep over, she was awakened at 10 pm by shouts and the noise of something breaking. Then Marivic came running into Ecel's room and locked the door. At this point her husband appeared outside the locked window shutters, waving a knife.

Ecel was also at the Genosa house on the night of the murder.

That afternoon Marivic had arrived home from work to find her husband not at home. Given it was payday, she assumed he would be out gambling his wages away. She was the main breadwinner in the household but her husband's smaller wage was still needed to support their two children. So she asked her cousin to help look for him around the various taverns of Isabel.

Failing to find him, the cousins returned to the Genosa home. Ben Genosa was there – drunk. Angry with his wife for looking for him, he began berating her. He was also particularly abusive that night, Marivic would later say, because he was "crazy" about the most recent of his long line of girlfriends. This one was a woman named Lulu Rubillos.

Fearful for her safety, Marivic asked her cousin to stay the night, but Ecel refused. Her father had heard what had happened on the last occasion she slept over and had forbidden her to spend the night there again when Ben was drunk.

The lead-up to Ben's death

Ben continued to harangue his wife. But she did her best to ignore him, focusing on their children, who were doing their homework.

She also directed her attention at the TV, which was on at the time.

Infuriated at being ignored, Ben first switched off the light. Then, fetching a large 46-cm-long Bolo knife, he cut the TV antenna wire.

The children were terrified, as was Marivic who was screaming for help as she ran out of the room and into the bedroom.

At that point, Ben left, possibly to have more to drink. Meanwhile Marivic set about calming the children and getting them to bed. She then started to pack up her husband's clothes, so she could get him to move out.

When he finally returned, the sight of his packed suitcase so enraged him that he grabbed his wife by the throat, shouting that he was going to kill her – to free himself from her nagging.

At the same time he dragged Marivic out of the bedroom and into the dining room. There was a special drawer in this room. It was where he kept a gun.

Fortunately it was locked and Ben didn't have the key. Enraged, he grabbed a three-inch-long blade cutter from his wallet and started jabbing the lock with it.

Marivic recognised that blade. In a previous fight Ben had held it against her throat. She was due to give birth the next month. Fearing she was fighting for her own life, as well as for the life of her unborn baby, she grabbed a lead pipe and smashed it down on her husband's arm. That caused him to drop both his wallet and the knife. But the pain from that blow failed to stop him.

Desperate, Marivic "smashed" (to use her word) him over the nape of the neck with the pipe. This time she succeeded in stunning him. She forced the drawer open, retrieved the gun, and shot her tormentor dead.

Marivic's escape

The next morning Marivic and her children boarded a Grand Air flight to Manila, where she rented a room and later took a job as a field researcher under the alias of "Marvelous Isidro".

Back in Leyte, two days passed before neighbours began noticing a foul odour emanating from the Genosa home. Police were called and Ben's body was found.

Marivic Genosa gave birth at the Rizal Medical Centre in Pasig City, 14 km southeast of Manila on December 1, 1995. She was suffering from eclampsia and hypertension, and her baby was born prematurely. Weeks later her in-laws tracked her down through her children's enrolment in a school in Laguna province, 50 km southeast of Manila.

The original physician's examination: hopelessly unscientific

There are two versions of how Ben Genosa actually died. There is the story presented by the prosecutor to the Regional Trial Court of Ormoc. And there's Marivic's own account.

The prosecutor told the court that Marivic had bashed her husband hard over the head with the same pipe she had used to hit his arm earlier, thereby causing his death.

This version of events was based on the medical evidence provided by the doctor who had examined Ben Genosa's body: physician Refelina Y Cerillo, aged 36, the local municipal health officer.

As previously noted, this examination was carried out in hopelessly unscientific circumstances. Dr Cerillo conducted her examination in the open air, just outside the house where the dead man was found. His body had been lying in the bedroom but had been taken outdoors for examination because of the terrible odour of decomposition inside.

According to Dr Cerillo's report there was only one injury to the body, which was decomposing by the time she examined it. This was damage to the occipital bone, the trapezoid-shaped bone at the rear of the cranium. She described it as a fracture "resulting [in] laceration of the brain, spontaneous rupture of the blood vessels on the posterior surface of the brain, laceration of the dura and meningeal vessels producing severe intracranial hemorrhage".

But when she presented this report in court, she gave no testimony on the actual cause of Ben Genosa's death. Disappointingly, Marivic's defence lawyer failed to cross-examine her on this point.

Marivic herself, on the other hand, continued to insist that she had shot her husband, after forcing open the drawer where the gun was kept.

It is amazing enough that this key detail of the accused's own version of events was dismissed by the prosecution. It was even more shocking that it was also ignored by her own defence lawyer.

Meanwhile, the prosecution produced witnesses who suggested that Marivic was a violent woman. Unsurprisingly, one of them was the accused's mother-in-law. The other was a workmate of Ben's who had known him for only a year but who was his regular companion at cockfights. He told the court he had been drinking and betting on a cockfight with the deceased on the night of his death. Later that night he happened to be walking past the Genosa house and was able to hear the exact words being spoken inside.

According to this witness's account, Marivic said, "I will never hesitate to kill you", with Ben replying "Why kill me when I am innocent?"

Interestingly the man's testimony covered a time during which two other witnesses were also in the vicinity. And they heard and saw entirely different things.

The first witness, a fisherman neighbour, overheard Ben and

Marivic quarrelling. He heard Marivic shouting for help, while the open shutters gave him a view of Ben grabbing Marivic in a chokehold.

This man's brother, another fisherman, also heard the shouting. From the window of his hut, adjacent to the Genosa house's window, he also saw Ben Genosa holding his wife's neck with both hands. After a while, as he told the court, he saw Marivic extricate herself and leave the room. He then went back to preparing for that evening's fishing.

Marivic Genosa's trial lasted 13 sitting days over the period from April 7, 1997, to August 6, 1998.

On September 23, 1998, Judge Fortunato L Madrona found Marivic guilty beyond reasonable doubt of the crime of "parricide" (murder of a close relative).

It's difficult not to feel pity for Marivic Genosa's situation, as she stood in the dock. She was an unhappily married woman living in the only country in the world, except the Vatican, where divorce is illegal. She was a battered wife and it was 1998. But while the phrase "Battered Wife Syndrome" was, by then, a familiar one in English-speaking courts in the UK, the US and Australia, her own defence lawyer didn't even raise it.

Yet she was fortunate in one respect.

The fact that she had been sentenced to death meant that her case would be subject to an automatic review, due in 2000.

Awareness of family violence rising

Meanwhile, after Marivic's conviction, public awareness of the issue of family violence had begun rising. The women's congressional group Abanse Pinay (Advance Filipina) took particular interest in her case.

Katrina Legarda, who would eventually take up Marivic Genosa's case personally, had founded this group herself.

Legarda succeeded in getting the courts to agree to have her client examined and evaluated by psychologists and psychiatrists to determine whether the abuse inflicted upon her would support a defence of "Battered Woman Syndrome".

This was an entirely new way of interpreting self-defence. It answers questions such as "Why didn't she just leave?" by explaining how repeated episodes of bullying break down a woman's psychological resistance and natural self-control. The bullying episodes induce a kind of psychological paralysis which can only be ended by an act of violence on her part.

It has to be noted that the appeal judgement did not completely accept Marivic's case as an example of "Battered Woman Syndrome". The judges certainly acknowledged that Ben Genosa had been a wife-beater. But they considered the violence that Marivic Genosa endured at the hands of her husband as only a "mitigating circumstance". Accordingly they lowered the imposable penalty from death to a prison sentence of 14 years and eight months. They also overturned the notion that the murder involved "treachery".

The decision remains a landmark, however, because the court had set a precedent by considering "Battered Woman Syndrome". It had defined it and allowed a woman's partial exoneration as a result of it.

After that judgement it was only a matter of months before Congress passed a new law, the "Anti-Violence Against Women and Their Children Act of 2004". Section 26 of it stated that "victim-survivors who are found by the courts to be suffering from battered wife syndrome do not incur any criminal and civil liability".

The Marivic Genosa case had made legal history. This would not have happened without the work of two exceptional women: forensic pathologist Dr Raquel Fortun and lawyer Katrina Legarda.

Case Fourteen
THE BALI BOMBING AND ITS "CSI MOMENTS"

The joint Indonesian-Australian investigation into the deadly 2002 terrorist attack on Bali was long, complex and difficult. But its Disaster Victim Identification work was a scientific success story on its own, while the forensic science achievements during the hunt for the bombers would not have been out of place in a Hollywood script.

Shortly before midnight on Saturday October 12, 2002, two bombs tore through the heart of the Kuta Beach tourist precinct on the Indonesian island of Bali. The first blast went off at 11.07 pm in Paddy's Bar, a popular drinking hole open to both locals and tourists. Less than a minute later, a second, far bigger explosion created a deadly inferno in the thatch-roofed Sari Club bar. Open only to tourists, it was located just metres away on the other side of the Legian Road nightclub strip. Forty-five seconds later a third bomb was detonated some 12 km away in Renon, on a deserted roadside between the US and Australian consulates.

The purpose of the Renon bomb was to send a clear message, via its location, about the intended political targets of the Kuta blasts. As planned by the bombers, who would later be revealed as hardliners from the local extremist group Jemaah Islamiyah (JI), the majority of the dead were Western tourists.

The death toll was 202, with a further 209 people horribly injured. From the beginning, the fate of the 88 Australians killed dominated the media narrative of this terrible event. In fact the bombing was often referred to as "Australia's September 11". But 38 of the dead were Indonesians. Two were from Japan, two were from South Korea and one was from Taiwan. A further 22 nations were represented in the death toll, including the UK, the US, Sweden, France and Germany. The destructive force of the horrific blasts was so powerful that it was estimated that about 70 per cent of the victims would need to be identified through DNA analysis.

Disaster Victim Identification (DVI)

The first flights into Bali after the bombing brought forensic pathologists, odontologists, crime scene investigators and mortuary staff. A "reconciliation room" (where experts compared ante-mortem dental records and medical reports with post-mortem X-rays and autopsy reports) was set up in Kuta's Kartika Plaza Hotel and a joint Indonesian and Australian Federal Police DVI team was established to identify the victims, using protocols that complied with international DVI standards. These excluded visual identification by relatives as proof.

In the immediate chaotic aftermath of the bombing, grieving relatives had been just walking into the mortuary of Denpasar's Sanglah Hospital and wanting to claim bodies they had identified as their family members so they could fly them home for burial.

That all came to an abrupt halt on October 15, the third day after the bombing, when it was announced that the Indonesian authorities had just decreed that dental or DNA information had to be used to confirm identities before bodies could be released.

Dr Tony Hill, the late Australian forensic odontologist, recalled walking into the hospital mortuary that day and being met by a group of angry relatives, all understandably desperate to leave Bali and take their loved ones' bodies home. All of them were frustrated with what they perceived as "bureaucratic" delays in releasing the bodies of the dead.

Dr Hill was appalled to learn that families had been making preliminary identifications on the basis of clothing. Other victims were being identified because of keys or jewellery found on their bodies, credit cards in their pockets, or the fact that their hair was braided. This was madness, given it was so common for young Australian tourists in Bali to have their hair braided, and to buy the same trinkets and clothing from cheap outlets near the beach.

While the forensic odontologist could feel sympathy for the resultant confusion and distress of relatives desperate to find a body to grieve over, he was only too aware of mistakes made in other mass disasters, where highly stressed families made misidentifications. In fact, of the eighteen cases of victims initially identified visually in the Sanglah Hospital mortuary, nine were subsequently proven to have been incorrect.

One of these identifications was done by an Australian man who had taken his fury with the authorities to the media. He was brandishing a photo of his wife and was sure he had found her in the mortuary. It later turned out that this particular woman's body had a pierced navel. His wife didn't. He then waited until his wife was finally identified through her dental records.

With all the correct protocols observed, this DNA and dentistry-driven identification process proved to be highly successful. Through the joint Indonesian and Australian Federal Police teams' DVI effort, 182 of the 221 missing or deceased in Bali were eventually identified, including all 88 Australians.

A long and complex investigation
Bali is renowned as an island paradise and mecca for international tourists. A catastrophe there gained immediate international media

attention. The Indonesians were flooded with offers of assistance by police agencies from around the world. Forensic experts from the FBI, Scotland Yard, Japan, Germany, France, the Netherlands, Sweden and the Philippines arrived en masse. In order to control this influx, the Indonesian National Police (INP) gave the Australian Federal Police (AFP) "lead agency" status. Now that the INP were under a spotlight on the international stage, the involvement of the Australians was a help to them.

The investigation was still a long, laborious and complex process, further complicated by the fact that it was a joint operation between Indonesian and Australian law enforcement officials.

Both police and scientists endured many periods of frustration and pessimism, especially in the first few weeks. But there were also several extraordinary scientific breakthroughs: the kind that tend to be featured in every single episode of shows such as CSI.

The presentation of such discoveries as a routine part of forensic work infuriates real-life forensic scientists. It is why most of them loathe these shows.

Forensic investigation, they explain over and over, can be a tedious and frustrating process. Literally hundreds of tests may be carried out on a single part of a crime scene, without a single one of them producing a helpful result.

"Light-bulb moments" do happen: when one scientific test produces a dramatic result that changes the direction of an investigation, or solves it. But most real-life scientists and forensic crime scene officers consider themselves lucky if they enjoy a handful of them in an entire working life.

Australian forensic biologist Steven Fowler actually coined a phrase to describe these rare and special experiences. He calls them "CSI moments". He had one of them at a murder scene where an old man had been brutally bashed over the head. Police had no clues to the weapon used. Judging from the injuries, it could have been a baseball bat, a sledgehammer or an axe. Fowler waited until nightfall to pick up his can of luminol. This chemical reagent is best used in darkness because it glows phosphorescent blue in the presence of blood or other substances containing iron. He then sprayed it over the grass where the man's body had been found. Within seconds, the telltale blue glow appeared. It was in the shape of an axe. The perpetrator had obviously put the implement down on the grass after using it on his victim. Still wet with blood, it had stained the grass underneath. Once the police knew what the murder weapon was, they knew where to start looking. And they were on their way to finding the culprit.

Amazingly, given the circumstances, the Bali bombing investigation featured several such "CSI moments".

Analysing the crime scene and identifying the bombers

The Bali bombing investigation was essentially a giant murder case: one with 202 victims and three crime scenes. As in any other homicide case, its aim was to uncover the identity of the perpetrators: the "whodunnit".

The "whydunnit" aspect was an important path to this aim. If you understand the motivation behind a crime, you are well on the way to finding its perpetrator. But in the immediate aftermath of the bombing the motivations of its organisers remained a mystery. No group claimed responsibility, although intelligence agencies were reported as suspecting that the perpetrators might be linked to Osama bin Laden's al-Qaeda. In this scenario, the deaths of Western tourists would have been seen as payback for Australia's role in backing the United States' "war on terrorism".

The key to solving this crime would be the "howdunnit". This is where the forensic scientists come in. If you can identify the materials used in the bombs and the methods used to explode them, you may well find a clue to the identity of one or more of the perpetrators.

Officially the "Labfor" (Pusat Laboratorium dan Forensik) forensic scientists from the Indonesian National Police were working together with their Australian Federal Police counterparts in a combined operation called Operation Alliance.

Operation Alliance came into being on October 18, six days after the bombing. On that day the AFP's Chief Commissioner Mick Keelty and the head of INP, General Da'i Bachtiar, signed an agreement formalising the existence of a Joint Indonesia-Australia Police Investigation and Intelligence Team to work together on the investigation. It would involve 120 AFP officers working alongside a similar number of their INP counterparts. But this agreement merely formalised what had begun happening within hours of the blasts.

The morning after the bombing, Keelty had been on the phone to Bachtiar to offer assistance. There were personal friendships involved here. General I Made Mangku Pastika, who had been appointed to head the investigation of the bombing, had been a classmate of the AFP's Chief Commissioner Mick Keelty at the AFP's "management of serious crime" course in 1993. The two men had been friends since.

By Sunday night October 13, less than 24 hours after the blasts, an AFP team of disaster victim identification, forensic, investigation, intelligence and bomb-blast experts were on their way to Bali. A dozen more disaster victim, bomb blast and forensic experts flew out of Canberra the following night, Monday October 14.

AFP forensic chemist David Royds was on this second flight – along with a group of Australian families whose young adult children were missing, feared dead, after the explosion. Royds was an experienced practitioner. He had joined the New South Wales police force as a science graduate and spent 13 years as a crime scene examiner, mostly in rural NSW. After being awarded a Rotary scholarship to do a masters degree in forensic chemistry in Scotland, he joined the AFP as a forensic chemist.

Royds and his colleagues had brought the contents of their mobile laboratory with them. Its bank of equipment ranged from microscopes to portable analytical instruments used for the tentative identification of commonly used explosives and/or their precursor ingredients. These included an ion mobility spectrometer and a portable infrared spectrometer. The aim was to do as much screening work as possible early in the investigation so as to provide "leads" for the investigators when they were most needed. Screening also allowed the "dross" to be culled so only a small number of the best samples, potentially rich in evidence, were brought back to the main laboratory for more in-depth analyses.

Royds' team had first deployed this mobile laboratory six months previously, as part of the AFP security for the 2002 Commonwealth Heads of Government Meeting in the Australian state of Queensland. And although no incidents occurred that required them to use it, the experience was valuable as it showed up some significant potential contamination issues. Strategies and procedures were then developed to address these risks.

By Tuesday night, after one change of hotels, the scientists had set themselves and their lab up in Kuta's Kartika Plaza Hotel. Their Indonesian counterparts, the 41 forensic experts led by Udayana University chemistry graduate Inspector Ngurah Wijaya Putra, were based in a suite of rooms at the INP Headquarters in the Balinese capital of Denpasar, 8 km away.

Finally, on the morning of Wednesday October 16, Royds and his colleagues made their first visit to the scene of the previous Saturday night's blasts. From the first moment of their arrival, the Australian scientists were made aware of their subordinate status in the Indonesian investigation. While they were working in a "team" effort, they were only to be allowed into the crime scenes after the Indonesian crime scene investigators had finished with them.

"Although everybody says we had this wonderful relationship with the Indonesian police, we really didn't," recalls Royds. "In fairness to them, it was their jurisdiction and from their perspective we were there to offer a second opinion, if asked. They had their investigation running but they were interested in what we, and our instruments, might come up with. They fed us 'selected' information."

The forensic experts had three scenes to examine: Paddy's Bar, where the first bomb went off; the Sari Club; and Renon, near the consulates. There had been no victims and little damage at the Renon site, but this crime scene proved to be rich in evidence. Analysis of damage and detritus indicated the use of high explosives, remains of a mobile phone and traces of TNT. This information helped them analyse the Paddy's Bar scene, where traces of TNT were also found.

A suicide bomber?

On that first day, the Sari Club was the place where the Indonesian team was focusing its efforts. Accordingly it was off limits to the Australians – as was Paddy's Bar, in theory. But with their Operation Alliance partners' attention elsewhere, the Australian scientists simply strolled into the scene of the first, smaller blast.

That morning Royds would make a discovery that was, in the end, absolutely crucial to the investigation. "I remember stepping over the barrier and walking into Paddy's Bar," Royds recalls. "Everyone was looking at the floor, the detritus and all the damage there." But Royds looked to the ceiling.

"There I saw a moment in time that had been captured in the form of spatter patterns in blood and soot," he says. "They were just waiting to be interpreted."

A photo taken in Paddy's Bar on that first day shows the scientist standing on a table in the bar, in his heavy blue cotton forensic overalls. Huge sweat stains bloom on his back and under his arms as he reaches up to take scrapings of blood and soot from the bar's concrete ceiling.

He was pretty sure that the soot he was sampling was TNT (trinitrotoluene). Unexploded, TNT has a yellow hue and looks like beeswax. When it explodes it gives off grey soot. Tests later confirmed his suspicions. A patch of this soot on the ceiling would usually correlate to the seat of an explosion below. Spatters of blood and tissue also indicated a trajectory back to this point. But there was no crater to be seen. How could this be? It seemed obvious that someone had been standing very close to the bomb, or possibly even carrying it, when it detonated. Might that person have been a suicide bomber?

Initially Royds was told to keep that theory to himself. At that point there was no acknowledgement that the bombing had even been a terrorist act. The official Indonesian government position was that, while the terrorist group Jemaah Islamiyah was known, it was not yet active in Indonesia. Yet the investigators knew it was in Asia and that it favoured suicide bombers. The year before it had planned a bloody attack aimed at Westerners in Singapore. Mercifully, it had been foiled.

Royds' theory continued to niggle at him. Meanwhile, at airports around Australia, members of the AFP were meeting survivors of the attack as they were flown back for treatment, and collecting their outer garments for forensic testing. The clothes were then submitted to the main forensic laboratory in Canberra. There, scientist Dr Sarah Benson would confirm the presence of TNT on victims who had emerged alive from Paddy's Bar.

So, where had the bomb been when it exploded? If it had been on the floor, it would have left a crater. It certainly hadn't been on the heavy table on which Royds had stood to swab the ceiling. It would have reduced that substantial piece of furniture to matchsticks.

"That's when I started thinking that the most plausible explanation was that it had been carried in by a human being," he says.

CSI moment (1)

On that very first day in Paddy's Bar, Royds had begun by swabbing the roof. He had then wandered around the room scanning the area for any other traces or remnants of an explosive device. He wasn't supposed to be collecting evidence. So he picked up a cup and pretended to be drinking water from it. When he spotted a couple of pieces of copper wire, they went straight into the cup: one for himself and one for his Indonesian colleagues if they wanted it.

The wire drew his attention because it was heat-damaged and distorted. It was also narrow and insulated. And it had a mono-core. Electronic devices use multi-strand copper wires. But detonator leg wires are always mono-cored.

Later, back at the Kartika Plaza Hotel, the scientist put the wires into a fresh white envelope, which he tucked into his overalls pocket.

Six hours later, physically and mentally exhausted, he was about to collapse into bed. But, after a day of "sweating like you wouldn't believe", the stench of his overalls was a palpable second presence in his room. He just had to wash them. Dumping them in the hotel sink, he turned on the water, scrubbed them thoroughly and hung them out to dry overnight.

It was only the next morning that Royds remembered the envelope – and the potentially vital evidence he had just laundered. Heading straight for the hotel room that had been transformed into the AFP lab, he swabbed one 3-cm piece of wire. He was relieved to detect the presence of TNT.

He then put the wire under a low-powered microscope. What he saw astounded him. As the wire came into focus at a magnification of 40 times larger than life, he could see tiny cotton fibres in strands of red, blue and white attached to it. This was a potentially momentous discovery. Yes, it was possible that it meant that the bomb had been wrapped in fabric to conceal it and this might also be a line of enquiry. Then he thought again of the spray of blood on the ceiling. He was keeping his suicide bomber theory to himself, as requested. But perhaps these fibres had come from the suicide bomber's clothing?

Just after Royds made his find in Paddy's Bar, the Australians were asked to leave. The Indonesian investigators then began their examination and it was more than a week before the AFP scientists were allowed back in.

They spent that week examining the Renon bomb scene and also working on the difficult job of trying to find useful samples of bomb residue around the area of the Sari Club blast site.

The Sari Club had been the scene of the biggest blast and the worst carnage. It was now waterlogged. The huge fire caused by the blast had been extinguished with water. And the crater in front of the club had been flooded with water from a burst water main. This made it very difficult to find samples that could be examined.

TNT does not dissolve in water. But it was already clear, from the small amount of it found, that it had not been the major explosive at this site.

The surfaces of two street lamp poles adjacent to and facing the crater were swabbed and found to contain traces of the oxidizing agent "chlorate". This is an inorganic salt that is very soluble in water. It also reacts rapidly with carbonaceous material such as smog and soot. Even high humidity can destroy it, so it was unlikely to survive more than a day or two in Bali's tropical environment.

There were a few other potential sources of good samples, however. AFP search teams scouring the surrounding rooftops had found parts of the bomb vehicle. These were particularly valuable because they had landed in high, dry and protected locations and could be carriers of explosive residue. Aluminium street signs were also of interest because microscopic particles travelling at high velocity could embed into the soft metal and stay there, protected and confined.

Meanwhile the question of the possible suicide bomber continued to weigh on Royds' mind. He couldn't wait to get back into Paddy's Bar. If a suicide bomber had been at work, and either wearing or carrying red, blue and white fabric, he might be able to find more traces of it.

Finally, eight days later, the Indonesian scientists completed their processing of the Paddy's Bar scene and allowed the Australians back in.

Although the Indonesian police had cleaned the place out, there were still piles of brick and rubble, while some nooks and crannies remained unexplored. The bar's interior designer had created a "tropical" décor. Painted forty-four gallon drums were wrapped around posts to make faux tree trunks, with branches and leaves "growing" out of them. Might bomb fragments and residue have fallen down inside them?

They had. After the drums had been cut away, the Australians found several pieces of red, blue and white tartan fabric, clumps of creamy "wadding", pieces of black fabric and bevelled-edged fragments of metal. Traces of these materials were also detected under the rubble and in various other locations in this area.

Might the black fabric, wadding and the tartan fabric have come from a padded vest? And who would wear such a garment in the tropics? Even the Balinese, famously sensitive to cold, would probably go no further than long sleeves. But what about a suicide bomber? Could this have been the remains of a vest bomb?

FBI scientists joined the team and set about tracing the different trajectories of blood spatter they had observed. They used string to locate the spot where all the trajectories converged. They came together in an area about 1-1.5 m above the ground and directly beneath the grey soot deposits on the ceiling.

"This was the first piece of strong evidence that it was a suicide bomber," Royds says. Meanwhile the Australians were busy mapping the locations of their finds of cloth and metal. They, too, centred on this point!

The results of DNA analysis of bloodstains on the roof above this point would be crucial.

"I wanted to see if more than one person was involved," Royds recalls. Scientists would expect to find several DNA profiles, if, for example, people had been standing over something on the floor when it went off.

If, on the other hand, all the blood and biological material came from one person, a suicide bombing would be a more plausible explanation.

Within a couple of weeks it was confirmed that all the staining on the ceiling contained the same DNA. Furthermore, it was not a match to any of the known victims from Paddy's Bar.

Royds' "suicide bomber" theory was still unofficial. Very unofficial. In fact, in a press conference given on November 1, three weeks after the bombing, the commander of the joint Indonesia-Australia police investigation, AFP Assistant Commissioner Graham Ashton made a point of hosing it down.

Ashton told the press that the Paddy's Bar bomb had been made of TNT, that it had been detonated by remote control, and that it had exploded between 80 and 120 cm above the floor. This, as David Royds had noted, was the height of a suicide bomber's waist.

The federal agent then went on to specifically scotch the suicide bomber theory.

"The bomb did not leave a crater so some of our initial thinking was that it may have been strapped to the body of, or held by, a suicide bomber," Ashton told the reporters. "It now appears likely the bomb was carried in a bag and left in the bar area on a table. It is likely that person left Paddy's Bar and set the bomb off remotely from a safe distance," he said.

"It exploded and sent people running out into the street and into the path of the Sari Club explosion, which we believe happened about 45 seconds after the Paddy's Bar bomb went off."

Yet Royds was sure he was right. He knew that the official denial of the "suicide bomber" theory was about political sensitivities, not science. At this point there was still no unassailable evidence that linked the bombing to either the Jemaah Islamiyah group or to al-Qaeda. So the Indonesian government was not keen to have its foreign partners in the investigation going public with any suggestion that there was.

Royds kept his mouth shut and waited.

In that same November 1 press conference in which Graham Ashton talked down the suicide bomber theory, he summarised the key details of the investigation's latest findings. One of them was the fact that the chassis number of the van carrying the Sari Club bomb had been identified. This discovery had only just happened and Ashton, along with all his Indonesian and Australian colleagues, was hoping that it would lead them to the bombers. But he couldn't count on it. If the van had been a stolen one, for example, information about its owners would have been useless.

Fortunately, luck was on the investigators' side.

Within a few days it would become clear that this find would be one of the great moments of the investigation. It would, on its own, lead to the discovery of the identities of six of the bombers, including their ringleader. And that ringleader would later confirm that David Royds had been right, and that the bombing of Paddy's Bar had been the work of a suicide bomber.

This finding of an identification number on the van was a true "CSI moment". It also took place at exactly the time that a TV scriptwriter would have suggested. It happened three weeks into the investigation, when the Indonesian crime scene investigators were in such despair that Bali police chief, General Made Pastika, a deeply religious Hindu, had taken himself off to a temple to pray for them.

CSI moment (2)

Twenty-one days earlier, the task of analysing the bomb debris had begun with huge energy and optimism. The morning after the blast the Indonesian crime scene examiners had started collecting and analysing debris from the Sari Club blast scene and its surrounds. Some burned chassis parts were even retrieved from the roofs of nearby buildings.

While there had been initial reports that the deadly firebomb had been caused by exploding gas cylinders, it was soon apparent that a huge bomb had gone off in a vehicle parked outside the Sari Club bar.

Within three short days, the Indonesian crime scene personnel had sorted through debris containing parts from 25 vehicles and 11 motorbikes, all of which had been damaged or destroyed in the blast. Crucially, they had established the make of the vehicle that had carried the bomb. It was a 1983 Mitsubishi L300 minivan.

But as the crime scene officers continued to sort fragments and piece them together, they reached the conclusion they had most feared. Like generations of car bomb makers before them, these bombers had ground off the vehicle's engine number and chassis. This van, the investigators feared, had no other secrets to tell. This conclusion cast a pall of gloom over the group. Vehicle and chassis numbers connect you to the person in whose name a car or truck was last registered. Even if the vehicle had been subsequently stolen, you have a place to start.

Fortunately one Indonesian Labfor officer wasn't ready to give up. Without his persistence, nothing more would have been learned from the van. In all likelihood, the identities of the bombers would never have been discovered.

Three weeks after the bombing, crime scene officer Rudi Aris David Puspito decided to take one more look at all the pieces of chassis that had been collected at the bomb scene.

He found his attention drawn to a twisted chassis rail, one that had been collected from the roof of a building across the road. It looked a little odd because there was a piece of metal welded into it. Perhaps the weld had been done to strengthen the chassis. But what if there was something underneath it? He just had to check.

Hammering off the extra piece of metal, Puspito experienced the same kind of excitement as Royds when he had seen the coloured cloth fibres on the bomb wire.

The unadorned chassis beam was now visible. It bore a number: DPR 15463. The Denpasar Motor Registry (DPR) always hand stamped an additional number behind the rear offside wheel of vehicles that could carry passengers. They needed to be able to check their roadworthiness.

Clearly the bombers had not known about this. And, as it turned out, the team member who had acquired the van had bought it in Java. He had no idea that it had ever spent any time in Bali.

Puspito's observation was only the first piece of outstanding investigative work to be done with this piece of charred metal.

The public transport registration number led the police to the vehicle's licence plate number. DK 1324 BS was registered to a Denpasar local by the name of Anak Agung Ketut Adi. A law-abiding citizen, he had registered the vehicle with authorities a few years earlier. He had then sold it, and its next owner had not bothered to register it.

When the investigators tracked that owner down, they found that he, too, had sold the van.

"Indonesian police then traced that number through six unregistered owners," says David Royds. "This was an outstanding achievement. They asked 'Whom did you buy this car from? Whom did you sell it to?' There was no paperwork. It was the most remarkable piece of 'feet on the ground' detective work that I have ever heard of."

The sixth name on the police list, Aswar Anas Prianto, lived in the village of Tuban in East Java. He had a very good recall of the man to whom he had sold the van. Not only had the sale taken place less than two months earlier, but the buyer had been flashing wads of foreign banknotes: United States dollars, Thai baht and Malaysian ringgit.

This buyer had visited Prianto twice, first to pay 10 million rupiah as a deposit and then, again, a few days later, to pay another 22 million rupiah. This made a total of about S$3500. His name was Amrozi and he lived in the village of Tenggulun, less than 50 km away.

Little more than 48 hours after the discovery of the public transportation registration number, police were watching Amrozi's house, waiting for the order to move in and arrest him.

When the officers searched his workshop, they found supplies of bomb-making chemicals and copies of speeches by al-Qaeda leader

Osama bin Laden and Jemaah Islamiyah headman Abu Bakar Bashir.

Back at the Denpasar headquarters of the investigation, Amrozi talked. And talked some more. He explained his own role in the bombing, which was to procure the car and drive it to the city of Surabaya. There he had bought the chemicals that would later be made into the bomb that the van would carry.

He also told police the names of six of the 17 people who would ultimately be identified as having planned and/or carried out the bombing. Two of them were his brothers! He also coughed up the name of the leader of the group behind the attack: Imam Samudra, an Indonesian cleric who had been named a few days earlier as a potential suspect.

It was November 5. Scarcely three weeks had passed since the bombing.

Another mystery solved: the Sari Club bomb

Amrozi's confession to having bought the chemicals used to make the Sari Club bomb brought resolution to an issue that had been causing tension between the Indonesian and Australian forensic teams since the bombing.

The receipt from the Surabaya shop where the chemicals had been purchased suggested a sale of cooking salts. But shop owner Silvester Tendean told police that he had sold Amrozi a tonne of potassium chlorate and had issued a false receipt: an act that would later earn him a seven-month jail sentence.

This information was the final confirmation that the Australian forensic scientists had been correct in their analyses of the few samples of residue that they had been able to obtain from the Sari Club site.

Flooding of the site had made sample collection difficult in the extreme. After testing the first few samples, Royds and his colleagues suspected that chlorate, an industrial salt that can be used to make both detergents and bombs, had been a key ingredient in the bomb. The chlorate in question was potassium chlorate, the oxidising agent on match heads that helps the chemical substances on them to ignite.

But because potassium chlorate is a salt, it is very soluble in water. So samples of unconsumed residue were very hard to find.

"We screened 2400 samples, and found chlorate on only six of them," the scientist recalls. "We were detecting chlorates in parts per billion concentration – minuscule traces." To underline his point, he produces a map of the Sari Club blast scene. Colour-coded dots indicate the location and result of tests. The majority of the dots are black, indicating that tests done returned negative results.

But his Indonesian counterparts were not getting the same results. It was their belief that the bomb had been a mix of many explosives, including the plastic explosive C4, ammonium nitrate, Tetryl and other substances with a long history of use in terrorist bombs.

This conflict had frustrated the Indonesian chief investigator Gories Mere to the point of tears – literally.

"Gories was insisting that their forensic people (and us) lock ourselves in a room until we achieve consensus," recalls Royds. "I said: 'You just can't do that. Evidence is evidence, not a consensus of opinions. I am not going to change my position'."

Royds responded by taking four samples from each of the samples that had tested positive to potassium chlorate. He gave one to the Indonesians, one to the Victoria Police lab in Melbourne, one to the AFP lab in Canberra and one to the UK government's Forensic Explosive Laboratories (FEL) at Fort Halstead.

"I am not the greatest chemist who ever walked," he says. "But if you have three labs using different techniques coming to the same conclusion, the public would have to be more confident with the conclusions – if they all align." His theory had correlated with information now coming to the Indonesian police from undercover sources and was finally accepted.

Then the other labs had confirmed Royds' results. And now, finally, so had the evidence of the chemical shop owner.

The search for the ringleader

While police were questioning Amrozi, Imam Samudra remained at large. But Indonesian police were closing in. They had held back the news of Amrozi's arrest for two days, until November 7. That way they could monitor calls made to and from the many numbers in Amrozi's mobile phone, and arrest the callers.

The investigators then used sophisticated AFP mobile phone signal triangulation software to track Samudra as he made quick calls from an ever-changing series of disposable mobile phones.

They were aided in their search by the fact that they had also arrested a man called Abdul Rauf, later revealed to have a reputation as a recruiter of suicide bombers. Samudra had emailed Rauf after the Bali bombing, thanking him for his assistance. The cleric had then been foolish enough to email his friend again, to tell him he was planning to flee to Sumatra, and would leave via the West Java ferry port of Merak.

This information gave the phone signal trackers an area to focus on. On November 21, their equipment "found" Samudra in a location that was going to make it hard for him to escape. He was talking on his phone from the back of a bus at the Merak ferry terminal.

The Indonesian police swooped. Just six weeks after the bombing, its mastermind was now in custody. Like his co-conspirator Amrozi, he was talking. And better than Amrozi, he was able to tell his interrogators exactly how the operation had been planned. He also confirmed a detail that had been the subject of intense behind-the-scenes debate since the bombing.

A suicide bomber had been involved, Samudra told General Da'i Bachtiar. A young man had carried a bomb into Paddy's Bar and detonated it himself. His name was Arnasan, but he was also known as "Iqbal 1". (An Arabic boy's name, *Iqbal* means "becoming successful", "facing problems bravely and getting things done".)

The suicide bomber: the proof mounts up

Samudra's information did not come as a surprise to Royds. But it gave him some professional satisfaction to have confirmation of a belief that he had held for more than six weeks.

Even before Samudra's shock announcement, the "suicide bomber" theory was still being quietly investigated, with forensic pathologists re-examining the body parts that had been brought into the Sanglah Hospital morgue in the aftermath of the bombing.

The focus of the investigation was "Body 006A": a dismembered head and two lower legs that, DNA testing had revealed, belonged to the same person.

There's nothing surprising in the fact that Body 006A had received so little attention before this. In the first weeks of the forensic investigation, no mention had been made of a "suicide bomber" theory. The forensic pathologists who were documenting the bodies were thinking only of victims. They were not on the alert for a body with the kind of catastrophic injuries you would expect to find in a suicide bomber.

In fact the pathologist who first looked at Body 006A would only have been asking one question. That was: "Is this person Australian or not Australian?" because forensic personnel from different countries were looking after the autopsies and identification processes for their own nationals.

Moreover, at a time of mass casualty, body parts "go to the end of the queue". Intact bodies are examined first, to speed the process up and reduce the anguish of relatives.

Now, with the benefit of a "suicide bomber" hypothesis to work with, Body 006A began to look very interesting. Royds assisted Dr Clive Cooke, a Western Australian government forensic pathologist, with the re-examination. Cooke has subsequently written a scientific paper on the identification of suicide bombers during autopsies and become an authority in the field.

"It was likely that these two feet and head belonged to each other and there had been a catastrophic failure in the middle," Royds says. "Cooke had also noted small skin flaps and a kind of black 'tattooing' on top of the feet, on the back of the calves, and under the chin. This 'tattooing' was caused by tiny particles of carbonaceous material actually penetrating the skin. All these characteristics were strong indicators of close contact with explosives at the time of detonation.

"There were signs that the bomb had damaged both the front and back of his body. And he had blast injuries into which some fragments of tartan fabric were recovered. So this had to be the suicide bomber.

"There were also bits of PVC embedded in his body parts – which we suspect were remnants of TNT-filled tubes that had lined his vest."

The DNA of Body 006A was also a match to the DNA profile taken from the bloodstains on the ceiling of Paddy's Bar. But who was its owner?

This is the kind of question that might have been easier to answer if Indonesia had had a forensic DNA database of the kind that the UK has had since 1995 and that different Australian states began compiling from 1997. These databases record the DNA of anyone convicted of an indictable criminal offence. Would any young man get involved in a deadly bomb plot like this one without having a few criminal offences under his belt first?

But Indonesia had no national DNA database.

Nevertheless, Imam Samudra's information appeared to solve the investigators' problem. He had given them the bomber's name. So they now knew the identity of the bomber. Or did they?

It goes without saying that neither the Indonesian nor the Australian investigators were going to merely accept Samudra's word that the bomber was a man called Arnasan. They knew that Body 006A had been the suicide bomber in the tartan vest. And they had Body 006A's DNA. But they needed to be sure that Body 006A's DNA was a match for Arnasan's DNA.

The final proof of identity

Indonesian and Australian police officers were immediately dispatched to the small village of Malingping, in West Java, where Arnasan (whose real name was Acong) had lived, to take samples of his parents' DNA.

His parents, Haji Sastra and Arti binti Saridan, were shocked by the arrival of police. They had last seen their son more than a month earlier when he told them he was heading for Jakarta to look for work. They later told a journalist that their son had been born in 1980 (they weren't sure of the month) and had only been educated to primary level because they could not afford fees for secondary schooling. But he was "a good boy", they said.

"He was quite devoted, prayed five times a day and always

observed Ramadan, but never expressed any extreme views," his mother said.

Illiterate as well as grindingly poor, she was unable to read his letter of apology for his "martyr's death". Written to her, reportedly by Arnasan, the letter was found in the house of one of his friends. "I want to say sorry to you, but all I want to do is commit myself to jihad," it said.

When the DNA results came back, police were stunned: the combination of Haji Sastra and Arti binti Saridan's DNA profiles could not have produced the profile that was supposed to belong to their son.

This may have sounded like a blow to the investigation. But it wasn't. The other information that Samudra had given police had been correct. Why would he implicate Arnasan, and his family, if Arnasan had had nothing to do with the bombing?

Arnasan was certainly nowhere to be found. But the investigators had another way to establish if he had died elsewhere at the blast scene.

The forensic scientists who had been working to identify all the victims had compiled a database that contained DNA from all the bodies and body parts found at the blast scenes.

If Arnasan had been a suicide bomber, then some of his body parts would have been found, and DNA profiled.

A check on the database revealed that the DNA found in two body parts found at the scene – body part number 30080 and body part number 30133 – was a match for the profile that would be expected from the union of Arnasan's parents.

Part number 30080, a section of a jawbone, had been found by AFP agent Kate Clifton on October 24, 2002, in an area 200 m south of the Sari Club. The other, part number 30133, had been found near the back wall of a surf shop near the club. This same DNA profile was later found at one of the houses in Denpasar used by the team of bombers. AFP forensic scientist Linzi Wilson-Wilde took swabs from three plastic drinking cups and a green comb found at 8 Kepanon St in the Balinese capital city of Denpasar. They all matched Arnasan's profile.

So Samudra had been telling part of the truth. He was right in saying that Arnasan had been a suicide bomber. But, as would later be revealed, there were two suicide bombers in action in Kuta on the night of October 12. Arnasan had driven the van carrying the Sari Club bomb, and had died while detonating it.

The Paddy's Bar bomber was someone else: a young man called Feri. Little was ever discovered about him, beyond his name and the fact that he was also known as Isa. To confuse matters even more, his co-conspirators also called him "Iqbal 2".

These details about Feri would finally come out in January 2003, when Amrozi's younger brother, Ali Imron was arrested. This arrest was just one more in the continuing chain reaction of arrests set off by the discovery of the registration number on the Mitsubishi van that was used in the Bali bombing and the consequent identification of Amrozi as the buyer of the van and the bomb ingredients.

Ali Imron and his other brother Mukhlas had been named by Amrozi as his co-conspirators. Mukhlas, allegedly the operations chief of the terrorist network Jemaah Islamiyah, had been arrested in early December in central Java, amid reports that he was also wanted in Malaysia, Singapore and Thailand in connection with several planned terrorist attacks, one being a plan to blow up water pipes in Singapore.

But Ali Imron had been harder to catch than either of his siblings.

The last key arrest: Ali Imron

Police had been tracking Ali Imron for months before finally running him to ground on January 14, 2003, on remote Berukang Island off Samarinda in East Kalimantan, Borneo.

When he was arrested, he admitted to training the two suicide bombers as well as helping build the giant Sari Club bomb. He told police that there had been a plan for a third suicide bomber: a man who was to have ridden a bomb-laden motorcycle into the Sari Club. But the stratagem was supposedly abandoned because the man chosen could not ride well enough.

Ali Imron confirmed that he had driven the Mitsubishi van with its deadly 1.1 tonne load to a point 400 m from the Sari Club. The two suicide bombers had then taken over. Arnasan had parked outside the Sari Club at around 11 pm, and waited until his colleague, who was wearing a tartan vest lined with 5 kg of TNT packed into six tubes, blew himself up inside Paddy's Bar. Arnasan had then detonated the vast load of explosives that had been packed into a series of filing cabinets in the back of his truck.

Within two days of his arrest Ali Imron had also led police to the Denpasar house where the bomb had been built. The house, at 18 Menjangan St, had been empty since the departure of the bombers, which meant there was a good chance of finding trace evidence that could be linked to the bomb.

Royds was back in Canberra when Imron pinpointed the house. But he flew back to process the scene. After having done exhaustive but fruitless testing of 23 other houses through Bali and Indonesia in an attempt to find trace evidence of the bombs, he wasn't going to miss this.

CSI Moment (3)

The bomb factory was in a suburban area, with the van kept in a garage behind a roller door.

"They had had one accidental explosion there," Royds says. "The potassium chlorate, sulphur and aluminium powder mixture is incredibly sensitive. You are supposed to mix it with a feather. Ali Imron had been immersing his whole arm in it."

The explosion scared the group and Umar Patek was brought in to show them how to mix the chemicals. Patek was finally arrested in January 2011 in Abbotabad, Pakistan (where Osama bin Laden lived until his death in May of that year).

To the naked eye, Royds recalls, the tiled floors of the house looked disappointingly clean. But using a special hand-held forensic vacuum cleaner, the scientists extracted dust caught in the cracks between the tiles.

"We came across the actual explosive mixture of potassium chlorate, sulphur and aluminium powder – unexploded," he says. "The particles were 0.2 mm in size. They were tiny but this was real trace evidence and it tied in beautifully." The scientists also found a drawing, done on a page of the *Bali Post* newspaper, showing the filing cabinet boxes (which would hold the 1150 kg of explosive mixture) and how they were to be loaded into the van. There was aluminium dust on the drawing.

"And in that aluminium dust, there was a footprint," says Royds. It was a good physical match to Amrozi's right foot.

Fingerprints matching those of Amrozi's fellow bombmaker Abdul Ghani were found on the back door of the house, while prints belonging to another bomb team member Sawad were found on the garage door frame and the back window of the living room. Ali Imron's right thumbprint was found on a set of scales, while tyre tracks matching those of a Mitsubishi L300 van were taken in the garage.

All these forensic results formed a crucial part of the briefs of evidence collected by Indonesian prosecutors in the bombers' trials. Within a year, 26 people had been convicted of involvement in the bombings.

By the middle of 2005, all the bombers had been identified, most had been arrested and the first trials had begun.

Aftermath

The trials of Amrozi, Mukhlas and Imam Samudra were held in 2003 in Denpasar. All three were sentenced to death that year and executed in November 2008.

Ali Imron, brother of Mukhlas and Amrozi, gave evidence against Amrozi, Mukhlas and Samudra at their trials and showed remorse for his actions. In September 2003 he received a life sentence for helping build the bombs. Mubarok, who channelled funds for the bombing and helped in the transport of the bomb materials to Bali, was arrested in January 2003 and sentenced to life imprisonment in October of that year.

Idris, logistics officer for the plot, was arrested in June 2003. He faced trial but avoided conviction on the legal technicality that the general terrorism laws under which he was charged had not yet been passed at the time of the Kuta bombing. He was later convicted for the 2003 bombing of the Jakarta Marriott and jailed for ten years but released after five.

The Muslim cleric, Abu Bakar Bashir, spiritual leader of Jemaah Islamiyah, met with Amrozi and Mubarok before the bombing. He was arrested and tried for terrorism offences in 2003, but acquitted. In March 2005 he was sentenced to 30 months' jail for his role in instigating the bombings.

Dr Azahari bin Husin, believed to be the technical expert behind the Bali bombing, was also involved in bombing attacks on the Jakarta Marriott Hotel in 2003 and the Australian consulate in Jakarta in 2004. He was shot and killed by police in the East Java village of Batu in 2005.

Dulmatin, an explosives engineer and planner of the 2002 bombs, was killed by Indonesian anti-terrorism police during a raid in Jakarta on March 9, 2010.

Umar Patek, who helped make the bomb, was arrested in 2011 in Pakistan and was extradited to Indonesia, where he received a 20-year jail sentence.

Afterword

So many of the forensic highlights of this story read as if they could have been written for television: a fact that award-winning Australian film and TV director Michael Jenkins recognised and acted upon. The filming of his TV drama based on the Bali bombing investigation began in late September 2005, with Australian star Richard Roxburgh playing chief AFP forensic scientist David Royds.

Being observed by the actor who was going to play him was an unnerving experience, Royds recalls. "I had a disconcerting feeling that he was studying me and my mannerisms," the scientist says.

But Royds never got to see himself portrayed on screen.

On October 1, the cast and crew were staying at Kuta Beach's Kartika Plaza Hotel, where Royds and his colleagues had been based in 2002, when terrorist bombs exploded at Jimbaran Beach Resort and at Kuta, within earshot of the production team. The Australians' permission to film was withdrawn and the project was never revived.

"I felt sorry for Michael Jenkins as he had invested a great deal in what could have been a really great production," says Royds.

"The actors, the street scenes, everything, had that real touch of authenticity.

"My understanding is that Made Pastika, former head of the Balinese police and later, Governor of Bali, recognised the potential damage to their tourism industry and put a stop to the whole show. He ordered cameras and equipment to be impounded. It was a tragedy from our perspective, but I can also see that he was protecting the livelihoods and lives of many of his people."

Case Fifteen
"UNKNOWN MALE ONE"

Five days after Noritta Samsudin was murdered in her shared KL apartment, police arrested her married boyfriend Hanif Basree Abdul Rahman. But had he killed her? At Hanif's trial, the prosecution argued that he had strangled his lover in a fit of jealousy over her involvement with another man. The defence, on the other hand, said that Noritta's killer was someone else altogether. In the end, the answer to the mystery lay in the forensic evidence.

Hanif Basree Abdul Rahman, a tall handsome city council engineer, met beautiful marketing executive Noritta Samsudin at the Crystal Club karaoke lounge in Kuala Lumpur in July 2003.

The attraction between them was mutual and immediate. Within three weeks they were lovers, meeting once a week and calling each other almost daily, just to chat and keep in touch.

By October Hanif's work schedule had become less hectic and the pair began seeing each other twice a week, a pattern that continued over the next two months.

The couple would spend their evenings together at a nightclub, staying out until after midnight. They would then return to Noritta's flat in the Puncak Prima Galleria, a condominium complex in the upper middle class residential area of KL's Desa Sri Hartamas. Noritta shared a three-room seventh floor apartment there with two friends: Nor Azora Hamid, a guest relations officer at the Crystal

Club, and Azora's boyfriend Kenneth Michael Yap, a DJ at the popular Nouvo Club.

Usually, on arriving at the flat, Hanif and Noritta would retire to Noritta's room and make love for an hour or two. Then Hanif would head home, passing the building's security guards on his way out.

But this is not the beginning of a conventional middle-class love story. Thirty-six-year-old Hanif was married and a father of three. Noritta, fourteen years his junior, had other boyfriends. Their relationship would last only five months. And it would end with her murder.

The night of the murder

The evening of December 3, 2003, was no different from any of the thirty-odd nights that the couple had spent together over the previous five months.

Later, however, Hanif would have cause to reflect on those few hours.

Looking back, it would seem that he had spent that evening in another universe: a simple, carefree place where he was free and blissfully anonymous. And where he could never have imagined the possibility that he would soon be seeing graphic details of his own sex life splashed across every single Malaysian newspaper.

Hanif arrived at his girlfriend's apartment at about 10.15 pm, with a few friends in tow. The group then headed to KL's Hard Rock Café, staying at the loud and busy club until 1.30 am when the lovers returned to Noritta's apartment at the Desa Sri Hartamas condominium. Hanif left the building at about 3.30 the following morning, Thursday December 4, and drove home.

He missed a call from Noritta at his office later that morning. But she had left a message and he called her back shortly before 1 pm. As usual, they just chatted. It was understood that they would see each other later in the week. There was no need to make a specific plan in advance.

Unsurprisingly, Hanif was feeling shattered after his late night. Leaving work at 4.30 pm, he drove home to his family's condominium in the satellite city of Shah Alam, 18 km from central KL. He went straight to the master bedroom and took a nap.

After a two-hour snooze he woke up ready to resume his life as a family man. First he drove one of his daughters to her tutor's office in the Shah Alam mall. Then he dropped his wife off at the nearby KTM Shah Alam commuter station. At around 8.30 pm, he collected his daughter from her lesson.

He returned home to find that relatives had arrived to visit. His brother-in-law and his fiancée were there, along with a friend. His brother's sister-in-law then joined the party and the group sat around chatting until 10.30 pm. After they left, he headed for bed, watching some television before falling asleep.

The phone call that came in at 10 am on Friday would change his life forever. It was his friend Jacky. "Mummy Celine" who worked with Noritta's flatmate Nor Azora Hamid at the Crystal Club had just called to pass on some terrible news. Noritta was dead.

The details were almost too unbearable to contemplate. Noritta's flatmates had returned home to find their friend in her bed, naked and tied up. Pieces of cloth were stuffed in her mouth.

Kenneth and Azora had arrived home at about 4.30 on Thursday morning after a big night out at the Eastin Hotel's dance club, Viva. It was the three flatmates' custom to leave the dining room light on for one another. But as the couple opened the front door they were surprised to find that light off. Fortunately the street lights outside cast a dim glow into the flat – enough for them to find their way in without turning on any inside lights.

A silhouette in the dark and a noxious smell

A dense cloud of repulsive body odour hung in the entrance area. Recoiling, they covered their noses and exchanged horrified glances. What could it be? Kenneth quickly checked the shoe rack area to see if a visitor's shoes were responsible. They weren't. Yet the noxious smell was human. Azora immediately assumed that Noritta had a visitor. It had to be someone who had never been to the apartment before. She certainly would have remembered that stink.

As they walked through the dim apartment, with Kenneth leading the way, the silhouette of a man appeared. He was only in Azora's peripheral vision. But he was there, somewhere to her right. And he was moving.

Although Azora had been drinking that night, the figure she saw was real. She had consumed two glasses of stout and some of Kenneth's beer but she still had her wits about her. She immediately asked Kenneth if he'd seen the man, but he shrugged the question off. Azora was just imagining things, he thought.

He ended the conversation by unlocking their bedroom door. Yet Azora still felt uneasy. Walking back out of the bedroom, she did a quick scan of the hall and the kitchen. Just to check. Like any nervous householder she also re-checked the front door although she had seen Kenneth lock it as they came in.

It was unlatched.

Both of them then began calling out Noritta's name but the apartment was quiet. Her stomach knotted with anxiety, Azora asked Kenneth to go to the guardhouse and ask if there had been any visitors earlier.

It was at that point that Azora noticed that Noritta's door was slightly ajar. Peeping into the room and flicking on the light, she thought the room was empty. Then she noticed items of clothing strewn across the floor – not a usual look for Noritta's room. Once again she called her flatmate's name, and pulled back the bed's duvet.

Her scream froze in her throat. Noritta was lying naked, face down on her mattress. Her head was covered with a pillow case and both her hands and legs were tied.

Rushing out of the room, and back into her bedroom, Azora leaned out the open window and shouted down to Kenneth, who was, by then, down at the guardhouse. She then ran to the neighbours' apartment but couldn't raise anyone. Leaning out her bedroom window again, she scanned the area in vain, unable to see Kenneth.

Instead she spotted a male figure moving in the darkness. He was walking towards the guardhouse, pulling on his shirt as he went. Was he the man she had seen earlier? She thought so.

"Bastard! Stop! I think you are a killer," she shrieked down at him.

The man kept walking. Seconds later, he had melted away into the darkness. Grabbing her mobile, Azora called her friend, Mikko. She had been drinking with him earlier and was sure he would be awake. She also shouted down to the guards at the guardhouse, asking them to stop the man she'd seen. There was no response.

Desperate to raise the alarm, Azora rushed to the lifts, meeting Kenneth who was just coming up with one of the security guards. Kenneth then walked into Noritta's room, and began calling her name.

"Ita!" he kept shouting. "Ita!" It was the name Noritta's close friends called her. But there was silence. Untying the pillow case covering his flatmate's head, Kenneth found a bolster case tied around her face. It covered her mouth and was knotted at the back of her head. As he undid that knot, a balled up piece of face towel fell out of her mouth.

Refusing to believe the young woman was dead, Kenneth's first reaction was to try and revive her, rather than call the police.

Rushing to the kitchen, he grabbed a knife so he could cut the cord tying her hands.

Then Azora's friend Mikko arrived. Pointing out that Noritta's lips were blue, the Finnish businessman suggested they try CPR. Kenneth didn't know how to do it and both men turned to the security guard, who had been watching impassively as Kenneth continued to call Noritta's name.

"Perhaps the guard knows?" Mikko suggested. The guard shook his head. Whether he knew CPR or not, he didn't want to get involved. Mikko then turned Noritta's body over and the two men tried to recall what they'd seen of CPR on television and apply it. They were undoubtedly too late and they failed to revive her. Kenneth then called the police.

Police dog hunts the fleeing man

By 5 am there were 10 police officers on the scene. Soon afterwards Noritta's body was taken away by ambulance officers, first to the Universiti Hospital (now the University of Malaya Medical Centre) and later to the mortuary at the Kuala Lumpur Hospital. There the Director of the Insititut Perubatan Forensik Negara, forensic pathologist Dr Abdul Halim bin Mansar, would carry out an autopsy examination.

Those first police officers made immediate efforts to track down the man whom Azora had seen fleeing the apartment. They called in the K-9 dog unit, based nearby at the Pulapol Police Training Centre. One of its handlers was at the scene by 5.25 am. After a briefing on the suspect's appearance (dark-skinned, 170 cm tall, in his 30s) he took his German Shepherd dog to the front of Noritta's apartment, for it to sniff around.

Finding a scent, the animal headed for the emergency exit. It then made its way down the staircase to the ground floor, snuffling along the drains beside some plants before reaching a fence. There it circled a spot several times before indicating that it had lost the trail and could go no further. A main road ran along the other side of the fence.

Had the dog actually detected the smell of the man with the foul body odour? The dog squad officer couldn't say.

By 6 am Assistant Superintendent of Police (ASP) Shahrul Lalli bin Masduki, who would be the chief investigating officer on the case, was on the scene along with two police forensic officers. Their focus was the gathering of evidence for later analysis. The officers took Noritta's bedding and cut out semen-stained sections of the mattress, bagging them for later testing. They also collected eleven pieces of tissue paper they found in the waste basket in the bedroom, along with the bra and electric cord used to tie Noritta up.

Meanwhile the police photographer accompanying them dusted Noritta's bedroom surfaces and door surfaces for fingerprints. But he found none of them distinct enough to be helpful.

The autopsy and collection of forensic evidence

By 12.30 that afternoon the autopsy was underway. Noritta's body lay on a stainless-steel dissection table in the Kuala Lumpur Hospital mortuary, as Dr Abdul Halim bin Mansar catalogued every mark and injury.

The forensic pathologist also collected blood samples, nail clippings, and anal and vaginal swabs from the dead woman. These would all be sent to Lim Kong Boon, the head of the Crime DNA Unit at the Government Chemistry Department in Petaling Jaya.

Lim held a masters degree in forensic science from the University of Strathclyde in Glasgow, UK, then the top university for forensics in the UK. He would extract the DNA from the biological samples, profile it and compare the results obtained to Noritta's DNA profile and the profile of any other suspects. In the case of Noritta's nail clippings, for example, it would be expected that the DNA obtained would be a mixture of her own DNA profile and the profile of any man with whom she had recently had close contact.

Over the next few days, police forensic officers delivered scores of samples to Lim. They sent him strands of hair found in Noritta's bedding, as well as samples from that bedding. From these, he extracted microscopic samples of human cells for testing. The officers also sent him the face towels that had been stuffed into Noritta's mouth; some electrical cord, cut from an iron, with which her hands had been tied; and several of her bras, including a black one. This garment had been used, along with a second piece of electrical cord, to tie her legs together at the ankles.

All in all, Lim Kong Boon received 116 samples, of which he found 112 suitable for DNA testing. The majority arrived in the first few days after the murder. A trickle of new samples followed in subsequent weeks, as police worked their way through a series of potential suspects, taking blood samples for DNA profiling.

Hanif's waking nightmare

Hanif Basree Abdul Rahman was living a waking nightmare. The engineer had seen enough crime dramas to know that the detectives always start with a murder victim's partner or romantic entanglements.

His relationship with Noritta had been no secret. She kept a photo of him in her mobile phone and her two flatmates both knew him. While he wasn't the only man to have been seen out and about with Noritta, his name would have been the first to come up when police questioned Kenneth and Azora.

Hanif had heard about Noritta's death on the morning of Friday December 5, only a matter of hours after it happened. The next day, he had opened the newspapers with trepidation, but there was nothing new about the investigation to read.

On Sunday December 7, however, when he picked up the paper, his name jumped out at him from an article about the crime. His cheeks burned and his heart thudded in his chest. Of course the police would want to discuss his movements on the night of the murder and his family would be dragged in to confirm them. At any moment his wife could be opening the door to a police officer with questions about her husband's girlfriend: a part of her spouse's secret life.

After work the next day, he drove to the Brickfields police station and presented himself for questioning. He received no reward or special treatment for being co-operative. Instead, he was arrested.

But he wasn't alone behind bars.

The police had obviously been very taken by the fact that there had been no signs of a forced entry to Noritta's apartment. They didn't seem to be exploring the possibility that a key to its front door might have fallen into the wrong hands, or had remained in the possession of a previous tenant.

Instead, they appeared to have decided that the young woman's killer would be found amongst her friendship group. So they arrested all her friends.

Friends all arrested

The first people to be taken into custody had been Noritta's two flatmates: Nor Azora Hamid and her boyfriend, Kenneth Michael Yap.

Then, along with Hanif, police arrested businessman Lim Sin Kean Childs and broker Shahfrul Azrin Azman, who would later sue several newspapers for defamation, on the grounds that they had portrayed him as the prime suspect. All three men had been seen out socially with Noritta.

On December 12 three more men were taken into custody. Two of them, Suhaimi Sanusi and Khairul Anuar, were also said to be boyfriends of the dead woman. The third was Mikko Kouko Johannes Jarva, a KL-based Finnish marketing manager. He was the friend of Azora's who had come over to the apartment when she phoned him after finding the body. If he had been a regular CSI viewer, he would have known that his CPR attempts would have left traces of his DNA on Noritta. He would also later sue several newspapers for defamation, on the grounds that they had implied that he was a suspect.

All the men detained had their blood samples taken, so their DNA could be compared to the profiles found at the crime scene.

But the police were paying Hanif special attention: the kind a key suspect receives. Shortly after his arrest he was examined by a forensic doctor. Kuala Lumpur Hospital's Dr Mohd Shah bin Mahmood scrutinised every square centimetre of his body. The expert was only able to find a scratch mark about 1.5 cm long behind Hanif's right shoulder. As he would later testify, the mark was about two to three days old.

Hanif knew that his DNA would be found on Noritta's body. After all, they had made love 24 hours before her murder. Twice. It was to be expected that traces of his semen would remain.

The police had accused him of tying Noritta up, raping her and killing her. He hadn't, as he kept telling them. But some other man had. That man's DNA should also be found on Noritta's body – unless the man had used a condom. If he did, then Hanif's semen would be the only human genetic material present, and things might start looking bad for him.

Could scientists tell the age of a DNA sample?

Could scientists, he wondered, tell the "age" of a DNA sample that they found? If it could be established that his DNA had been left on Noritta more than 24 hours before her death, then he would be in the clear.

While the doctor had been examining him and taking a sample of his blood, Hanif had asked whether DNA tests on semen could also indicate the time that had elapsed since ejaculation. The doctor had given him the impression that it wasn't possible.

It was a reasonable and practical question from an engineer who didn't know anything about the science of DNA. Later on, however, when he was on trial for Noritta's murder, it would be interpreted by the prosecution as an indicator of guilt. So would the fact that he had cleaned his nails and clipped his pubic hair before surrendering to police, although such hygiene measures are routinely observed by Muslim men. In fact they are regularly discussed in "Muslim men only" chat groups where it is explained that such grooming is part of *fitrah* – a Muslim's obligation to cleanliness.

The gossip begins

Within days of the murder, the death had become fodder for gossip in the coffee shops of KL. It was served up with accompanying salacious stories about Noritta's many male friends and unconventional lifestyle.

The known details were widely repeated, such as the absence of any signs of a break-in. Did that mean that Noritta's killer had been known to her? And what about the rumour that she had been tied up? Had there been some kind of sex game going on? Wouldn't that mean the death might not have been murder, but an accident? Her mobile phone was also supposed to be missing. Had her killer taken it because his number was in it?

Echoing the gossip, newspapers were also reporting the theory that the death might have been "misadventure". Angry police spoke out to slam this explicit newspaper coverage for focusing only on the "character" of the victim rather than her murder. Yet the officers who made these public comments did not attempt to defend the dead woman or correct any of the media assumptions.

They were certainly in the position, early on, to clarify that this was a murder case, not an accidental death caused by a "game" of erotic asphyxiation – the deliberate induction or enhancement of orgasm by self-hypoxia. But they did nothing to stem the tide of rumours.

Forensic pathologist Dr Abdul Halim bin Mansar certainly believed that Noritta Samsudin had been murdered, and the investigators would have known the content of his report immediately.

It was Dr Abdul Halim's opinion that Noritta Samsudin had died of asphyxia or suffocation. He also ruled out death by sexual asphyxia or any other kind of accidental death. In his view, her death had been caused by the forcing into her mouth of a face towel – one of the two that fell out of her mouth when Kenneth untied the bolster case around her head.

The doctor had noted congestion in the young woman's thyroid gland, bruises on her tongue and a haematoma (a solid swelling of clotted blood) at the left side of the epiglottis, the tissue at the base of the tongue. These injuries were caused, he believed, by something being pushed into her mouth. This had made her tongue roll back and collapse, causing her to choke and then suffocate.

None of this information made it into the newspapers in the first weeks after the murder. And in the absence of any real information, reporters focused on the few details available to them: the names of all the people who were being arrested and held for questioning.

Multiple arrests and DNA tests

One newspaper report of these arrests explained that all the people involved were being DNA tested. It put the most salacious slant possible on the exercise, stating that samples had been obtained from the eight "as this would enable them to ascertain who, among them, had engaged in sexual activity with Noritta prior to her death".

Certainly the testing of samples taken from Noritta's body cavities was a crucial aspect of the DNA comparison exercise. But DNA testing isn't only about sex. The narrative of a crime can be read in the DNA evidence collected at the scene. DNA profiles tell investigators about the people present: who and where they were, and what they touched. Good investigators do not want to find themselves stuck with the DNA profile of an unidentified person on a crucial piece of evidence. Noritta had been found with face towels stuffed in her mouth. If her killer had taken them from the apartment's only bathroom, then there would be others' DNA on them. In fact, depending on the flatmates' laundry and personal habits, the DNA of any of the flat's occupants or their visitors might be expected to be found on any towel in that bathroom.

By Wednesday December 17, twelve days after the murder, the only three suspects still in custody were the three who had been seen out and about with Noritta: Hanif, businessman Lim Sin Kean Childs and broker Shahfrul Azrin Azman. Hanif, of course, had admitted to having had sex with Noritta. The other two men maintained, later swearing to it on oath, that their relationships with Noritta had been platonic. All three denied having killed her.

Two guards arrested and released before Hanif is charged

That night two more men were arrested, both of them security guards from the Puncak Prima Galleria. The investigators on the case had spoken to these two men before. But, as would become clear later, police had not yet obtained from them the information they wanted.

By the end of Saturday night, December 20, those two guards had been released. On Monday, December 22, the "remand" orders on Hanif, on Lim Sin Kean Childs, and on Shahfrul Azrin Azman, were due to expire.

Something changed over the weekend, however. Lim Sin Kean Childs and Shahfrul Azrin Azman were released and only Hanif Basree Abdul Rahman remained in custody. On the morning of December 22, he was taken to the Magistrates' Court and charged with the murder of Noritta Samsudin. Four days later he appeared in the High Court, where he formally entered his plea of not guilty.

By then he had been in custody for two and a half weeks. A large media contingent was present at the High Court hearing, during which his hands were cuffed in front of him. The reporters noted that he was wearing the same clothes that he'd worn to the Magistrates' Court on Monday and that his wife and his parents were there to support him.

The journalists recorded the fact that he had to ask a policeman for permission to call his father over while they were waiting for the hearing to start. They described the tears he shed as his mother hugged and kissed him, and the tears his wife Noraidah Mohamed wiped away as she walked back to her seat after exchanging a few words with him.

Devastated by the police allegations, Hanif's family had hired eminent criminal lawyer Dato' V Sithambaram to defend him.

"To them it was surreal that Hanif was undergoing this ordeal," the advocate recalls. "The family was even more shocked when the charge read to Hanif in court showed that he was accused of the murder on a day that (they knew) he had spent at home with his family."

His trial was scheduled for the following May. But had Hanif actually killed Noritta Samsudin? The officer in charge of the case, ASP Shahrul Lalli bin Masduki was certain he had.

But, as far as Hanif's lawyer was concerned, the police case against his client didn't comprise much more than Shahrul's certainty.

An overzealous officer

Reflecting on the case recently, Dato' Sithambaram describes Shahrul as "an overzealous officer trying to secure a conviction".

"I was convinced of Hanif's innocence as he was at home on the night of Noritta's murder. Hanif had four credible witnesses from whom the police had taken statements even before they had recorded Hanif's own statement."

Certainly, at that point, Shahrul did not yet have the results of the DNA investigation, in which samples taken from Noritta's body were compared to the DNA of any man she had been linked with.

The Assistant Superintendent of Police charged Hanif without them. In fact Lim Kong Boon's report would not be ready until April 5. It appeared that the police officer wasn't expecting that report to tell him anything he didn't know already.

After all, Hanif's DNA was certain to be found in Noritta's body. The police had his testimony on that point. In a statement he had made after his arrest, he had said that Noritta was his girlfriend, with whom he had last had sex early on the morning of December 4, 2003.

And it seemed that Hanif's DNA was the only sample that the ASP cared about.

After reporting Hanif's "not guilty" plea, the newspapers left the case alone. In late December the police had successfully applied for a "gag" order on the reporting of any details of the case.

The trial opens

The trial of Hanif Basree Abdul Rahman for the murder of Noritta Samsudin opened on May 7, lasted 28 days and heard from 34 of the 80 witnesses who had made statements. Noritta's father and younger sister were among them. As was his wife, who would testify that he had been at home on the night of the murder.

Throughout, Dato' Sithambaram remained convinced of his client's innocence. When the trial opened, he had no inkling of any of the evidence that the prosecution might have against his client. Although he knew that the DNA report was now back, the prosecution had refused to give it to him.

"There was deliberate suppression of the DNA report, which only became available in the course of the trial," he recalls.

The lawyer knew that the lynchpin of the prosecution's case would have to be a claim that Hanif had been the last person to have been seen with the victim before her death. Of course, he also expected that the DNA report would record the presence of his client's DNA in the victim's body. They were lovers. The man's DNA would have to be there.

But, like the general public, he had to wait until the trial began to find out what other evidence, if any, the prosecution had against his client.

It was only when the trial began and Deputy Public Prosecutor Stanley Augustin began outlining the case against Hanif, that it finally became clear why ASP Shahrul Lalli bin Masduki had charged Hanif before he had the DNA results back.

Two star witnesses are unveiled

The chief investigating officer believed he had something better than mere DNA. He had two "star" eye-witnesses: two men who were both prepared to testify that they had seen Hanif at the Puncak

Prima Galleria on the night of the murder.

These witnesses were the two security guards, Suzaki Supok and Thanabalan Kobal. They had both been in the guardhouse of the condominium over the night of December 4 and into the wee hours of December 5 and had, in theory, been in a position to see everyone visiting the premises. Both had been questioned repeatedly in the days afterwards about what – and whom – they had seen on that night. During interviews in the first days after the murder, when neither was under arrest, both had told police that they had not seen any man entering or leaving the premises with the dead woman on the night she was killed.

Both had shared their clear recollection of having seen Hanif with Noritta late on December 3 and in the early hours of December 4, the night the duo spent at the Hard Rock Café, just over 24 hours before Noritta's death. The guards both knew Hanif by sight as he was a regular visitor, and told police that they had often seen him arrive home with Noritta at about 2 am.

All that changed when they were arrested. The three nights spent in custody dramatically "improved" their memories of what they had seen a fortnight earlier. Apparently they had been feeling "confusion" earlier. That feeling had evaporated and both had been able to summon up a new and very detailed memory of seeing Hanif and Noritta together at around 1 am on December 5.

These new unconfused memories were recorded in statements that the guards made to police when they were in custody. They then repeated this evidence at Hanif's trial.

Guards "saw Hanif on the night of the murder"

Only four hours before Noritta's body was found, as Suzaki Supok told the court, he had seen the pair together in the street, outside the guardhouse. At the time, the lovers were chatting to two Malay couples who had arrived in a white Kancil car. Then, after ten or fifteen minutes' conversation, Noritta and Hanif had headed back up to Noritta's apartment. The guard never saw Hanif leave. But police were able to come up with an explanation for that. Hanif was six feet, three inches tall: tall enough to climb over the fence and into the car park, and escape without passing through the gate.

Suzaki's colleague, Thanabalan Kobal, told the court the same story.

This evidence was, initially at least, devastating to the defence. Hanif had been seen with Noritta less than hour before she was murdered.

Hanif was visibly aghast when he heard it. It was bad enough that the guard had told the court that he had seen Hanif visiting Noritta five or six times a week. That was untrue but harmless.

But this was devastating. "How could he say that?" he asked his lawyer, distraught, so loudly that the newspaper reporters heard him and included this detail in their stories.

Hanif had not been at the Puncak Prima Galleria condominium that night. He knew it, and his wife and family could testify to it.

Fortunately, his defence lawyer was soon on his feet to cross-examine both Suzaki and Thanabalan. Within a short time their credibility was in tatters as the lawyer drew attention to the timeline of their changing statements. When first questioned by police, neither man had said anything about seeing Noritta with Hanif on the night of her death. Then, after being arrested and kept in custody, their stories had changed.

DPP Stanley Augustin appeared unworried by the fact that the lawyer had destroyed his two star witnesses' testimonies. But a few days later the newspapers published a plea by police, asking "the four people who met murder accused – Hanif Basree Abdul Rahman – and Noritta Samsudin at 1 am on December 5 outside the Puncak Prima Galleria" to come forward. It is hard to interpret this as anything else than a face-saving exercise. Perhaps those four people were there that night. But they could not have seen Hanif.

A motive: jealousy

Meanwhile DPP Augustin pressed on with impressive confidence. Although proof of motive is not required in order to prove a murder charge, Augustin told the court he could also present a motive that would explain why Hanif Basree Abdul Rahman had killed his lover.

That motive was jealousy. Hanif had killed Noritta Samsudin because he couldn't bear the fact that she was seeing someone else on the side. That other man, the prosecutor said, was businessman Lim Sin Kean Childs.

Lim told the court that he had met Noritta in July 2003 at the Crystal Club, the karaoke lounge where Azora worked – and where Noritta had also met Hanif for the first time. They had exchanged phone numbers and started seeing each other about two or three times a week.

Called as a witness for the prosecution, Lim gave evidence that certainly confirmed that he and the deceased had been close friends.

The businessman had even met Noritta's family, driving her to Perlis to see her grandmother. The previous November he had gone to Singapore with Noritta, her sister and mother, and stayed there for two nights.

He consistently denied having had a sexual relationship with Noritta. But, given that sexual jealousy tends to be the least "evidence-based" of the human emotions, his denials did not mean that Hanif might not have viewed him as a rival. They certainly didn't stop the prosecutor from stating, in his summing up, that Noritta had had "two boyfriends": Hanif and Lim.

Evidence "a series of threads that make a strong knot"

The evidence against Hanif, DPP Augustin told the court, was like a series of threads.

"When tied together, it can be a knot strong enough to hang the accused," he said.

There were many of these threads, he continued. They included the following: the fact that there was no break-in at the scene of the crime, meaning that the killer was known to Noritta; the fact that the accused had an intimate relationship with her; the fact that the accused had easy access to her rented apartment; and the fact that the time of the murder was consistent with the time that Hanif usually visited Noritta. Another thread was the fact that Hanif, according to the two security guard witnesses, was the last person to be seen with Noritta, having been observed to arrive on December 5, 2003, between about 1 am and 1.30 am. (The prosecutor was ignoring the fact that the defence had destroyed the star witnesses' credibility on this point.)

The court also heard evidence in support of Hanif's insistence that he had been home at the time of the murder. ASP Shahrul had personally interviewed all the people present at Hanif's home that night, taking statements from his wife, their maid, his sister-in-law and his wife's brother. They had all confirmed that he had been at home all evening.

Other information available also appeared to support Hanif's version of events. It was a 30-minute, 31-km drive from his place in Shah Alam to Noritta's apartment. Checks on Hanif's Touch n' Go card (a pre-paid electronic cash card which Malaysians use to pay tolls on highways and expressways) and on his SmartTAG tollway cards showed that Hanif had not driven his car again after arriving home on the evening of December 4.

This important information had not been shared with the defence, who only received it during the trial. It surfaced when DPP Rosianayati Ahmad, who was sharing the presentation of the prosecution arguments with DPP Stanley Augustin, was questioning ASP Shahrul about how long it would have taken Hanif to get home from the crime scene.

Determined to cast Hanif as a killer, the police had come up with the theory that Hanif had not used his own car on the fateful night. One of the first of the prosecution's witnesses was Hanif's friend Gan Sem Hua, who often lent his two-door Mercedes CLK to the accused. But, try as they might, the prosecution was unable to establish that Hanif had borrowed his friend's car on the night in question.

Hanif's DNA was everywhere, but that meant nothing

This left the prosecution with the scientific evidence against Hanif. DPP Augustin sounded supremely confident when presenting it.

Indeed, when this evidence was presented out of context it could sound damning.

After all, there were so many places where Hanif's DNA had been found. The DNA analysis done on the duvet, bedsheet, and three pieces of cut mattress showed only his DNA profile. Then there was the DNA test done on one of the face towels stuffed into Noritta's mouth. It also contained his DNA. This meant, the prosecutor said, that Hanif had stuffed it in.

It didn't, of course. In fact the DNA on that towel was a mixture of "at least three persons", the scientist had said. Most of the DNA on it was Noritta's own, because it was her towel. And Hanif was a regular visitor to the apartment – and one who had been there the day before the murder. So it could be expected that Hanif's DNA would also be there.

Hanif's DNA was also found in Noritta's vagina. Lots of it. Again, that was no surprise.

But scientist Lim Kong Boon had made another discovery. This result was not listed as one of the "threads" in the prosecution case. Yet it was in the report that the scientist had given to the prosecution.

It came out in court while DPP Augustin was questioning him about the contents of the report.

The DNA of another man found

The fact is that the DNA of Hanif Basree Abdul Rahman was *not* the only male DNA that Lim Kong Boon found on the vaginal swabs taken from Noritta Samsudin.

The scientist had found the DNA of another man in Noritta's body. In fact he had found it all over the crime scene.

It had taken some time for the scientist to clarify all the DNA results. Mixed samples take much longer to profile than a simple blood or buccal sample (a swab of the cells inside the cheek) from one person.

The test results, when complete, were unambiguous. The swabs taken from both the upper and lower vaginal region of the deceased contained a DNA profile that was a mixture of three individuals. Noritta's DNA was there, as it had to be. Hanif's DNA was present, as expected.

But there was also the DNA of a male to whom the police could attach no name and whom the scientist called "Unknown Male One".

If Unknown Male One's DNA had been found only on Noritta's vaginal swabs, the investigators might have been justified in not allowing it to change their interpretation of the crime scene material.

Male DNA may be detected in a woman's vagina for up to seven days after intercourse. On its own, the finding would have been meaningless, because there would have been no indication of *when* Noritta had had sexual contact with Unknown Male One. Or *where*.

Unknown Male One's DNA on the cord that bound Noritta's legs

But Unknown Male One's DNA was in all the crucial places. It was found in clippings from the fingernails of Noritta's left hand (where it was detected alongside Hanif's while her right hand nail clippings only contained Hanif's DNA). It was found in strands of hair collected from Noritta's duvet and bedsheet. It was in a semen stain on the bolster from Noritta's bed; and it was on a black bra that had been used, along with electrical cord, to tie her legs. Significantly, it was found in the victim's anus – a place where Hanif's DNA was not found.

Most crucially, it was identified on the electrical cord that had been used to tie Noritta's legs together.

Unknown Male One, it appeared, had at least touched the cord around her legs. And if he hadn't tied it, who had?

According to an Australian police scientist, the DNA on the cord and bra was the evidence that the investigators should have been focusing all their attention on.

"We know that, with DNA from skin, the person that last touched the item is (usually) the main DNA source detected. Therefore, finding it there should have been a signal to the forensic scientist that Unknown Male One was the last person to touch the cord, and therefore probably the person that tied it around her legs."

The prosecution ignored it.

"They had a biased interpretation of the scientific evidence," recalls Dato' Sithambaram. "They refused to view the evidence objectively; it appeared they wanted to 'solve' the case with the conviction of Hanif. This was a high profile case and 'solving' the case appeared paramount."

The key to the mystery: injuries inflicted after death

There was even more information available in connection with this electrical cord. It came from forensic pathologist Dr Abdul Halim. He was able to provide a crucial piece of information that would unlock the mystery of Noritta's death – although, once again, the police appeared to have chosen to ignore it.

The key was the difference that an expert can ascertain between the look of injuries sustained by a living body and injuries inflicted on a dead body. Blood is still circulating around a living body, meaning that tiny injuries will still cause bleeding or blood spots under the skin. That process does not occur after death.

Examining the injuries on Noritta's body, Dr Abdul Halim had effectively given the police a timeline of Unknown Male One's activities in the moments before and after the murder.

The forensic pathologist had examined the places on Noritta's arms and legs where the knots had been fastened. Knotted ligatures tied around living limbs cause bleeding, bruising or blood spots. There were no such "vital signs" documented on Noritta's arms and legs.

One conclusion could be drawn here: by the time Unknown Male One was tying the electrical cord around Noritta's wrists and ankles, she was already dead.

Dr Abdul Halim had also noted the appearance of some tiny anal tears and fissures, presumably inflicted by Unknown Male One, whose DNA had been detected on a swab of the victim's anus. In his opinion, these tiny injuries had been sustained during sexual intercourse while Noritta was still alive.

The forensic information gained by the combination of the DNA results and the forensic pathologist's report pointed both to the timeline of the murder and its perpetrator.

It should have been enough to make ASP Shahrul and his team re-think their commitment to the belief that Hanif was the killer.

Unfortunately it wasn't.

A DNA manhunt might have found the killer

If they had re-considered that commitment, it is possible that Noritta's murderer could have been found. But first the team would have had to release Hanif, re-open the investigation and launch an immediate hunt for Unknown Male One.

This would have meant finding every man that Noritta Samsudin had been in contact with and DNA-testing him: every man who had phoned her, every tradesman who had ever worked in the condominium, every man in the many photos taken at the Crystal Club.

Although it would have been a gargantuan task, it could have been done. Several similar manhunts have been conducted over the last 30 years.

The world's first DNA-based manhunt took place between 1986 and 1988 in the UK, during the investigation of two rape-murders in 1983 and 1986 in the Leicestershire village of Enderby. In this case, the prime suspect had confessed to the second crime but refused to own up to the first. Using the then newly-discovered technique of DNA profiling, police realised he was innocent of both. The actual killer was found during the testing of 5,000 local men. The man had avoided being tested but was caught after the friend who took the test for him was heard boasting about cheating the system.

Since then, police forces across the world have undertaken similar exercises. Police officers in the UK city of Bristol DNA-tested 5000 men in the area where an 18-year-old girl was raped and murdered on Christmas Day, 1995. Her 21-year-old killer was caught 14 months later when it was noticed that he had avoided giving the DNA sample requested.

In the year 2000 police questioned and DNA-tested 470 men after a 91-year-old woman was raped in the tiny Australian town of Wee Waa, 500 km from Sydney. The perpetrator was one of those tested. He handed himself in afterwards, knowing the result would unmask him.

ASP Shahrul may have believed that a mass screening like this would be impossible to carry out in Malaysia.

Who was Unknown Male One?

Yet he did not entirely ignore Unknown Male One. A small, secret effort was made to find the owner of this DNA. It came out during the trial that more DNA tests had been ordered *after* Hanif had been charged. DNA profiles were obtained from five of the security guards and from Noritta's boss. These tests look like an attempt to put a name to Unknown Male One.

So who was this man? Nor Azora Hamid had seen a mysterious "dark-skinned" man leaving their apartment on the night of the murder.

Early in the investigation the police appeared to have taken some notice of what Nor Azora had told them about that individual.

An official "Wanted" notice for a dark-skinned man aged about 30, 170 cm in height and with long tied-back hair had been placed in the newspapers, at the behest of KL's officer in charge of criminal investigations.

ASP Shahrul had never actively ordered a search for this man. He had seen the notice in the paper, he would later tell the court. But he had made no effort to follow it up.

Once the trial had started, however, the prosecution tried to suggest that the man Azora had seen and smelled had actually been Hanif, sweating as he escaped the murder scene.

This was in clear contradiction to Kenneth's evidence that Hanif never smelled bad. He was "a smart and well-groomed person", he had told police. In fact he recounted an episode, only two days before Noritta's death when Hanif had given him a ride in his air-conditioned car – and he had not noticed any body odour or unpleasant smell.

Kenneth had also echoed Azora's description of the 6-foot, three-inch fair-skinned engineer as an imposing figure – well-built and "easy to spot" at a distance. The man Azora had seen fleeing the apartment was short.

The prosecution tried to excise this mystery man. They alternatively ignored him and merged him with Hanif.

But he had suddenly re-appeared during the trial, labelled Unknown Male One, with his movements documented in the pages of Lim Kong Boon's report. A few of his long hairs had been collected from the bedding. And, as noted above, his DNA was all over the crime scene.

He had tied Noritta up after her death – because he had killed her. Most certainly he, not Hanif, had been the last person to see Noritta alive.

The prosecution had all this information well before Hanif's trial began. But they went ahead with the prosecution anyway, setting out a case supported by such a highly edited version of the available evidence that it was entirely misleading.

The defence lawyer

Hanif was a fortunate man. In hiring Dato' V Sithambaram, he had acquired a thorough, dedicated and articulate defence lawyer.

After the prosecutor had spent weeks weaving a web of circumstantial evidence around his client, the barrister's message was short and sharp.

"The wrong man has been charged with killing Noritta Samsudin," he told the court.

Instead of focusing attention on engineer Hanif Basree Abdul Rahman, Dato' Sithambaram told the court, the police should have searched for the unknown man whose DNA had been found on the body of the deceased, on the electrical cord used to tie her up, and on a duvet and mattress in her bedroom. Meanwhile the prosecution's star witnesses – Suzaki and Thanabalan – had proven unreliable.

"A criminal trial is not a fairy tale wherein one is free to give flight to one's imagination and fantasy," he said. "It concerns the question of whether the accused arraigned is guilty of the crime with which he is charged. In arriving at the guilt of the accused, the court has to judge the evidence by the yardstick of probabilities, its intrinsic worth and animus of witnesses."

He urged Justice Abdull Hamid Embong to acquit his client.

As one would hope, the judge had looked at all the evidence available, rather than at the highly edited version of the facts that the prosecution had used to argue its case. On July 1, 2004, he acquitted Hanif without even requiring him to enter a defence.

The judgement frees Hanif

In his judgement he said that the prosecution had failed to establish that Hanif had murdered Noritta Samsudin. It had not even established that Hanif was the last person to have been with her.

On the contrary, he said, it was most likely that the last person with Noritta was the man identified as Unknown Male One.

The judge also rejected the story presented by the prosecution's two "star witnesses", finding them both untruthful and unreliable.

It was a day that Dato' Sithambaram would never forget. All Malaysia had been following the case, and he had become increasingly aware of the number of people who believed Hanif was innocent.

Walking out of court into the hot KL afternoon he saw a crowd of almost 200 people waiting. Hanif's family were all there, crying and embracing.

"More spectacularly, there were shouts of 'long live Hanif'," the lawyer recalls. "This kind of reception for an ordinary civilian acquitted of a criminal charge is unheard of. One can conclude that the public felt relieved that justice had been served and an innocent man wrongly prosecuted had been rightly acquitted."

On July 13, 2004, Hanif went back to work, with an audience of reporters in pursuit, noting that he was dressed in a white long-sleeved shirt and wearing a chequered blue tie when he reported for duty at the Shah Alam City Ccouncil.

The prosecution fights on

Yet Hanif still wasn't free of the case. The prosecution's response to his acquittal was to lodge an immediate appeal, arguing that the trial judge should have called for the defence to answer the prosecution case.

In December 2006 the Court of Appeal upheld Justice Abdull Hamid Embong's decision.

The prosecution then made an appeal to the Federal Court for the dismissal of that appeal. Hanif's wife, mother and other family members were with him in the Federal Court on March 28, 2008, to hear Federal Court judge Tan Sri Zaki Azmi pronounce that the prosecution's appeal was dismissed.

Outside the court Hanif told reporters he was relieved to no longer have an appeal hanging over him.

"I thank Allah that this is finally over. I have always believed that justice will triumph under whatever circumstances," he said.

A case where the forensic details told the story

Public Prosecutor versus Hanif Basree Abdul Rahman was one of those few real-life cases where the solution to its central mystery was to be found only in the minutiae of its forensic evidence.

It remains a difficult case to write about with any delicacy because so many of its important details relate to evidence of acts of sexual intercourse, both vaginal and anal.

The local press reported all these sexual minutiae with apparent relish. In fact the coverage of the trial was so explicit that it prompted a stream of letters to the editor from parents worried that their children were being exposed to excessive sexual detail. This trend had begun in 1998 with the reporting of the first of several trials of former Malaysian Deputy Prime Minister Anwar Ibrahim on charges of sodomy. It had reached a new low point with this case.

The worried parents wanted the media to reflect the conservative cultural mores of Malaysia's Muslim majority by censoring the content. It wasn't a surprising expectation.

The country's films and television shows, for example, are regularly censored to remove scenes of men and women or same-sex couples kissing or having sex. Conversations about sex may also be cut.

But there were different rules for newspapers, it seemed, and the politicians kept out of the debate about salacious court reports. The advisor to the prime minister on Islamic issues, Datuk Abdullah

Mohamad Zain, suggested that cases which could embarrass family members should be held behind closed doors. But the Information Minister Abdul Kadir Sheikh Fadzir remained neutral.

"The media must decide. They are led by people who can think," he said.

Salacious reporting and a father's ordeal

The newspaper coverage created even more suffering for Noritta's parents.

The headlines were awful: lines such as "Noritta sexually active, possibly kinky" (*The Star*); "Hanif had sex with Noritta twice a week" (*Nation*); and "Noritta had sex with more than one person before death, court told" (*New Straits Times*). But at least the articles that followed set out to report the evidence of the trial.

The Internet was worse, offering up material portraying their daughter as more villain than victim. There were even reports of photos and sex DVDs, falsely claiming to contain footage of Noritta, being sold online. Even more upsetting were the stories of their dead daughter's restless spirit returning to their home village of Kampung Utan Aji, Perlis, where they had buried her.

On the first day of the trial Noritta's father, Samsudin Ahmad, had to endure the ordeal of identifying his daughter from postmortem photographs. He broke down and wept in the witness box as he did so. Afterwards he continued to read the daily court reports; it was the only way he could find out how the case was proceeding. Noritta's mother stopped reading the papers after the opening of the trial. The explicit details, she later told a *New Straits Times* reporter, were too upsetting.

The prosecution's poor science

The material in some of these articles needs to be summarised, if only to record the desperation – and poor science – displayed by the prosecution. They needed 74 to make the results in Lim Kong Boon's DNA report fit their argument that Hanif had been the last person to have had sex with Noritta. To do so, they ran an argument that was, scientifically speaking, nonsense.

The scientist had noted that there was more of Hanif's DNA found on the accused's vaginal swabs than the unknown male's DNA.

In fact, as he told the court, the composition of the DNA mixture was 60 to 70 per cent from Hanif, while 20 to 25 per cent came from Noritta and 10 to 15 per cent from the unidentified man.

The prosecutor then asked what it meant that Hanif was "the major contributor" and the chemist had replied that it meant that he was the last person to have had sex with the victim. In fact, it meant no such thing.

In the first place, a person with common sense might have factored in Hanif's evidence that he and Noritta had made love twice on their last night together, possibly producing a larger volume of DNA than that produced by Unknown Male One.

To be fair to the chemist, he had noted in his report that many variables had to be taken into account when trying to make these kinds of judgements, such as the amount of semen ejaculated (which varies between individuals). Importantly, when challenged by the defence, he recanted and agreed that he could not say that Hanif was the last man to have had sexual intercourse with Noritta.

It cannot be emphasised too much that this whole debate about the meaning of the semen mixture, all reported in excruciating detail in the newspapers, was of no scientific value at all.

Any independent forensic biologist with experience in sexual assault cases will testify that the volume or amount of semen found in a woman's body bears no relation to the "last person to have intercourse" with her. It is possible to get an estimation of the time since intercourse, but even then, the time windows are vague. The longer the amount of time that sperm spends in the vagina, the more it will degrade, with sperm progressively losing their tails over the course of several days. But 24-hour-old sperm, as Hanif's was, would have been intact.

It was bad science to use an argument about the amount of semen to try to establish a timeline and say that Hanif was the last person to have had sex with Noritta.

According to Dato' Sithambaram, this line of argument ultimately caused the prosecution to lose its case.

"My feeling is that once the DNA expert could not confirm after cross-examination that Hanif was the last person to have had sex with Noritta, the prosecution case collapsed."

There was a similarly low standard of science on show in the attempt by the prosecution to draw a major conclusion from a pile of tissue paper recovered from under a pile of clothing in a waste basket and supposedly still damp when collected.

The pieces of tissue paper, which were semen-stained, had yielded a mixture of Noritta's and Hanif's DNA. To "prove" that this meant that the tissues had been used only a matter of hours earlier rather than 24 hours or so earlier, the prosecution commissioned testing in which tiny amounts of semen from the lab refrigerator were dropped on a couple of tissue papers in the laboratory.

According to Lim Kong Boon, it took between 60 and 90 minutes in an air-conditioned room for these tissues to dry up. The prosecution used this evidence to argue that the dampness of the tissues found in Noritta's room meant they had been used only one-and-a-half hours before they were collected by the forensic officers.

Again, this was bad science – a fact underlined by Federal Court judge Tan Sri Zaki Azmi in the judgement in which he rejected the prosecution's final unsuccessful appeal.

"It did not need an expert," he said, "to know …(that) tissue papers that were dripped with semen and spread out in an air-conditioned room would dry very much faster than if kept in a form of a ball under a stack of clothing. There was also no evidence as to the amount of semen used by the chemist in his experiment compared to that found on the contaminated tissues."

Postscript

At the time of writing in 2017, Unknown Male One may still be at large and living in Kuala Lumpur. Perhaps he has been emboldened by the fact that he got away with murdering Noritta Samsudin. He may still be raping women and tying them up.

Back in 2003 if Malaysia had had a DNA database, of the kind pioneered by the UK in 1995, and emulated in the Australian state of Victoria in 1997 and in the US by the FBI in 1998, Unknown Male One might very well have been caught. At the very least he may have been linked to another unsolved sexual crime.

DNA databases contain all the "unknown" DNA profiles police forensic officers have collected at crime scenes, along with the DNA profiles of all convicted criminals and all suspects for serious crimes (although these latter samples are often supposed to be deleted after a year).

These databases have proven to be the most dramatic and effective crime-solving measure of the 21st century because they allow police to check DNA profiles left at crime scenes against their existing library of DNA profiles. Links are then discovered between apparently unrelated crimes and suspects.

A "cold DNA hit" – where there is no suspect for a crime until the database produces one – is now a common occurrence. Over the last 15 years or so, police forces across the world have reported many "cold case" successes in which the DNA of perpetrators arrested for relatively minor offences in the 21st century has been matched to horrific unsolved crimes from the 1990s, 1980s and even 1970s.

Since 2013, Malaysia has been building its own forensic DNA database. An initiative from Malaysia's Inspector-General of Police Tan Sri Khalid Abu Bakar, it was made possible by the passing of the 2009 DNA Act, which allowed the collection of DNA profiles from prisoners, suspects, people detained under terrorism laws, drug addicts and volunteers and their cross-referencing with data already on the Government Chemistry Department's database.

Once long-haired and slim, Unknown Male One may now be bald or grey and very fat. But his DNA profile will not have changed.

In 2017, Malaysia's Department of Chemistry's DNA database team was still in the process of checking and uploading profiles. The profile of Unknown Male One had not yet been uploaded.

Once his profile is uploaded to the database, it may yet identify him. He may commit another offence. Or he may be linked to another crime. Either way, a new set of circumstances may contain clues to his identity. There is still time for the killer of Noritta Samsudin to be brought to justice.

Case Sixteen
THE MURDER OF CANNY ONG

Reports of the rape and murder of IT analyst Canny Ong, who was abducted from a car park in a Kuala Lumpur shopping mall in 2003, struck real fear into the hearts of women all over Malaysia. Her assailant was caught but, after initially confessing, continued to plead not guilty. So the forensic evidence tying him to the crime became crucially important.

It is almost unbearable to think about Canny Ong's last few hours of life. The 28-year-old IT analyst was abducted from a shopping mall car park in Kuala Lumpur and endured hours of terror before she was raped, stabbed and strangled. Her body was then set on fire. Even more upsetting to contemplate is the fact there were three separate opportunities – three – where, with the tiniest bit of luck, she might have been saved.

Canny Ong didn't actually live in KL. Raised in the Malaysian capital, she had gone to university in the US and lived in San Diego with her husband, Brendan, whom she had married in 2001.

She had flown back to KL to visit her father who had been diagnosed with cancer. But he was recovering and she had decided to have one last night out in her hometown before returning to her life in the US.

Her ordeal began on the evening of Friday June 13, 2003, as she walked alone through the dark underground car park of Kuala

Lumpur's upmarket Bangsar Shopping Centre.

She had just finished a dinner of crabs and steak with her family and friends in Restoran Monte, one of the luxury shopping centre's many eateries. It had been a night full of joy and laughter – and the younger members of the party were ready to kick on. At about 10.30 pm, Canny noticed that her mother, Pearly Viswanathan, was looking tired. Always considerate and dutiful, Canny offered to drive her parent home before returning to continue the party with her friends.

Queuing to pay for parking, she realised she had left the ticket back in the car. Her mother had commented on the eerie darkness of the car park when they arrived. But Canny dashed off to retrieve the ticket before either her mother or sister Elsie could stop her.

When the young woman failed to reappear after twenty minutes, her relatives began calling her mobile. Their calls went to message bank. Then the phone was turned off.

Viewing the CCTV

Pearly and Elsie had noticed CCTV cameras all over the car park. They rushed to the shopping centre's security office and begged the guards to show them the footage.

Just before midnight Pearly, Elsie and a group of Canny's friends stood watching, aghast, as the grainy footage showed a Proton Tiara car, registration number WFN 6871, on the move in the car park. It was Canny's. They could see a stranger at the wheel and a woman cowering in the passenger seat as the vehicle sped towards the exit and smashed through the exterior boom gate.

Like any shopping centre in an affluent upper-middle class area, the Bangsar Shopping Centre had plenty of security guards.

Canny's first piece of bad luck was that none of those guards happened to be watching the CCTV screens at the moment when her kidnapper smashed her car through the exit barrier. If they had seen the incident they would have called the police immediately.

Instead the first call to police was made more than an hour after her abduction, as the horrified guards watched the footage with Canny's mother.

The kidnapper almost caught

At 11.45 pm, just before that report was made, Canny's kidnapper was almost in police custody. He was actually being questioned by a police officer near Subang, more than 15 km away. But undercover motorcycle cop Lance Corporal Subramaniam Ravichandran let the man slip away. Ravichandran and a colleague had been in the area on "crime prevention patrol". At 11.15 pm the two plainclothes officers had noticed a Proton Tiara stop by the roadside. Half an hour later, they had ridden past again, and noticed the car still in that same spot. It was time to check if its occupants were dealing drugs.

Pulling his motorbike over and switching off its engine, Ravichandran knocked on the driver's window and introduced himself as a police officer. Noting that the driver was a Malay male and the passenger a Chinese woman, he showed them his police ID and asked for their names and identity cards. The pair obeyed. Examining the driver's card, the policeman asked the man to take off his cap. The man complied but then refused the officer's request for him to get out of the car.

Hearing the officer's request, Canny had moved as if to open her door. But the driver stopped her.

"They're crooks, not cops," he snapped. Apparently believing him – or perhaps trying to keep her captor calm – Canny remained still. When Ravichandran once again asked the man to open his door, the woman began making a puzzling series of gestures in his direction.

As the officer would later tell the High Court, Canny pointed to herself and pressed her palms together in a prayer-like gesture. She did this while her male companion's attention was on the policeman. But as soon as the man sensed her movement and looked back at her, she dropped her hands.

How could the police officer have failed to get the message that Canny was so desperately trying to send him?

Did it all happen too quickly? Or, less comfortable to contemplate, perhaps some bias was at work – conscious or unconscious. The policeman would later tell the High Court that the woman was wearing "tight clothing that revealed her upper chest and revealed her navel". Perhaps he had already made some kind of a judgement on her morals, unconsciously classifying her as someone undeserving of his empathy.

Maintaining his focus on the driver's refusal to get out of the car, Ravichandran tried to open the car door. Unfortunately the man at the wheel was too quick for him. Starting the car, he floored the accelerator and sped off. The police officer was left standing on the spot, open-mouthed, the two ID cards in his hands. Collecting his wits, the officer pulled out his pistol and fired at the car's tyres, hitting the front right one. Both policemen then jumped on their motorbikes and attempted to follow. But they soon found themselves lost in a maze of narrow streets, their quarry gone.

A second opportunity for rescue

Less than 15 minutes later there was another potential opportunity for rescue.

Clerk Aminah Isahak was on the way to the airport to collect her sister. Her brother-in-law was driving along Jalan Sungai Way and had pulled over to the side of the road to wait for another car carrying family members who were also going to the airport. As they waited she saw a man get out of a Proton Tiara parked about twenty feet in front of them. He came over and asked to borrow a jack but was unable to turn the wheel nuts and loosen his right front tyre. While the man struggled with the wheel, Aminah's glance was drawn to the female passenger who remained sitting in the car. The woman was in "a sexy black net dress", and looked frightened. She was pulling odd faces, as if she were trying to signal to Aminah in some way. But when the man looked up from his struggle with the tyre, she stopped.

Certain that something was dangerously amiss, Aminah took a piece of paper to jot down the Proton's number and give it to the police. Sadly, this being real life and not a movie, that was all she did. She did not grab her brother-in-law as back up, walk over to the woman, open her car door, and ask her if she needed help.

Instead she sat passively in her own car and wrote down the car registration number. She did it just in time. The man was growing increasingly frustrated because he couldn't get the tyre off the car. Moments later he gave up, got back into the vehicle, and drove off.

Aminah and her brother-in-law then went straight to the Subang Jaya police station and reported the incident.

A third potential rescuer

Canny's last potential chance for rescue came an hour later, in the unprepossessing form of Azizan Ismail. The technician was on his way to his employer's office, more than half an hour's drive away. He was driving his van along Jalan Klang Lama, about 20 km from the spot where Aminah Isahak had spotted the Proton Tiara – and he was in desperate need to "take a leak". So he stopped in a road construction area. While he was there, he took a walk around, in the hope of finding a piece of wood that he could use to support the broken back seat of his van.

That was when he saw the parked Proton Tiara. It had a deflated front tyre and a topless woman was stretched across its back seat. As he watched he saw a man standing outside the car. Sadly Azizan had no idea that he had just stumbled on to a sexual assault. Instead he assumed that the man and the woman inside had been making love. While he watched, the man got back in the car, started the engine and drove off.

Some time later, driving back the same way, Azizan noticed the car back in the same area, but in a slightly different spot. This, the killer would later confess, was the place where he would rape Canny Ong for a second time and stab her twice in the stomach.

Stopping his van, Azizan could see that there was no one in the Proton. He had no idea that, at the time, its driver was only a short distance away. As Canny Ong's killer would later tell police, he had panicked at the sight of his bleeding victim and had dragged her body over the barrier that separated the road from the construction site. Then, spotting an open manhole, he had dumped her body inside. Later he had returned to try and burn the body, to cover the crime.

Burgling the car

Azizan Ismail knew nothing of this. He was too busy burgling the car. He snatched a shoulder bag bearing a "Maybank Yippie" logo and pocketed Canny Ong's phone, which he later used to call his wife. He then set off for Penang. On the way he sold the phone's SIM card to a man he met at an Esso petrol station in Sungai Buloh. He stopped again in Ipoh to sell the handset to a phone shop. And then he put the incident out of his mind ... until the police came knocking on his door.

Canny Ong's burned out Proton Tiara was found at 8 pm on Saturday night June 14, less than 24 hours after she was kidnapped.

There were bloodstains on the back seat, but the absence of a body gave investigators hope that the missing woman was still alive. Her phone therefore was of urgent interest.

It remained so, even after the following Tuesday when workers on a Jalan Klang Lama flyover construction site found charred human remains. The workers had noticed planks with burn marks on them lying across a manhole. Removing the planks, and two tyres, they found the burned body of a woman with brown shoulder-length hair. Her hands were bound in front of her, and a piece of cloth was around her neck.

While police feared that the remains were Canny's, they needed to await the results of DNA and dental tests to be sure.

In the meantime they were even more interested in locating her phone. For all they knew, Canny's abductor (a man likely to also be her killer) might have been ignorant enough of police investigative procedure to be still using it.

But who was he?

The search for forensic evidence

From the moment the Proton Tiara was discovered, the police focused on the search for forensic evidence in the car – anything that might offer clues to the man's identity.

Eminent crime scene examiner Amidon Anan, then head of the Selangor Police's forensic unit, and later a guest lecturer at the National University of Malaysia's forensic science programme, was in charge of the forensic analysis of the car. He cut fabric from the front and back seat so that the bloodstains on it could be analysed.

The car wasn't the only crime scene. The burned body in the manhole was another potential source for material that might identify the killer. The forensic pathologists who performed the autopsy on it were able to establish that this female victim had been strangled before her body was set ablaze.

The investigators still had to establish that the body was Canny's. Once they could do so, the body would be an important "silent witness" to this crime, conveying important information about Canny's attacker. Semen, for example, could very well have survived after the victim's body had been set on fire.

The year was 2003; Malaysia had not yet established a national forensic DNA bank, in which the DNA profiles of convicted criminals would be stored. The legislation to set one up was still six years in the future. Therefore there was no chance of any DNA profile from the crime scene being matched to a killer who was not already on the detectives' radar.

But male DNA taken from the body could be compared to the DNA of any suspect in custody. On the day the body was discovered Canny's family had taken part in a press conference in which they appealed to the public for help. The police were hoping that someone might come forward with information that could provide a hint as to the identity of Canny 's abductor.

Canny's phone tracked

Investigators already had one clue. Or so they thought. Their tracking of Canny's phone revealed that it had been used to make calls between June 14 and June 16 – after her abduction. They were soon talking to three men: Farizal Shapei, who had bought the SIM card from Azizan in the early hours of Saturday June 14; Mohamed Yusri Mohamed Yusof who was with him at the time; and to Azizan himself.

All three men were arrested and taken into custody.

Soon investigators had another suspect. He was most certainly Canny's abductor. And they even had his name!

The sudden burst of publicity linking a missing woman, a charred body and burned out Proton Tiara had made undercover motorcycle cop Lance Corporal Subramaniam Ravichandran recall the couple in the Proton Tiara he had questioned on the night of Friday June 13. The couple whose identity cards he had been left holding.

Within hours, those cards were in the hands of the chief investigator on the case, Abu Bakar Mustafa, head of Criminal Investigations for Selangor. Now his team had a photo and a name: Ahmad Najib bin Aris, aged 27.

The address on that card was false. As the investigators started scouring the many records that every citizen accrues throughout adult life, they found more false addresses, and fictitious employment records as well. But the Malaysian national social security registry and marriage registry brought up an address for the man's wife.

Surveillance of the wife, and then the husband

Covert surveillance officers staked out the woman's workplace and followed her home to suburban Pantai Dalam. Her husband was a supervisor with a cleaning company that serviced aircraft.

Police then set up surveillance of their house. Finally, shortly before 6 am on the morning of Friday June 20, a taxi pulled up outside the house. Ahmad Najib got out. And the police officers pounced. His wife later told police that her husband regularly visited brothels and returned home in the wee hours.

Later that afternoon the cleaner appeared before a magistrate who granted the police request to have him held in custody for ten days to help with their investigations. The next day, the man spent three hours in front of a magistrate at the Petaling Jaya Magistrates' Court, during which time he recorded a full confession.

The day after that, a media pack followed as the investigators took the man on a tour of the various crime scenes associated with the horrific rape/murder. Further forensic evidence, including strands of hair, an earring and bloodstains, were collected near the culvert where Canny Ong's body was found.

At this point it might have looked as if the case was solved. Of course the detailed forensic analysis of the various crime scenes still had to be done. Police also had to ensure that the man in custody was in fact the man who had committed the crime and not, as sometimes happens in cases attracting huge media attention, somebody offering up a false confession.

The police certainly had reason to feel pleased. They had a suspect in custody and he had confessed. Moreover, the prosecution had eyewitnesses who could testify to having seen Ahmad Najib with a terrified-looking Canny Ong in her blue Proton Tiara.

They also had forensic scientists who could testify that the DNA profile extracted from the semen found in Canny Ong's dead body was a match to Ahmad Najib's. The three men who had been held in jail over the possession of Canny Ong's phone had been released. They would still have a useful role to play in the case, however. Ultimately they would serve as three of the 69 witnesses the prosecution would assemble to make its case.

Case solved. But not yet resolved

But the case was far from closed. On August 5, 2003, when Ahmad Najib faced the High Court on the rape and murder charges, he pleaded not guilty.

The man had a good defence lawyer, Mohamed Haniff Khatri Abdulla, an articulate advocate supported by a team of three other lawyers. And, like any good lawyer, his approach was to question everything about the prosecution case.

The trial opened on September 15, 2003, and Mohamed Haniff began with a challenge to the validity of his client's confession. It had been given, he suggested, "under duress".

The main trial was then halted so a "trial within a trial" could be held to assess the admissibility of this confession. It was, after all, the key to the prosecution case.

Muhammad Rushdan, the magistrate who had taken the confession, was the first to testify. He told the court that Ahmad Najib had appeared relaxed and showed no sign of having been physically coerced to confess.

The magistrate said that he had carefully examined the man's head, upper body and legs and had found no injuries, cuts, or swelling and that the accused had told him that his confession was "voluntary and sincere". He had also cautioned the man that whatever he said would be recorded and could be used against him at trial. Ahmad Najib had replied that he understood and wanted to make a confession.

A confession that fitted some of the facts

The confession, recorded non-stop from 12.14 pm to 1.30 pm on June 21, 2003, ran to ten pages. It told a story that fitted all of the events on the evening of Canny Ong's disappearance that had been witnessed by others.

Ahmad Najib confessed to having gone to the shopping centre car park late on the night of June 13. He told the magistrate he had been looking for a woman he had a grudge against. Supposedly she was a former employer of his. Mistaking Canny Ong for the woman, he had followed her to her Proton Tiara. When she opened the door, he had pushed her in and driven off.

He only realised his mistake, he claimed, when he checked his captive's ID card. He then maintained that he had intended to release her. But the encounter with motorcycle cop Subramaniam

Ravichandran had spooked him. He also confessed to stopping, as witnesses had confirmed, to check the front wheel of the car before driving to the road construction site.

It was there, he said, that he told Canny Ong that he wanted to have sex with her. He then claimed that, after he had placed his knife on the car dashboard, she agreed. She had only started to struggle, he said, after they had had sex. That was when he had stabbed her twice in the abdomen.

He said that he had seen "a man with a stick" approaching the car (obviously the technician Azizan who had been looking for a piece of wood to support his van's broken back seat) and had sped off.

Ahmad Najib then claimed to have helped Canny, still alive at that point, to dress before carrying her to an embankment. There he tied her feet and hands and gagged her. He also said he had seen his car being ransacked.

He admitted to placing his victim in the drain. In fact he claimed to have held her hand and apologised before telling her he was going to burn her body. He then hid the Proton Tiara 3 km away and took a taxi home to Pantai Dalam at about 6 am. The following day he bought petrol, returned to the manhole and set Canny Ong's body on fire.

During this "trial within a trial" Ahmad Najib attempted to support the case against the use of this confession by claiming that he had been threatened with violence. He also said he had been coached by a police officer on how to confess to the crime of rape and murder. He insisted that he had been kicked in the face and groin and had endured a lot of pain. Oddly enough this supposed beating had not caused him to shed any blood. Nor had he sustained any bruises.

Setbacks for the defence lawyer

The mini-trial ran for ten days. But it ended badly for Mohamed Haniff Khatri Abdulla, with the trial judge admitting the confession.

That setback didn't appear to faze the lawyer in the slightest. He had limited material at his disposal, but he worked it very hard.

It would have been difficult to argue against the array of prosecution witnesses who had seen Ahmad Najib with Canny, so his main approach was to run the theory that his client wasn't the only person responsible for the abduction and murder.

The defence lawyer first flagged this theory when Canny's father, Ong Bee Jeng, was giving evidence. He began by mentioning the fact that a rich Malaysian lawyer had apparently funded the young woman's education in the US. He then proceeded to ask Canny's father so many questions about the family's finances that Deputy Public Prosecutor Salehuddin Saidin protested to the judge about their relevance.

The judge then ordered the lawyer to ease off. But Mohamed Haniff explained that the defence wanted to establish the possibility that others could be responsible for Canny Ong's abduction and murder. He then brought up the issue of the two-carat diamond ring, worth about RM80,000, that the victim had been wearing on the night she disappeared.

The ring was missing when her body was found. Might not this mean, the lawyer suggested when cross-examining Assistant Superintendent of Police Muniandy, that other parties might have been involved in the murder?

The investigator said he had not looked into this possibility.

The lawyer also worked hard on the issue of the weight of the cement-filled tyres on the victim's body in the manhole. The police superintendent had conceded that they were very heavy and would require strength to move. But he refused to agree with the lawyer that this meant that more than one person was involved in placing them on Canny Ong's body.

The defence lawyer's other approach, so common in rape trials, was to undermine the victim's dignity. University Malaya Medical Centre consultant forensic pathologist Professor Dr Kasinathan Nadesan had given evidence on the cause of Canny Ong's death.

He had pointed to the cloth ligature around her neck, and explained her death as a result of strangulation – although he could not dismiss the theory that her death may have been a result of abdominal bleeding caused by a sharp weapon.

The only skin on the victim's neck that had escaped charring, he had pointed out, was under the ligature around her neck. As the expert explained to the court, this was an indication of how brutally tight it had been knotted.

But the defence lawyer used the fact of the ligature as an opportunity to suggest that the cloth found around the unfortunate victim's neck had been placed there as part of consensual "sexual asphyxia".

This is an act performed by couples but more commonly by men who, while masturbating, put ligatures around their own necks. This reduces the flow of oxygen to the brain, producing a state of helplessness that is believed to be sexually erotic. It also occasionally results in accidental death by strangulation.

Mohamed Haniff asked Dr Kasinathan if he could completely exclude the possibility that the cause of Canny Ong's death was sexual asphyxia.

The pathologist replied that this sort of sexual asphyxia or mechanical asphyxia usually occurred "in places away from the public eye and not in a car, on the roadside or the wayside". But when further pressed by the lawyer, he had to agree that, in theory, he could not rule it out.

The prosecution called 44 witnesses including the victim's parents in the 46-day hearing.

Overwhelming forensic evidence

The circumstantial evidence against Ahmad Najib was already powerful. But the forensic evidence against him was, Deputy Public Prosecutor Salehuddin Saidin told the court, overwhelming. Most damning was the fact that the DNA profile extracted from live sperm found in Canny Ong's body was a match to the accused man's DNA.

Sperm can survive up to five days. The fact that these sperm were still alive was, as Salehuddin told the court, proof that the accused had had intercourse with the victim between the night of June 13 and the morning of June 14, 2003.

There was also Ahmad Najib's "Jack Blue Classic jeans", found in his house and stained with his victim's blood. The blood was also consistent with his confession that he had stabbed Canny with a knife.

Then there was the cloth. The autopsy report indicated that Canny Ong had died of strangulation by a cloth ligature. Forensic expert evidence confirmed that the colour, type and composition of the muslin cloth ligature found around the victim's neck was similar to the muslin cloth used for cleaning aircraft. Meanwhile witnesses had confirmed that, as the team leader of an aircraft cleaning crew, Ahmad Najib had access to this kind of cloth.

DPP Salehuddin said the defence had failed to cast a reasonable doubt on the prosecution's case and had merely relied on bare denials. These were not a defence.

"The defence's contention (among others) that there was someone else that impersonated Ahmad Najib who committed the crime does not make any sense," the deputy public prosecutor said.

Ahmad Najib still had the option to defend himself by giving sworn testimony from the witness stand or by making a statement from the dock. But he chose to remain silent.

On February 23, 2005, High Court Justice Datuk Muhamad Ideres Muhamad Rapee sentenced Ahmad Najib to death for the murder of Canny Ong. For the rape he received the maximum sentence of 20 years, with ten strokes of the rotan.

But this tragic saga still had many years to run.

An appeal, the first of several

In May 2005 Ahmad Najib filed notice of his appeal against his conviction and death sentence.

Once again the key issue was his confession. The convicted man claimed that the trial judge had erred in accepting the confession made at the Petaling Jaya Magistrates' Court. He claimed that the evidence against him was circumstantial and that several witnesses' identification of him was inconclusive. He even brought up the forensic evidence, querying the DNA findings and claiming that the cause of death, whether by stabbing or strangling, had not been established.

During the four-day appeal in January 2006, Ahmad Najib's lawyer Mohamed Haniff once again ran the accusation that his client had been threatened by police. He raised doubt over the ownership of the blood-stained jeans found in his client's house because the man had not been asked to try them on to confirm they were his. He also alleged that the prosecution had not conclusively proved that the seminal fluid obtained from a vaginal swab of the victim was Ahmad Najib's.

"The chemist relied on equipment to come to his conclusions," he told the court. "But the machine was not calibrated and there was no certificate to show that it was in working order."

The lawyer repeated the allegation made in the trial, that the victim had consented to sex after Ahmad Najib picked up a knife from underneath his seat and placed it on the dashboard without threatening her.

On March 5, 2007, three judges of the Court of Appeal were unanimous in rejecting the appeal. Mohamed Haniff did win one point. The judges agreed that the confession was inadmissible (they said there was a strong suspicion that the appellant had been pressured by the police into making the confession). But after examining the rest of the prosecution case, they accepted it. They also accepted the evidence on the identification of the accused, the chemist's evidence and the DNA evidence. Their conclusion was that Ahmad Najib, and no one else, was responsible for what happened to Canny Ong on the night she died.

Yet the case was still not over. Six months later, Ahmad Najib's hardworking defence lawyer managed to get leave to add an additional ground to his client's petition for appeal. It was highly technical, and it had to do with the appeal judges failing to identify that they had the power to assess the evidence without having to refer to the High Court judgement. The case was then adjourned.

When the court reconvened in May 2008, this time with five judges on the bench, Ahmad Najib's lawyer asked to have crucial exhibits produced.

The first exhibit requested was a photo of the closed-circuit television camera image allegedly showing the accused and his victim in her Proton Tiara, speeding out of the Bangsar Shopping Centre car park.

Mohamed Haniff said he intended to dispute the identity of the driver of the car, meaning that the photographs had to be produced in court. He also wanted to see the tyre that had been placed on top of Canny Ong's charred body in the manhole. He wanted to demonstrate how the accused would not have been able to lift it over a shoulder-height wall. The lawyer then won an adjournment of the hearing, due to the unavailability of the exhibits.

The appeal was finally heard over two days in October 2008. On March 27, 2009, the court once again rejected the appeal.

By then Ahmad Najib bin Aris had spent two years on remand and four years on Death Row. During this period Malaysian shopping malls reformed their security procedures. Round-the-clock patrols were introduced, along with women-only parking spaces near entrances, and high-definition digital security cameras.

In October of 2009, Ahmad Najib made one last application to the Federal Court, asking it to invoke its discretion under Rule 137 of the Rules of the Federal Court 1995 to review its previous decision on the basis that it was unjust. It was dismissed.

Finally on September 23, 2016, Ahmad Najib bin Aris was hanged at Kajang Prison and his body was buried at the nearby Sungai Kantan Muslim cemetery in Kajang.

By then, more than eleven years had passed since he had been sentenced to death.

ABOUT THE AUTHOR

Liz Porter is an Australian writer best known for her prize-winning books about "the real CSI" – the way forensic science is used to solve crime.

Crime Scene Asia: when forensic evidence becomes the silent witness is her latest book. Her first book, *Written on the Skin: an Australian forensic casebook*, was joint winner of the 2007 Ned Kelly award for the best true crime book. Porter also won the Australian Sisters in Crime's 2012 Davitt Award (best true crime category) for her book, *Cold Case Files: past crimes solved by new forensic science*.

She is an open water swimmer and a member of a pop music choir.